Hans Magnus Enzensberger

CRITICAL ESSAYS

The German Library : Volume 98

Volkmar Sander, General Editor

Hans Magnus Enzensberger

CRITICAL ESSAYS

Edited by
Reinhold Grimm and
Bruce Armstrong

Foreword by John Simon

CONTINUUM · NEW YORK

1982

The Continuum Publishing Company
575 Lexington Avenue, New York, NY 10022

Copyright © 1982 by The Continuum Publishing Company

Foreword © 1982 by John Simon
Introduction © 1982 by Reinhold Grimm

Printed in the United States of America

Library of Congress Cataloging in Publication Data

Enzensberger, Hans Magnus.
Critical essays.

(The German library; v. 98)
Includes bibliographical references.
I. Grimm, Reinhold.   II. Title.
PT2609.N9A24   834′.914   81-19612
ISBN 0-8264-0258-5   AACR2
ISBN 0-8264-0268-2 pbk

For acknowledgments of previously published material, see
page 250, which constitutes an extension of the copyright page.

Contents

Foreword

Renaissance men (or women) are in short supply these days. Rare indeed is the writer who can hold his own as poet, translator, critic, playwright, polemist, anthologist, and editor of two remarkable—and very different—periodicals. But Hans Magnus Enzensberger is all of those things (and probably a few others I forgot to mention), and manages them with a wit and polish that belie their profundity. Yet what makes him so extraordinary is that even within each individual field he is a bit of a Renaissance man.

Thus there is no end to the themes and forms that Enzensberger's poetry, for example, has espoused; yet from volume to volume, and even from poem to poem, it is able to be as various as verse can get, without losing, however, the feel and scent of its author's unmistakable identity. There seem to be, as when a ball of mercury is rolled across a smooth surface, a great number of glittering little Enzensbergers that in the end coalesce all the same into one dazzling mind and sensibility.

We are presented here with a selection of Enzensberger's essays that, of necessity, cannot encompass the full range of the man. Even so, they do give a generous inkling of his diversity, and attest to the benefits of a complex literary sensibility's latching on to political matters, and, conversely, of a historically and politically astute mind's addressing itself to our arts and culture. As Reinhold Grimm points out in his Introduction, Anglo-American reference books—and, presumably, the English and American readership—

seem to consider this sort of searching, far-ranging, well-informed, intellectually and morally challenging essay the monopoly of French literature and blithely ignore the contribution of such distinguished German essayists of all periods as Professor Grimm adduces. But much as I deplore the other omissions, the absence of Enzensberger from Anglo-American awareness seems to me particularly unfortunate.

The reason is plain enough. In fact, it is plainness itself. For Enzensberger knows how to deal with complicated ideas and fine discriminations in a style that, though anything but inelegant, is nevertheless stunningly straightforward and plain. We live in an age—need I remind you of this melancholy truth?—when plain statement in any field, but particularly in the critical, cultural, or political essay, is extremely hard to come by. For this, the French and their Anglo-American emulators are especially to blame. Not so Enzensberger. He may have begun as an adherent of Marxism, but by now even that -ism—at least in its doctrinaire form—has been left behind. With the more modish and obscurantist ones he never had any truck. The only -ism that persists in his work is humanism. There are no hobby horses; only horse sense.

What Enzensberger can do with the essay, you will find out as you turn the pages. Here, however, I should like to quote a poem of his; partly in order to remind you of a very important other aspect of his talent, but even more so as to give you a sense of the essential Enzensberger expressed most tersely, yet with those persistently, understatedly reverberating ironies that I urge you to notice in the prose as well. The poem is called "Remembrance."

> Well now, as concerns the seventies
> I can express myself with brevity.
> Directory assistance was always busy.
> The miraculous multiplication of loaves
> was restricted to Düsseldorf and vicinity.
> The dread news came over the ticker tape,
> was taken cognizance of and duly filed.
>
> Unresisting, by and large,
> they swallowed themselves,
> the seventies,

without guarantee for latecomers,
Turkish guest workers and the unemployed.
That anyone should think of them with leniency
would be asking too much.

The tone, *mutatis mutandis,* is very much the one of Enzensberger's best essays: the chiseled mockery of a civilized man who has not given up the fight, but who chooses his weapons fastidiously: the implication-drenched detail, hearty irony, incitement to thought.

This is in the best tradition of the German essay. Besides the authors with whom Professor Grimm brackets Enzensberger, we should also invoke Heine and Kleist, Karl Kraus and Frank Wedekind. Their mode, except for Heine's, may be harsher than that of Enzensberger, but they are ironists all, and quite as much his ancestors or mentors. And here it behooves us to recognize how few of our English and American essayists had this kind of sardonic acumen to apply equally to culture and politics: George Orwell, of course, and Edmund Wilson, and doubtless a few others. But they are precious few, and Hans Magnus Enzensberger, in good English translations, readily assumes a place beside them as their equal. For what gives him the finishing touch of the Renaissance man is his internationalism. However much we might wish, defensively, to relegate him to otherness—to being German, European, Continental, or whatever—it won't wash. He stands right beside us, whoever we are. He is one of us.

JOHN SIMON

Introduction

It happened nearly two decades ago, yet I can recall it as vividly as if it had occurred yesterday. The scene: Frankfurt University; the year: 1964. A slender, fair-haired, almost boyish-looking man of thirty-five was mounting the rostrum. He was greeted with a veritable uproar of applause. His first public address as the newly appointed poet-in-residence had been the talk of the town; in fact, town and gown—both students and scholars, critics and fellow writers, the representatives of the big publishing firms and of the mighty media, as well as the city's dignitaries—all were in attendance. Not even the largest lecture hall could hold this crowd: the event had to be broadcast by short-circuit to an adjacent hall. The late Theodor W. Adorno, editor of Walter Benjamin and West Germany's leading philosopher, sociologist, and aesthetician, had volunteered to present the speaker. Adorno declared, to cheers: "All we have in German literary criticism, nay, in criticism as such, is Hans Magnus Enzensberger . . . and a few scattered attempts" (*Wir haben ihn und Ansätze*). This is precisely what the great scholar Ernst Robert Curtius had once stated in regard to the seminal critic and essayist Friedrich Schlegel, and what Schlegel himself had said of Gotthold Ephraim Lessing, founder of a comparable literary criticism.

When Enzensberger was hailed in the mid-sixties as a latter-day Lessing or Schlegel by his friend and mentor, only two volumes (albeit weighty and sizable ones) of his critical and essayistic output had appeared, but he had already brought out three volumes of poetry, containing some of the finest post-war verse written in German. His lyrical breakthrough in 1957 had been likened to the meteoric rise and lasting fame of Heinrich Heine, and in 1963 he had been awarded the prestigious Büchner Prize which commemorates Heine's contemporary, Georg Büchner. More achievements were to follow: a documentary play and a documentary novel, a pair of libretti, an epic, another three volumes of poetry, and two more volumes of essays and criticism. Enzensberger was also active as a prolific and conscientious editor who enjoyed that rarest of editorial gifts: serendipity. With his two journals alone, *Kursbuch* (timetable or railroad guide—a title abounding in ambiguities and allusions) and *Transatlantik*, founded in 1965 and 1980 respectively, he might safely boast of having ensconced himself as the most innovative and stimulating literary promoter and critical mediator of his generation.

Born at Kaufbeuren, a small town in the Bavarian Allgäu region, in 1929, Enzensberger grew up in Nuremberg, the atmosphere of which, during the thirties and early forties, was a strange and often stifling mixture of provincial remoteness and drowsiness touched with faint recollections of a magnificent past, and the deafening din and foaming bombast of Hitler's party rallies and bloody warmongering. Enzensberger lived through the musty idyll and the pandemonium, as well as the devastating air raids that soon began to sweep the city. Toward the end of the war, he was drafted by the Nazis' desperate conscription of shaky old men and underfed teenagers, the *"Volkssturm."* Later he dabbled awhile in the black market and tried his hand at the theater; he also finished high school. Having attended various German universities, as well as the Sorbonne, where he studied literature, languages, and philosophy, he earned his degree at Erlangen near Nuremberg. Enzensberger's dissertation analyzed the techniques of the Romantic poet Clemens Brentano. It was eventually published. He graduated with honors, receiving his doctorate summa cum laude at the age of twenty-six.

Enzensberger could easily have entered an academic career, but his aims were different. Immediately after finishing his studies, he joined the Stuttgart Radio and was assigned to the section dealing with essays; later, he served as a reader for the Suhrkamp Verlag, which became his publisher. In between, he was a visiting lecturer.

Since 1961 Enzensberger has lived and worked as a freelance writer and has gained spectacular success and great stature. In 1970 he founded a publishing house of his own.

Enzensberger traveled a great deal and, in fact, sojourned for long periods abroad. As a student he toured Europe, emerging in Spain and Greece, in Finland and Italy—wherever the torn and ravaged continent was accessible then. Subsequently, he took a good look at North and South America, at Australia, China, and the Soviet Union. There is hardly a country of importance that he has not inspected. ("Fieldwork" is a favorite term of his, applicable in both a literal and a figurative sense, if we think of documentary works like *Der kurze Sommer der Anarchie: Buenaventura Durrutis Leben und Tod* [*The Short Summer of Anarchy: Life and Death of Buenaventura Durruti*], 1972, his novel on Spanish anarchism; *Das Verhör von Habana* [*Hearings from Havana*], 1970, his play on the abortive Bay of Pigs invasion; or even poetic works like his monumental epic *Der Untergang der Titanic: Eine Komödie* [*The Sinking of the Titanic: A Comedy*], 1978; and his equally momentous collection *Mausoleum: Siebenunddreissig Balladen aus der Geschichte des Fortschritts* [*Mausoleum: Thirty-Seven Ballads from the History of Progress*], 1975, about the progress of barbarism.)

Enzensberger has also lived in Southern Norway, at times retreating to a tiny island in the Oslo Fjord, and in the insular yet cosmopolitan city of West Berlin, a place of strangely extraterritorial climate and yet somehow also a hub of things. In 1980 he moved to Munich, probably because of responsibilities arising from his new editorship. Before 1980, Enzensberger spent at least a year at Lanuvio near Rome and nearly a year—a crucial, searching, and disappointing one—in Castro's Cuba. He appears regularly in New York and the Eastern U.S., although in 1968 he gave up his fellowship at the Center for Advanced Studies at Wesleyan University and left the United States in open protest against the war in Viet Nam. The letter in which he explained his decision, a scathing piece of criticism published jointly by the *New York Times* and the West German weekly *Die Zeit,* is still held against him by a number of people.

But controversies are inevitable for Enzensberger, since he is not only a widely traveled and highly intellectual, but also a deeply committed and boldly experimental author. His childhood nightmares and adult forebodings, as well as his spontaneous outbursts, whether romantic, revolutionary, or both, constitute a pattern, a pattern of life and personality, of work and opinions, issuing in his achievements and reputation as a critic and essayist.

Enzensberger's very concept of art and literature and their function is reflected in this pattern of steady development and restless change. Since his first publications in the mid-fifties, he has expanded his horizons, but he also became absorbed in nearly insoluble problems—he has proceeded from local and national to global and international and therefore ever graver concerns. His earliest collection of essays, *Einzelheiten* [*Odds and Ends; Details*], first published in 1962, was soon after brought out as a two-volume paperback comprising *Bewusstseins-Industrie* (*The Consciousness Industry*) and *Poesie und Politik* (*Poetry and Politics*). The collection featured an acid polemic against the *Frankfurter Allgemeine Zeitung*, the foremost West German newspaper, and an unmasking of *Der Spiegel*, West Germany's equivalent of *Time* Magazine, and its jargon. On the other hand, his last such collection to date, *Palaver: Politische Überlegungen* [*Palaver: Political Considerations*], which appeared in 1974, contained a broad and strongly self-critical satire on the leftist intelligentsia of all countries and their cherished "tourism of the revolution." It analyzes their traveling and fellow-traveling to socialist paradises and tellingly culminates with the penetrating "Critique of Political Ecology," which is scarcely Marxist in any orthodox sense, but is certainly Marxian. The two earlier collections of 1964 and 1967 reveal in their choice of titles, *Politik und Verbrechen* (*Politics and Crime*) and *Deutschland, Deutschland unter anderm* [*Germany, Germany Among Other Things*], that duality of centrifugal expansion and centripetal absorption, entanglement though never total engulfment, which distinguishes Enzensberger's manifold and seismographic oeuvre. As controversies are unavoidable, so are contradictions. Enzensberger's widening gyre reveals itself as a deepening vortex as well.

Yet precisely this complexity makes him exemplary for our present age; it elevates his writings—with their unceasing dialectic of past and future, closeness and distance, commitment and resignation, hope and despair, even utopia and apocalypse—to an outstanding contribution to world literature and modern life. His essays can perhaps be best summed up by drawing on their author's own binary formula: they treat, basically, either "poetic" or "political" issues, just as his creative work at large consists, for the most part, of either poetry or critical prose. The texts assembled here represent the scope and topicality of Enzensberger's approach to questions of art, literature, culture, to history, sociology, ecology. His volumes of poetry can only be listed: they are *Verteidigung der Wölfe* [*In Defense of the Wolves*], 1957; *Landessprache* [*Vernacular*], 1960; *Blindenschrift* [*Braille*], 1964; and *Die Furie des Verschwindens* [*The Fury of Disappearance*], 1980; also a 1971 selection from the first three volumes entitled *Gedichte 1955–1970* [*Poems 1955–1970*], as well as a bilingual anthology *Poems for People Who Don't Read Poems*, 1968.

Enzensberger is also a sovereign and versatile translator. Enviably gifted in languages and exceptionally well read, he is both a polyglot writer and a *poeta doctus*. By 1970 he had completed and published, as separate works or whole books, translations from the French, English, Italian, Spanish, Swedish, and Russian; he had also translated and edited a volume of selected poems by William Carlos Williams, the American poet whose work had been an important influence on him. There exist as well virtually dozens of prefaces, commentaries, and the like, all of which appeared during the same relatively short span of time. With equal fervor and skill, he combats both poetic provincialism and political illiteracy, as amply illustrated by his famous anthology *Museum der modernen Poesie* [*A Museum of Modern Poetry*], 1960, on the one hand, and by his provocative collection *Freisprüche: Revolutionäre vor Gericht* [*Acquittals: Revolutionaries on Trial*], 1970, on the other. "Poetry and politics," to be sure.

For the structure and style of his essays, however, a convenient formula is harder to find. But is not the essay, as indicated by its very name, the experimental and, as a consequence, open and elusive genre par excellence? The reference book I consulted does not list even one German title or author under the heading "Essay." Do not Lessing and Schlegel deserve mention, not to speak of Goethe, Schiller, Heine, Nietzsche? And what about such widely divergent modern classics as Thomas Mann, Gottfried Benn, and Bertolt Brecht? What about Brecht's friend Walter Benjamin and, in his train, Adorno? The German tradition offers a wealth, not only of genuine essays worth reading, but also of pertinent insights well worth pondering. For example, Schlegel's aphorism has it that it is as detrimental to a writer to have a solid system as to have no system at all; he must sustain a dialectical unity, if not balance, of contradictions. This definition illuminates both the content and structure of Enzensberger's work in the genre as well as that of many other writers.

It is to be hoped that the essays of Hans Magnus Enzensberger will succeed in redressing the general state of neglect and ignorance of German achievements in the essay form from the time of Lessing and Schlegel. These essays preserve and enliven a rich tradition. In form and essence, and for all the tentativeness and subjectivity peculiar to their kind, they partake of much of Lessing's humanistic verve and straightforwardness, much of Schlegel's literary urbanity and wit—to mention again two of Enzensberger's earliest ancestors. Steadfastly, Enzensberger continues to take up and face, more than any other essayist I know of, the burning issues of our time.

All texts are complete and unabridged, except for sections 28 through 38 of "Berlin Commonplaces," which have proved too specialized for the American reader. Also, apart from a minimum of explanation, mostly in the form of footnotes, nothing has been added. All translations, including the author's own, have been carefully checked and, wherever appropriate, revised to make them conform as much as possible to the German original. The texts in the present selection are arranged in chronological order.

R.G.

Part One

LITERATURE
AND
THE MEDIA

1

The Industrialization
of the Mind

All of us, no matter how irresolute we are, like to think that we reign supreme in our own consciousness, that we are masters of what our minds accept or reject. Since the Soul is not much mentioned any more, except by priests, poets, and pop musicians, the last refuge a man can take from the catastrophic world at large seems to be his own mind. Where else can he expect to withstand the daily siege, if not within himself? Even under the conditions of totalitarian rule, where no one can fancy anymore that his home is his castle, the mind of the individual is considered a kind of last citadel and hotly defended, though this imaginary fortress may have been long since taken over by an ingenious enemy.[1]

No illusion is more stubbornly upheld than the sovereignty of the mind. It is a good example of the impact of philosophy on people who ignore it; for the idea that men can "make up their minds" individually and by themselves is essentially derived from the tenets of bourgeois philosophy: secondhand Descartes, rundown Husserl, armchair idealism; and all it amounts to is a sort of metaphysical do-it-yourself.

We might do worse, I think, than dust off the admirably laconic statement that one of our classics made more than a century ago: "What is going on in our minds has always been, and will always be, a product of society."[2] This is a comparatively recent insight.

3

Though it is valid for all human history ever since the division of labor came into being, it could not be formulated before the time of Karl Marx. In a society where communication was largely oral, the dependence of the pupil on the teacher, the disciple on the master, the flock on the priest was taken for granted. That the few thought and judged and decided for the many was a matter of course and not a matter for investigation. Medieval man was probably other-directed to an extent that our sociology would be at a loss to fathom. His mind was, to an enormous degree, fashioned and processed from "without." But the business of teaching and of indoctrination was perfectly straightforward and transparent—so transparent indeed that it became invisible as a problem. Only when the processes that shape our minds became opaque, enigmatic, inscrutable for the common man, only with the advent of industrialization, did the question of how our minds are shaped arise in earnest.

The mind-making industry is really a product of the last hundred years. It has developed at such a pace, and assumed such varied forms, that it has outgrown our understanding and our control. Our current discussion of the "media" seems to suffer from severe theoretical limitations. Newsprint, films, television, public relations tend to be evaluated separately, in terms of their specific technologies, conditions, and possibilities. Every new branch of the industry starts off a new crop of theories.[3] Hardly anyone seems to be aware of the phenomenon as a whole: the industrialization of the human mind. This is a process that cannot be understood by a mere examination of its machinery.

Equally inadequate is the term *cultural industry,* which has become common usage in Europe since World War II. It reflects, more than the scope of the phenomenon itself, the social status of those who have tried to analyze it: university professors and academic writers, people whom the power elite has relegated to the narrow confines of what passes as "cultural life" and who consequently have resigned themselves to bear the unfortunate label cultural critics. In other words, they are certified as harmless; they are supposed to think in terms of *Kultur* and not in terms of power.

Yet the vague and insufficient label *cultural industry* serves to remind us of a paradox inherent in all media work. Consciousness, however false, can be induced and reproduced by industrial means, but it cannot be industrially produced. It is a "social product" made up by people: its origin is the dialogue. No industrial process can replace the persons who generate it. And it is precisely this truism of which the archaic term *culture* tries, however vainly, to remind us. The mind industry is monstrous and difficult to understand because it does not, strictly speaking, produce anything. It is an intermediary, engaged only in production's secondary and tertiary derivatives, in transmission and infiltration, in the fungible aspect of what it multiplies and delivers to the customer.

The mind industry can take on anything, digest it, reproduce it, and pour it out. Whatever our minds can conceive of is grist to its mill; nothing will leave it unadulterated: it is capable of turning any idea into a slogan and any work of the imagination into a hit. This is its overwhelming power; yet it is also its most vulnerable spot: it thrives on a stuff it cannot manufacture by itself. It depends on the very substance it must fear most, and must suppress what it feeds on: the creative productivity of people. Hence the ambiguity of the term *cultural industry*, which takes at face value the claims of culture, in the ancient sense of the word, and the claims of an industrial process that has all but eaten it up. To insist on these claims would be naive; to criticize the industry from the vantage point of a "liberal education" and to raise comfortable outcries against its vulgarity will neither change it nor revive the dead souls of culture: it will merely help to fortify the ghettoes of educational programs and to fill the backward, highbrow section of the Sunday papers. At the same time, the indictment of the mind industry on purely esthetic grounds will tend to obscure its larger social and political meaning.

On the other extreme we find the ideological critics of the mind industry. Their attention is usually limited to its role as an instrument of straightforward or hidden political propaganda, and from the messages reproduced by it they try to distill the political content. More often than not, the underlying understanding of politics is extremely narrow, as if it were just a matter of taking sides in everyday contests of power. Just as in the case of the "cultural critic," this attitude cannot hope to catch up with the far-reaching effects of the industrialization of the mind, since it is a process that will abolish the distinction between private and public consciousness.

Thus, while radio, cinema, television, recording, advertising, and public relations, new techniques of manipulation and propaganda, are being keenly discussed, each on its own terms, the mind industry, taken as a whole, is disregarded. Newspaper and book publishing, its oldest and in many respects still its most interesting branch, hardly comes up for serious comment any longer, presumably because it lacks the appeal of technological novelty. Yet much of the analysis provided in Balzac's *Illusions Perdues* is as pertinent today as it was a hundred years ago, as any copywriter from Hollywood who happens to be familiar with the book will testify. Other, more recent branches of industry still remain largely unexplored: fashion and industrial design, the propagation of established religions and of esoteric cults, opinion polls, simulation and, last but not least, tourism, which can be considered a mass medium in its own right.

Above all, however, we are not sufficiently aware of the fact that the full deployment of the mind industry still lies ahead. Up to now it has not managed to seize control of its most essential sphere, education. The industrialization of instruction, on all levels, has barely begun. While we still indulge in controversies over curricula, school systems, college and university reforms, and shortages in the teaching professions, technological systems are being perfected which will make nonsense of all the adjustments we are now considering. The language laboratory and the closed-circuit TV are only the forerunners of a fully industrialized educational system that will make use of increasingly centralized programming and of recent advances in the study of learning. In that process, education will become a mass medium, the most powerful of all, and a billion-dollar business.

Whether we realize it or not, the mind industry is growing faster than any other, not excluding armament. It has become the key industry of the twentieth century. Those who are concerned with the power game of today—political leaders, intelligence men, and revolutionaries—have very well grasped this crucial fact. Whenever an industrially developed country is occupied or liberated today, whenever there is a coup d'état, a revolution, or a counterrevolution, the crack police units, the paratroopers, the guerrilla fighters no longer descend on the main squares of the city or seize the centers of heavy industry, as in the nineteenth century, or symbolic sites such as the royal palace; instead, the new regime will take over, first of all, the radio and television stations, the telephone and telex exchanges, and the printing presses. And after having entrenched itself, it will, by and large, leave alone those who manage the public services and the manufacturing industries, at least in the beginning, while all the functionaries who run the mind industry will be immediately replaced. In such extreme situations the industry's key position becomes quite clear.

There are four conditions which are necessary to its existence; briefly, they are as follows:

1. Enlightenment, in the broadest sense, is the philosophical prerequisite of the industrialization of the mind. It cannot get under way until the rule of theocracy, and with it people's faith in revelation and inspiration, in the Holy Book or the Holy Ghost as taught by the priesthood, is broken. The mind industry presupposes independent minds, even when it is out to deprive them of their independence; this is another of its paradoxes. The last theocracy to vanish was Tibet's; ever since, the philosophical condition has been met with throughout the world.

2. Politically, the industrialization of the mind presupposes the proclamation of human rights, of equality and liberty in particular. In Europe, this threshold was passed by the French Revolution; in the Communist world, by the October Revolution; and in America, Asia, and Africa, by the wars of liberation from colonial rule. Obviously, the industry does not depend on the realization of these rights; for most people, they have never been more than a pretense or, at best, a distant promise. On the contrary, it is just the margin between fiction and reality that provides the mind industry with its theater of operations. Consciousness, both individual and social, has become a political issue only from the moment when the conviction arose in people's minds that everyone should have a say in his own destiny as well as in that of society at large. From the same moment any authority had to justify itself in the eyes of those it would govern, coercion alone would no longer do the trick; he who rules must persuade, lay claim to people's minds and change them, in an industrial age, by every industrial means at hand.

3. Economically, the mind industry cannot come of age unless a measure of primary accumulation has been achieved. A society

that cannot provide the necessary surplus capital neither needs it nor can afford it. During the first half of the nineteenth century in Western Europe, and under similar conditions in other parts of the world, which prevailed until fairly recently, peasants and workers lived at a level of bare subsistence. During this stage of economic development the fiction that the working class is able to determine the conditions of its own existence is meaningless; the proletariat is subjected by physical constraint and undisguised force. Archaic methods of manipulation, as used by the school and by the church, the law and the army, together with old customs and conventions, are quite sufficient for the ruling minority to maintain its position during the earlier stages of industrial development. As soon as the basic industries have been firmly established and the mass production of consumer goods is beginning to reach out to the majority of the population, the ruling classes will face a dilemma. More sophisticated methods of production demand a constantly rising standard of education, not only for the privileged but also for the masses. The immediate compulsion that kept the working class "in its place" will slowly decrease. Working hours are reduced, and the standard of living rises. Inevitably, people will become aware of their own situation; they can now afford the luxury of having a mind of their own. For the first time, they become conscious of themselves in more than the most primitive and hazy sense of the word. In this process, enormous human energies are released, energies that inevitably threaten the established political and economic order. Today this revolutionary process can be seen at work in a great number of emergent nations, where it has long been artificially retarded by imperialist powers; in these countries the political, if not the economic, conditions for the development of mind industries can be realized overnight.[4]

4. Given a certain level of economic development, industrialization brings with it the last condition for the rise of a mind industry: the technology on which it depends. The first industrial uses of electricity were concerned with power and not with communications: the dynamo and the electrical motor preceded the amplifying valve and the film camera. There are economic reasons for this time lag: the foundations of radio, film, recording, television, and computer technologies could not be laid before the advent of the mass production of commodities and the general availability of electrical power.

In our time the technological conditions for the industrialization of the mind exist anywhere on the planet. The same cannot be said for the political and economic prerequisites; however, it is only a matter of time until they will be met. The process is irreversible. Therefore, all criticism of the mind industry that is abolitionist in its essence is inept and beside the point, since the idea of arresting and liquidating industrialization itself (which such criticism implies) is suicidal. There is a macabre irony to any such proposal, for it is indeed no longer a technical problem for our civilization to abolish itself. However, this is hardly what conservative critics have in mind when they complain about the loss of "values," the depravity of mass civilization, and the degeneration of traditional culture by the media. The idea is, rather, to do away with all these nasty things and to survive, as an elite of happy pundits, amidst the nicer comforts offered by a country house.

Nonetheless, the workings of the mind industry have been analyzed, in part, over and over again, sometimes with great ingenuity and insight. So far as the capitalist countries are concerned, the critics have leveled their attacks mainly against the newer media and commercial advertising. Conservatives and Marxists alike have been all too ready to deplore their venal side. It is an objection that hardly touches the heart of the matter. Apart from the fact that it is perhaps no more immoral to profit from the mass production of news or symphonies than from that of soap and tires, objections of this kind overlook the very characteristics of the mind industry. Its more advanced sectors have long since ceased to sell any goods at all. With increasing technological maturity, the material substrata, paper or plastic or celluloid, tend to vanish. Only in the more old-fashioned offshoots of the business, as for example in the book trade, does the commodity aspect of the product play an important economic role. In this respect, a radio station has nothing in common with a match factory. With the disappearance of the material substratum the product becomes more and more abstract, and the industry depends less and less on selling it to its customers. If you buy a book, you pay for it in terms of its real cost of production; if you pick up a magazine, you pay only a fraction thereof; if you tune in on a radio or television program, you get it virtually free; direct advertising and political propaganda is something nobody buys. On the contrary, it is crammed down our throats. The products of the mind industry can no longer be understood in terms of a sellers' and buyers' market, or in terms of production costs: they are, as it were, priceless. The capitalist exploitation of the media is accidental and not intrinsic; to concentrate on their commercialization is to miss the point and to overlook the specific service the mind industry performs for modern societies. This service is essentially the same all over the world, no matter how the industry is operated: under state, public, or private management, within a capitalist or a socialist economy, on a profit or nonprofit basis. The mind industry's main business and concern is not to sell its product; it is to "sell" the existing order, to perpetuate the prevailing pattern of man's domination by man, no matter who runs the society and no matter by what means. Its main task is to expand and train our consciousness—in order to exploit it.

Since "immaterial exploitation" is not a familiar concept, it might be well to explain its meaning. Classical Marxism has defined very clearly the material exploitation to which the working classes have been subjected ever since the industrial revolution. In its crudest form, it is a characteristic of the period of the primary accumulation of capital. This holds true even for socialist countries, as is evident from the example of Stalinist Russia and the early stages of the development of Red China. As soon as the bases of industrialization are laid, however, it becomes clear that material exploitation alone is insufficient to guarantee the continuity of the system. When the production of goods expands beyond the most immediate needs, the old proclamations of human rights, however watered down by the rhetoric of the establishment and however eclipsed by decades of hardship, famine, crises, forced labor, and political terror, will now unfold their potential strength. It is in their very nature that, once proclaimed, they cannot be revoked. Again and again, people will try to take them at their face value and, eventually, to fight for their realization. Thus, ever since the great declarations of the eighteenth century, every rule of the few over the many, however organized, has faced the threat of revolution. Real democracy, as opposed to the formal façades of parliamentary democracy, does not exist anywhere in the world, but its ghost haunts every existing regime. Consequently, all the existing power structures must seek to obtain the consent, however passive, of their subjects. Even regimes that depend on the force of arms for their survival feel the need to justify themselves in the eyes of the world. Control of capital, of the means of production, and of the armed forces is therefore no longer enough. The self-appointed elites who run modern societies must try to control people's minds. What each of us accepts or rejects, what we think and decide is now, here as well as in Vietnam, a matter of prime political concern: it would be too dangerous to leave these matters to ourselves. Material exploitation must camouflage itself in order to survive; immaterial exploitation has become its necessary corollary. The few cannot go on accumulating wealth unless they accumulate the power to manipulate the minds of the many. To expropriate manpower they have to expropriate the brain. What is being abolished in today's affluent societies, from Moscow to Los Angeles, is not exploitation, but our awareness of it.

It takes quite a lot of effort to maintain this state of affairs. There are alternatives to it. But since all of them would inevitably overthrow the prevailing powers, an entire industry is engaged in doing away with them, eliminating possible futures and reinforcing the present pattern of domination. There are several ways to achieve this end: on the one hand we find downright censorship, bans, and a state monopoly on all the means of production of the mind industry; on the other hand, economic pressures, systematic distribution of "punishment and reward," and human engineering can do the job just as well and much more smoothly. The material pauperization of the last century is followed and replaced by the immaterial pauperization of today. Its most obvious manifestation is the decline in political options available to the citizen of the most advanced nations: a mass of political nobodies, over whose heads even collective suicide can be decreed, is opposed by an ever-decreasing number of political moguls. That this state of affairs is readily accepted and voluntarily endured by the majority is the greatest achievement of the mind industry.

To describe its effects on present-day society is not, however, to describe its essence. The emergence of the textile industry has ruined the craftsman of India and caused widespread child labor in England; but these consequences do not necessarily follow from the existence of the mechanical loom. There is no more reason to suppose that the industrialization of the human mind must produce immaterial exploitation. It would even be fair to say that it will eventually, by its own logic, do away with the very results it has today. For this is the most fundamental of all its contradictions: in order to obtain consent, you have to grant a choice, no matter how marginal and deceptive; in order to harness the faculties of the human mind, you have to develop them, no matter how narrowly and how deformed. It may be a measure of the overwhelming power of the mind industry that none of us can escape its influence. Whether we like it or not, it enlists our participation in the system as a whole. But this participation may very well veer, one day, from the passive to the active and turn out to threaten the very order it was supposed to uphold. The mind industry has a dynamic of its own that it cannot arrest, and it is not by chance but by necessity that in this movement there are currents that run contrary to its present mission of stabilizing the status quo. A corollary of its dialectical progress is that the mind industry, however closely supervised in its individual operations, is never completely controllable as a whole. There are always leaks in it, cracks in the armor; no administration will ever trust it all the way.[5]

In order to exploit people's intellectual, moral, and political faculties, you have got to develop them first. This is, as we have seen, the basic dilemma faced by today's media. When we turn our attention from the industry's consumers to its producers, the intellectuals, we find this dilemma aggravated and intensified. In terms of power, of course, there can be no question as to who runs the business. Certainly it is not the intellectuals who control the industrial establishment, but the establishment that controls them. There is precious little chance for the people who are productive to take over their means of production: this is just what the present structure is designed to prevent. However, even under present circumstances, the relationship is not without a certain ambiguity, since there is no way of running the mind industry without enlisting the services of at least a minority of men who can create somthing. To exclude them would be self-defeating. Of course, it is perfectly possible to use the whole stock of accumulated original work and have it adapted, diluted, and processed for media use; and it may be well to remember that much of what purports to be new is in fact derivative. If we examine the harmonic and melodic structure of any popular song, it will most likely turn out to employ inventions of serious composers of centuries ago. The same is true of the dramaturgical clichés of mediocre screenplays: watered down beyond recognition, they repeat traditional patterns taken from the drama and the novel of the past. In the long run, however, the parasitic use of inherited work is not sufficient to nourish the industry. However large a stock, you cannot sell out forever without replenishment; hence the need "to make it new," the media's dependence on men capable of innovation, in other words, on potential troublemakers. It is inherent in the process of creation that there is no way to predict its results. Consequently, intellectuals are, from the point of view of any power structure bent on its own perpetuation, a security risk. It takes consummate skill to "handle" them and to neutralize their subversive influence. All sorts of techniques, from the crudest to the most sophisticated, have been developed to this end: physical threat, blacklisting, moral and economic pressure on the one hand, overexposure, cooptation into star cult or power elite on the other, are the extremes of a whole gamut of manipulation. It would be worthwhile to write a manual analyzing these techniques. They have one thing in common: they offer short-term, tactical answers to a problem that, in principle, cannot be resolved. This is an industry that has to rely, as its primary source, on the very minorities with whose elimination it is entrusted: those whose aim it is to invent and produce *alternatives*. Unless it succeeds in exploiting and manipulating its producers, the mind industry cannot hope to exploit and manipulate its consumers. On the level of production, even more than on the level of consumption, it has to deal with partners who are potential enemies. Engaged in the proliferation of human consciousness, the media proliferate their own contradictions.

Criticism of the mind industry that fails to recognize its central ambiguities is either idle or dangerous. It is a measure of their limitations that many media critics never seem to reflect on their own position, just as if their work were not itself a part of what it criticizes. The truth is that, nowadays, no one can express any opinion at all without making use of the industry, or rather, without being used by it.[6]

Anyone incapable of dialectical thinking is doomed as soon as he starts grappling with this subject. He will be trapped to a point where even retreat is no longer possible. There are many who feel revolted at the thought of entering a studio or negotiating with the slick executives who run the networks. They detest, or profess to detest, the very machinery of the industry and would like to withdraw into some abode of refinement. Of course, no such refuge really exists. The seemingly exclusive is just another, slightly more expensive style within the same giant industrial combine.

Let us rather try to draw the line between intellectual integrity and defeatism. To opt out of the mind industry, to refuse any dealings with it, may well turn out to be a reactionary course. There is no hermitage left for those whose job is to speak out and to seek innovation. Retreat from the media will not even save the intellectual's precious soul from corruption. It might be a better idea to enter the dangerous game, to take and calculate our risks. Instead of innocence, we need determination. We must know very precisely the monster we are dealing with, and we must be continually on our guard to resist the overt or subtle pressures that are brought to bear on us.

The rapid development of the mind industry, its rise to a key position in modern society, has profoundly changed the role of the intellectual. He finds himself confronted with new threats and new opportunities. Whether he knows it or not, whether he likes it or not, he has become the accomplice of a huge industrial complex that depends for its survival on him, as he depends on it for his own. He must try, at any cost, to use it for his own purposes, which are incompatible with the purposes of the mind machine. What it upholds he must subvert. He may play it crooked or straight, he may win or lose the game; but he would do well to remember that there is more at stake than his own future.

Translated by the author

2

Poetry and Politics

The state decides what poets may or may not write—that is a nightmare as old as the Occident. Decency and good behavior must be observed. The gods are always good. Statesmen and officials may not be disparaged in public. Praise be to heroes, no matter what. The crimes of our rulers are not fit subjects for poetry but for committee meetings behind closed doors. Protect our youth! Therefore, there must be no portrayal of unbridled passion unless it is authorized by the state. Irony is forbidden. There must be no effeminacy. Poets, being born liars, are to be assigned to the public-relations detail. The control commission not only assigns topics; it also decrees what forms are admissible and what tone of voice is desired. The demand is for harmony at all costs; this means "good language and good harmony and grace and good rhythm"—in a word, affirmation. Nuisances will be exiled or eliminated, their works banned, censored, and mutilated.

These familiar maxims, formulated in a small Balkan state more than two thousand years ago, can be found at the root of all European discussion of poetry and politics.[1] They have since spread across the entire world. Dully, monotonously, brutally, they clang through history with the terrible regularity of a steam hammer. They do not question what poetry is, but treat it simply as an instrument to influence those held in subjugation, as something to be used at will in the interests of authority. Hence the tenacious life of these maxims, for they are tools of power—the selfsame

15

thing into which they are trying to turn poetry. For this reason they are passed from hand to hand through history, like bludgeons, fungible, easily detachable from the philosophy from which they were hewn. Not only do they serve Platonism as cudgels against Aeschylus and Homer, but they serve every political administration. Christianity, feudalism, absolute monarchy, capitalism, fascism, and communism have all adapted Plato's doctrine; even in our own day and in the freest countries not a month goes by in which poetry is not put on trial, according to the Platonic prescription, for blasphemy, licentiousness, or as a danger to the state. In fact, this trial has lasted since Plato's day, and the variety of works incriminated proves that the trial was initiated not against this or that individual poem, but against poetry as a whole. It continues to drag on from case to case, from court to court, and there is no sign that it is approaching its end. The same old speeches are exchanged between prosecution and defense, and the trial is still heard before incompetent tribunals and commissions. Self-defense prompts us to intervene in these proceedings, as a sad necessity. It is utterly tedious to refute for the thousandth time the Platonic theses that have long since fallen into decay and sunk to the level of third-rate editorials. Poetry and politics always has been and still is, especially in Germany, a disagreeable and sometimes bloody theme, clouded by resentment and servility, suspicion and bad conscience.

This gives us even less excuse to leave the matter where it is. Indeed, the time seems to have come when we can filter the poisoned ideas and guide the old questions into new channels. Self-defense is not enough. Refuting the bailiffs with their writs still does not explain the relationship between poetry and politics. It may be more to the point to question not only poetry's prosecutors and defenders, but poetry itself, which is likely to be more articulate than either. The more obscure the theme, the more transparent should be the methods of investigation. For the moment, therefore, let us content ourselves with what is simplest by looking at the surface of the matter and discussing the most obvious example: the political poem. We must first seek guidance where poetry does not immediately reject the Platonic and all subsequent simplifications, where it manifests its political nature.

Poetry, no less than political administrations, claims to be of divine origin. Both have roots in mythology. The earliest poems immortalize gods and heroes, the notion of whose immortality comes from the obscurity of the death cult. Poetry alone can procure their salvation by casting on them the light of fame, a fame invented by the Greeks. The Romans first made political profit from poetry's unique ability to immortalize what is transient. With Virgil and Horace the history of poetry as political affirmation starts in earnest; henceforth rulers seek to ensure posthumous fame for themselves so that their subjects continue to toe the line. And to this end the poet has to be subservient to them. As a result there emerges a specific genre of poetry, the so-called eulogy of the ruler, a literary institution that has persisted to our day. Strangely, though perhaps not by accident, no one has ever undertaken a thorough investigation of this phenomenon. Here we have space only for a few hints about its history. Ancient literary theory, as we know, derived from rhetoric; after the Hellenistic period the eulogy occupied a central place in it. In accordance with the practice of professional rhetoricians, the eulogy can be traced back not to mythological origins, or to the old art of the hymn, but to the public utterances of the Sophists—that is, in essence, to funeral orations and speeches in court. "It acquired political importance at the time of the Emperors. Latin and Greek eulogies of those in power were one of the sophists' main tasks. The eulogy of the ruler ($\beta\alpha\sigma\iota\lambda\iota\kappa\grave{o}\varsigma$ $\lambda\grave{o}\gamma o\varsigma$) was introduced as a separate genre at that time."[2]

This had certain consequences for poetry. By the second century A.D. Hermogenes of Tarsus, one of the most important of the didactic rhetoricians, could define the genre straightforwardly as a panegyric. The technique of the eulogy of the ruler was built into a scholastic system of recurring figures of speech that, as we shall see, can be traced right into the twentieth century. The rule books of rhetoric passed on to the Middle Ages the tradition of the eulogy of the ruler. The genre spread throughout Europe, became interwoven with feudal ideas, and endured at court almost until today. The office of poet laureate still exists in England and Sweden.

In what relation does poetry stand to politics? It is obvious that anyone asking this question will find it instructive to look at the history of the eulogy of the ruler (and at its much rarer opposite, censure of the ruler), for of all the forms this relationship may take, it is in the eulogy that it appears most explicit, concrete, and undisguised.

The maxims of Walther von der Vogelweide, the earliest political poems in the German language, are a classic example of this. In the course of barely twenty years the author served three emperors: first the Hohenstaufer Philipp, then the Guelph Otto, and finally the Hohenstaufer Friedrich II. The double switch in political loyalty seems to have caused Walther little concern: without visible strain on his conscience he is ever ready to sing the praises of the victorious prince. He never hides the fact that his homage is opportunistic; on the contrary, he openly declares the fact.

> Wie solt ich den geminnen der mir übele tuot?
> mir muoz der iemer lieber sin der mir ist guot,

he writes in the service of Friedrich[3]: "How shall I pay court to him who treats me ill? I cannot help preferring him who treats me well." Or in plain English, I shall praise the one who knows how to reward me suitably. Such frankness must not be mistaken for naiveté; tactically it is very shrewd. *"Wirf von dir miltecliche!"* (Scatter thy bounty freely!); even the crudest poetic beggary is not adequately explained by the poet's economic dependence on the ruler whose praises he sings.[4] The shamelessness of such lines, their lack of restraint, the easy conscience with which they are uttered, all the qualities in fact that we find painful or incomprehensible in them, are characteristic. Not only do they express very clearly a fundamental relationship of feudal society—that between the lord and his vassal, a mutual dependence based on give and take—but the threatening, not to say extortionary, undertone of certain verses tells us still more: the poet, despite his economic dependence, was by no means politically powerless. The prince had a fief to bestow, but the poet had fame—or the disgrace of slander, which was not to be borne lightly. The lord was quite simply dependent on the poet's praise, not out of vanity, but on political grounds, as if his overlordship needed the confirmation of poetry. However incontestable the proverb that art goes a-begging, it is inadequate to explain the age-old custom of patronage, which rulers have assumed and traditionally maintained toward the fine arts, and toward poetry in particular. This patronage certainly does not owe its existence to any special liking for poets on the part of the rulers. The Maecenas-like gesture always has about it something of the pious fraud when exercised ex officio, since the reason for it is not the overlord's appreciation of art, or his generosity, but the fact that in the last resort it protects the protector from the protégé, from the threat to his rule inherent in poetry itself. Feudal society never lost its awareness of this, as can be seen in even the most vapid eulogistic routine, and trashiest and most servile dedicatory verses. This awareness reaches its apotheosis in a great saying, coined at the end of the feudal era. Writing to his principal, a certain Friedrich Wilhelm, who had returned some memorial verses with the comment that they were as "good as poetry," Count von Gneisenau said, "The security of the thrones is founded on poetry."

The day of this security was soon to pass. The writer of the sentence was as unaware of its historic irony as was the man to whom it was addressed; it lay in the fact that when the sentence was written it was already too late. Henceforth poetry disclosed the reverse side of that power to found and secure that it had been demonstrating since the days of Virgil—that reverse side that its patrons had always mistrusted and secretly feared: instead of the power to found, the power to shatter and overthrow; instead of affirmation, criticism. This turning point manifests itself in the crisis of the eulogy of the ruler.

Goethe did not entirely abstain from writing traditional court poetry. He undertook it as an exercise. The smooth, cold, humble verses he addressed to ruling princes (to the emperor and empress of Austria, for instance) betray no emotion, unless it be secret contempt; he did not include one of them in the definitive edition of his works, the *Ausgabe letzter Hand*. They were the result of an arrangement that exempted him from all public or political obligation and were intended to insulate his own private existence from feudal society. Insofar as it was not motivated by his friendship with the young Carl August, Goethe's eulogy of the ruler is an altogether nebulous production, in which we can already sense the sovereign reservations of the posthumous works:

> Leider lässt sich noch kaum was Rechtes denken und sagen
> Das nicht grimmig den Staat, Götter und Sitten verletzt.[5]

> (Unfortunately there's scarcely a damn thing worth saying or thinking that doesn't in some way violate the state, the gods, or morality.)

In Germany the last poetically legitimate verses composed as eulogies of the ruler were written at the same time that Count von Gneisenau sought to draw the attention of his ruling prince to the political importance of poetry to the *ancien régime*. They are by Heinrich von Kleist. In his poem "*An Franz den Ersten, Kaiser von Österreich*," written in 1809, we find joined once more, and for the last time, the purest forces of the genre, which the poem transcends:

> O Herr, du trittst, der Welt ein Retter,
> Dem Mordgeist in die Bahn;
> Und wie der Sohn der duftgen Erde
> Nur sank, damit er stärker werde,
> Fällst du von neu'm ihn an!

> Das kommt aus keines Menschen Busen
> Auch aus dem deinen nicht;
> Das hat dem ewgen Licht entsprossen,
> Ein Gott dir in die Brust gegossen,
> Den uns're Not besticht.

> O sei getrost; in Klüften irgend
> Wächst dir ein Marmelstein;
> Und müsstest du im Kampf auch enden,
> So wirds ein anderer vollenden,
> Und dein der Lorbeer sein![6]

(Sire, by taking a stand against the spirit of evil, you have become the savior of the world; and, like the son of this fragrant earth of ours who fell but to grow in strength, you strike the murderer anew!

Your actions don't originate in any human breast, not even your own; they spring from eternal light, and it is a god who, moved by our need, has instilled it in your breast.

Be of good courage! Somewhere in some rocky cleft a block of marble bears your name; and even if it is your lot to fall in the fight, another will take your place and bring us victory—and the laurel crown will still be yours!)

The poet makes use in various ways of the aids and artifices that the rhetoric of the eulogy of the ruler has at hand: he names marble and laurel as the insignia of fame, he does not shun the obligatory mythological comparison (in this case with Antaeus), and he proclaims the prince, whom he addresses as a Messiah on whose appearance depends the salvation, not of a few petty European states, but of the whole world itself. To all appearances Kleist incorporates yet another figure of speech in the poem: overlordship, like poetry, owes its existence to inspiration; both have the same origin, namely God's grace. But the God Kleist refers to has nothing in common with the ancient gods. He is not named, but he is none other than the God of history. The ruler no longer appears in person at all; not one of the verses alludes to his ancestors, his life, or his personality. Who Franz I is, the poet neither knows nor cares. The ruler is no longer Caesar, whose secret resides in his person; he is simply the viceroy of history, the executor of the *Weltgeist*. When he goes, *wirds ein anderer vollenden* (another will take your place), no matter what his name or his dynasty. Kleist's poem is a finale; it both consummates and destroys the eulogy of the ruler. Twenty-five years later Georg Büchner wrote in *Der Hessische Landbote*, "The Prince is the head of the leech that crawls over you."

This is the end of the eulogy of the ruler in German literature. The remainder of the genre, which is considerable, is either farcical or obnoxious. The countless numbers who have tried to continue it during the last 150 years have done so at the expense of their authorship. Since Kleist, every poem written in homage to those in power has backfired and exposed its author to derision or contempt. One of the many victims, and probably the most naive, was Fontane who, shortly before the turn of the century, wrote his "Wo Bismarck liegen soll":

> Nicht in Dom oder Fürstengruft,
> Er ruh' in Gottes freier Luft
> Draussen auf Berg und Halde,
> Noch besser: tief im Walde;
> Widukind lädt ihn zu sich ein:
> "Ein Sachse war er, drum ist er mein,
> Im Sachsenwald soll er begraben sein."
>
> Der Leib zerfällt, der Stein zerfällt,
> Aber der Sachsenwald, der hält;
> Und kommen nach dreitausend Jahren
> Fremde hier des Weges gefahren
> Und sehen, geborgen vorm Licht der Sonnen,
> Den Waldgrund im Efeu tief eingesponnen
> Und staunen der Schönheit und jauchzen froh,
> So gebietet einer: "Lärmet nicht so!—
> Hier unten liegt Bismarck irgendwo." 7

(No cathedral, no royal vault, shall be his resting place; he shall rest in God's fresh air, in the open on a mountain, on some hillside, or better still, deep in the forest. Widukind claims him for his own: "He was a Saxon, therefore he is mine, let him be buried in the Saxon forest."

The body decays, stone decays, but the Saxon forest lives on; and if in three thousand years strangers passing this way shall see the forest glade, sheltered from the sunlight and embedded deep in ivy, and shout for joy, astonished by its beauty, a voice will command them: "Do not shout so!— somewhere beneath this spot lies Bismarck.")

The unintended humor of these verses, particularly of the *irgendwo* (somewhere) of the last line, is proof of the disastrous impossibility of the task that Fontane, in all good faith, set himself: the task of writing a modern eulogy of his ruler. Later attempts to revivify the genre have been less ingenuous. In face of these, irony is powerless; they are dreadful, and not only because they obliterate their authors as thinking people. There is no lack of examples. The following specimen earns an immediate place alongside the Hitler hymns of Gaiser, Seidel, and Carossa:

Als es geschah an jenem zweiten März,
Dass leiser, immer ferner schlug sein Herz,
Da war ein Schweigen wieder und ein Weinen,
Um Stalins Leben bangten all die Seinen.

Und als verhaucht sein letzter Atemzug,
Da hielt die Taube ein auf ihrem Flug
Und legte einen gold'nen Ölzweig nieder.
Die Völker sangen stille Lieder.

Den Namen Stalin trägt die neue Zeit.
Lenin, Stalin sind Glücksunendlichkeit.
Begleitet Stalin vor die Rote Mauer!
Erhebt Euch in der Grösse Eurer Trauer!

Seht! Über Stalins Grab die Taube kreist,
Denn Stalin: Freiheit, Stalin: Frieden heisst.
Und aller Ruhm der Welt wird Stalin heissen.
Lasst uns den Ewig-Lebenden lobpreisen.[8]

(When, on that second of March, Stalin's heartbeats grew fainter and more distant, a silence fell and there was weeping as all his people waited anxiously.

And when he had breathed his last, a passing dove, stopping in its flight, set down a golden olive branch. Meanwhile the people all sang hymns of praise to the departed.

The new era bears the name of Stalin. Lenin and Stalin stand for boundless happiness. Follow Stalin to the Red Wall! Arise in the extremity of your grief!

Look! The dove is circling Stalin's grave, for Stalin is the name of freedom, Stalin is the name for peace. And Stalin shall be the name for glory throughout the world. Let us extol him who lives eternally.)

These lines are not quoted for the disgust they are likely to arouse; for our purposes, even the author, a man named Becher, is irrelevant. The lines are of interest only as a symptom. They follow Plato's precepts exactly:

> And again, even if the deeds of Cronus, and his son's treat-ment of him, were authentic facts, it would not have been right, I should have thought, to relate them without the least reserve to young and thoughtless persons: on the contrary, it would be best to suppress them altogether. . . . Then let us not believe, any longer, or allow it to be said, that Theseus the son of Poseidon, and Peirithous the son of Zeus, went forth to commit so dire a rape; nor that any other god-sprung hero could have ventured to perpetuate such dreadful impie-ties as at the present day are falsely ascribed to them: rather let us oblige our poets to admit, either that the deeds in ques-tion were not their deeds, or else that they were not children of gods. . . . You must not forget that, with the single ex-ception of hymns to the gods and panegyrics on the good, no poetry ought to be admitted into a state.[9]

In the second place, Becher's lines obey, and in no less zealous and absurdly precise a way, the old rhetorical precepts for the pane-gyric poem; the clichés of which it consists have one and all been played out in the course of two thousand years' usage: the olive branch, the dove, eternal life, *die Völker alle.* "An enhancement of the virtues of the person to be extolled is achieved (and has been since the early Middle Ages) by announcing that everyone joins in the admiration, joy, grief. . . . One is tempted to assert that all peoples, lands, and epochs sing X's praise." The formula "the whole world praises him" became established usage. The Carolingian poets often applied it to Karl.[10] The copybook care with which Becher, presumably unawares, has transcribed third-rate hagiographers and grammarians of the Latin middle ages is bewildering. But it cannot explain the scandal that Becher's work even exists. This scandal has nothing to do with craftsmanship; the text cannot be saved by any trick or artifice, by eliminating the stupid comparisons and falsely inflated metaphors, for in-stance, or by syntactical assistance. It is not the blunders that are offensive; what offends us is the actual existence of these lines.

Why? This is a question that must be thoroughly gone into, because it is fundamental. Moreover, it is a question that hitherto has never been seriously asked or answered, probably because no critical effort is required to dispose of effusions that express this all-too-familiar fawning. They are self-condemned. One is tempted to leave it at that and save oneself the trouble of seeking a reason for this verdict. Even those who make the effort seldom go far enough. The root of the scandal does not lie where it is usually sought: it lies neither in the person of him who is praised nor him who praises.

A phenomenon such as the end of the eulogy of the ruler cannot be explained by analyzing the opinions and motives of the author, which is the method adopted everywhere during recent decades when the relationship of poetry to politics has been discussed. This method itself needs explanation. In view of the experience we have had with our literature, it is understandable that we have grown accustomed to questioning the political "reliability" or even the "respectability" of a writer; but the very terminology of such questioning shows that it threatens to infect criticism with the to-talitarian stuff of its mortal enemies.

To point to the party badges, loyal addresses, and public posi-tions of certain authors can provide data for criticism, but nothing more; it doesn't enable us to form a judgment of their work. No poem by Benn, not a single Heidegger sentence, can be refuted in this manner—which statement doesn't excuse the slightest act of barbarity. We have not made it to exonerate from criticism Hit-ler's and Stalin's spokesmen. On the contrary, our intention is first and foremost to subject them to a criticism that does not take its task too lightly. We have only to question the motives that prompted Becher, for instance, to write his hymn to Stalin to for-get all claim to critical acumen. Whether he wrote it out of stupid-ity or opportunism, voluntarily or under duress, is completely be-side the point. The same applies to the sentiments in Becher's heart: pious conviction or cynical winking, laborious self-deception or augurlike humbug—it is of equally small importance. Eulogy of the ruler and poetry are incompatible: this proposition is as true of Fontane as it is of Becher, and it is independent of the person of the author who violates it, whatever his motives or sentiments.

It is also independent of the subject of eulogy. Any explanation that concentrates on the person praised is also inadequate. Becher's lines are not disqualified by Stalin's crimes: it is enough that they are addressed to a ruler at all. Comparison with Fontane's harmless and labored production is instructive also in this respect. Poetry can no longer be addressed to any statesman, no matter what our opinion of him. Poetry addressed to Adenauer is equally unimaginable, as much a contradiction in terms as if it were addressed to Hitler, Kennedy, or de Gaulle. The phenomenon in question cannot be grasped in ideological or moral terms. It is not merely the fact that no writer of any importance has made such an attempt of his own free will that supports this conclusion. The argument can be demonstrated *ex contrario*: with the possibility of eulogizing the ruler has also gone the possibility of defaming him. Heine realized this.[11] No legitimate poetic work exists in which Hitler's name has been preserved. Even Brecht came to grief in his attempt to defame him in verse, as he also did in his poem *"Die Erziehung der Hirse,"* in which Stalin is mentioned, and in *"Kantate zu Lenins Todestag."*[12]

This failure is first and last of a political nature. It is not because of a general compulsion toward abstraction, for instance, that true poetry resists both eulogy and defamation of the ruler. Nor is it the fact that they are mentioned by name, which renders worthless all the poems on Hitler and Stalin; poetry does not reject names in general, but only the names of those exercising authority. Poems addressed to anyone else are as possible today as ever—poems to a wife, a friend, a taxi driver, a greengrocer. Many modern poems are addressed to people: Lorca lamented the bullfighter Ignacio Sanchez Mejías in an oratorio, Supervielle wrote an ode to Lautréamont, and Auden a memorial to Yeats. None of these names is rejected by the language of poetry; they are all incorporated in the text without breaking it up.[13]

What have we accomplished with these reflections? The end of the eulogy of the ruler, that is, of an extreme political element in poetry, defies all political, psychological, or sociological explanations. We are concerned with an objective fact: the language of poetry refuses its services to anyone who uses it to immortalize the names of those exercising power. The reason for this refusal lies in poetry itself, not outside it. With this conclusion we have reached a decisive stage in our discussion and we can now drop the example of the eulogy of the ruler, which we have used to pry open the surface beneath which lies the secret of what binds poetry to politics and what divorces it from it.

Our example teaches us that the political aspect of poetry must be immanent in poetry itself and cannot be derived from outside it. This completely condemns Marxist literary doctrine as it has conceived of itself up to this point. That doctrine's attempts to isolate the political content of a poetic work resemble sieges. The poem is encircled from without; the stronger the poem, the more difficult it is to force it to surrender. What are the author's class origins? How has he voted? What marks do his ideological utterances earn? Who has paid him? What public has he written for? Has he spent his life in castles or hovels? Were his friends millionaires or stevedores? What has he supported, what has he opposed? Justifiable questions, highly interesting questions, frequently neglected questions, instructive, useful questions—only they do not touch the heart of the matter, don't even want to. The literary critic who writes from the standpoint of literary sociology is blind to his subject and sees only what lies at the surface, and he betrays his opinion of the quality of the works he criticizes at once with the choice of his categories. Hence his predilection for the classics; this enables him to avoid the vexing question of the status of the work into which he is inquiring. From its beginnings, Marxist criticism has unhesitatingly accepted the judgments of the bourgeois literary canon, contenting itself with using them for its own purpose. The reverse of this "cultivation of our heritage" is disastrous uncertainty in the face of contemporary production. Marx expressed a considered opinion on only one novel of his day, a fairly trivial work by Eugène Sue called *The Secrets of Paris*.[14] The theory of realism developed by Engels starts with a discussion of a long-forgotten English penny dreadful.[15]

Only in connection with Ferdinand Lassalle's play *Franz von Sickingen* do Marx and Engels have anything to say on the subject of tragedy; they make no mention of Büchner's work, which appeared during the same decade.[16] A hundred years later Georg Lukács was to treat the literary output of his day with the same lack of discrimination: on the chessboard of his theory of realism he valiantly compares Romain Rolland and Theodore Dreiser to Proust, Joyce, Kafka, and Faulkner, without even suspecting that such a match of pawns against kings might expose the promoter to ridicule.[17] Fortunately, neither Marx nor Lukács has expressed his opinion on poetry, and we can only guess what the world has been spared. For, while orthodox literary sociology can at least enter halfway into the heart of a novel or play by way of the *pons asinorum* of its plot, poetry excludes such an approach from the outset. The only approach to poetry is via language, and this is why Lukács ignores poetry.

Such obtuseness plays into the hands of the bourgeois esthetic that would like to deny poetry any social aspect. Too often the champions of inwardness and sensibility are reactionaries. They consider politics a special subject best left to professionals and wish to detach it completely from all other human activity. They advise poetry to stick to such models as they have devised for it, in other words, to high aspirations and eternal values. The promised reward for this continence is timeless validity. Behind these high-sounding proclamations lurks a contempt for poetry no less profound than that of vulgar Marxism. For a political quarantine placed on poetry in the name of eternal values itself serves political ends. Poetry is to be made surreptitiously serviceable to these ends precisely where its social relevance is denied, as decoration, as window dressing, as a stage set representing eternity. Both sides, both Weidlé and Lukács for example, agree that poetry in essence, and especially modern poetry, is disturbing and that it does not fit into the plans of either of them because it is no one's handmaiden.

The confusion of ideas is general and almost total. In the search for enemies or allies, the diaries and letters, opinions and lives of the poets are gone over with a fine-tooth comb, and the fact that they have also been engaged in writing poetry becomes practically superfluous. The following are examples of this hopeless confusion.

Insofar as it is possible to speak of progressive literary criticism in our country, those practicing it have always regarded German romanticism as a purely reactionary movement.[18] These critics have heard that the romantics counted landed gentry and anti-Semites among them, but they remain unaware that Novalis and Brentano, those politically irresponsible sons of the German middle class, gave birth to a poetic revolution that was the beginning of modernity, a revolution without which the writings of Trakl, Brecht, Heym, and Stadler, Benn, Arp, Apollinaire, Éluard, Lorca, Neruda, Esenin, Mandelstam, Eliot, and Thomas cannot be imagined. These critics have been content to interrogate romanticism ideologically, to denounce it as a counterrevolutionary movement, and thus to deliver an indispensable and powerful element of modern tradition to nationalism and subsequently to fascism. On the other hand, they have given high progressive marks to Herwegh, Freiligrath, and Weerth, to men, that is, whose poetry was mediocre and epigonous. The results can still be seen in the handsomely bound, allegedly revolutionary lyric writing practiced in Dresden and Leipzig today.

Or take the opposite case of a German right-wing critic who mistakes for a general world condition the sluggish intellectual climate of the Federal Republic (he calls it "postrevolutionary," thereby indicating that his notion of revolution is limited to Hitlerism); in 1961 this bourgeois critic tried to claim Baudelaire and Eliot as good conservatives for his dwindling company by playing off the reactionary views of these writers against their revolutionary works. It is true that in his diary Baudelaire wrote the horrifying phrase, *"Belle conspiration à organiser pour l'extermination de la Race Juive,"* [19] but does this turn *Les Fleurs du Mal* into a collection of SS sermons? T.S. Eliot acknowledged the monarchy and the Anglican Church; does *The Waste Land* thereby become an edifying plea for a literature of the day before yesterday? Can a confining political viewpoint of the author cast the poetic revolt of these verses into chains? Since Plato's day, of course, the self-appointed ideological watchdogs have always considered viewpoints more important than the objective social content of poetry. This content can be found only in the language of poetry, the discovery of which presupposes an ear.

Under such auspices the expression "political poem" becomes suspect to the point where it is no longer of any use. Everyone imagines he knows what it means, but on closer examination we find that it is applied almost exclusively to writings serving the ends either of agitation or of the establishment. But what we have learned from the example of the eulogy of the ruler holds true in this instance too. The results can be classified under battle songs and marching songs, poster rhymes and hymns, propaganda chants and manifestoes in verse—irrespective of whose or what interests they are intended to promote. Either they are useless for the purposes of those who commission them or they have nothing to do with poetry. No national anthem written in the twentieth century is a legitimate poem; it is impossible to write such an anthem. The attempt is punishable by ridicule. If we are unwilling to admit this, we have only to compare two such attempts from the recent German past:

> *Auferstanden aus Ruinen*
> *Und der Zukunft zugewandt,*
> *Lass uns dir zum Guten dienen*
> *Deutschland, einig Vaterland.*[20]

(Risen from ruins, turned toward the future, let us serve your welfare, Germany, common Fatherland.)

This is a verse from the East German national anthem, composed by Johannes R. Becher in 1950. For the Federal Republic, on the other hand, Rudolf Alexander Schröder proposed the following lines, although in fact they were rejected by the authorities in favor of the proven and ever-topical words of Fallersleben:

> *Land der Liebe, Vaterland,*
> *Heilger Grund, auf den sich gründet,*
> *Was in Lieb und Leid verbündet*
> *Herz mit Herzen, Hand mit Hand:*
> *Frei wie wir dir angehören,*
> *Schling um uns dein Friedensband,*
> *Land der Liebe, Vaterland!*[21]

(Land of love, Fatherland! Sacred ground on which everything is founded that unites us in love and sorrow, heart to heart, hand to hand: Free as we belong to you and pledge ourselves to you, wrap your band of peace around us, land of love, Fatherland!)

Despite the ideological differences that separate the two authors, their works are interchangeable. Phrasing, prosody, and vocabulary are identical. In neither case can one really speak of a political poem, since these anthems bear no more relation to poetry than does an advertising slogan for margarine. They fulfill their political mission by lies. Contrast with them a poem by Brecht, *"Der Radwechsel"* (Changing the Wheel):

Ich sitze am Strassenhang.
Der Fahrer wechselt das Rad.
Ich bin nicht gern, wo ich herkomme.
Ich bin nicht gern, wo ich hinfahre.
Warum sehe ich den Radwechsel
Mit Ungeduld? [22]

(I sit by the roadside. The driver changes the wheel. I don't
like where I came from. I don't like where I'm going. Why
am I impatient as I watch him change the wheel?)

A political poem? The mere question shows how little is to be
gained by the use of that category. A wheel is being changed—six
lines in which neither the Fatherland nor any other regime is mentioned, six lines before which the zeal of the ideological carpers
falters. They too regard *"Der Radwechsel"* with impatience, because they cannot use the poem for their purposes. It says nothing
to them, because it says too much. It was written in the summer
of 1953. A political poem or not? This is a verbal quibble. If politics means taking part in the social conditions that men create for
themselves in history, then *"Der Radwechsel,"* like every poem
worthy of the name, is political in essence. If politics means the
use of power for the purposes of those who wield it, then Brecht's
lines, in common with poetry of any kind, have nothing to do
with it. The poem expresses in an exemplary way the fact that it
is not at the disposal of politics: this is its political content.

Which proves what? That we cannot exhaust this turbid theme
by resorting to clear-cut linear theses. Looking at the subject of
poetry and politics as a whole, and not from the view of an individual poem, we do not have much to go on that is simple. It is
necessary to insist on what there is, not because it is new but
because, being well known, it is constantly being forgotten: poetry
and politics are not "specialized fields" but historic processes, one
in the medium of speech, the other in the medium of power. Both
are integral parts of history. As sociology, literary criticism cannot
see that language constitutes the social character of poetry, and
not its entanglement in the political battle. Bourgeois literary esthetics is blind to, or else conceals, the fact that poetry is essentially social. The answers offered by the two doctrines to the question of the relationship of the poetic to the political process are

correspondingly clumsy and useless: complete dependence in one case, complete independence in the other. On the one hand is the party calendar, on the other timelessness. The real question at issue remains unexamined and indeed unasked; for what remains to be said we are forced to rely on conjectures and postulates; we have no scholarship to help us.

"Owing to inclement weather the German revolution occurred in music."[23] This bitterly sarcastic remark of Tucholsky's, urgently recommended as a motto for our political historians, reveals more than is apparent at first sight—more perhaps than its author intended. It is not only in politics that revolutions take place.

> "The overseers of the state must hold fast to . . . the principle . . . which forbids any innovation, in either gymnastics or music, upon the established order, requiring it, on the contrary, to be most strictly maintained. . . . For the introduction of a new kind of music must be shunned as imperilling the whole state; since styles of music are never disturbed without affecting the most important political institutions. . . ."
>
> "Then to all appearances," I continued, "it is here in music that our guardians should erect their guardhouse."
>
> "At any rate," said he, "it is here that lawlessness easily creeps in unawares."
>
> "Yes, in the guise of amusement, and professing to do no mischief."
>
> "No, and it does none, except that gradually gaining a lodgement, it quietly insinuates itself into manners and customs; and from these it issues in greater force, and makes its way into mutual compacts; and from compacts it goes on to attack laws and constitutions, displaying the utmost impudence, Socrates, until it ends by overturning everything, both in public and in private."[24]

No enemy of poetry has described its effects with greater insight than Plato: unpredictable effects, calculable by no one, not even by the poet, like those of a trace element or a shower of tiny spores. Plato's warnings are more perceptive than any literary scholarship to date; they relate not to manifest political opinions and content, but to the heart of the poetic process, which threatens to elude the guardians' control; its political consequences are never more dangerous than where they don't even try to serve as a guideline for poetic conduct.

Despite their barbaric ignorance, Plato's totalitarian followers have displayed a surer instinct for this connection than have the professional estheticians; their official bodies have forbidden, as a danger to the state, not only tendencies and contents but, to use Plato's language, "styles" and "modes," that is, deviations in poetic language itself. Only a few years ago, the politburo of a small Central European state rendered a poet the macabre homage of forcing him to alter the punctuation he had chosen for his writings; he was enjoined, for reasons of state, to put back the full stops and commas he had left out. We are ill-advised to laugh at this. The incident, however unimportant it may seem, brings to our attention something that, while literally true, often remains unnoticed, although it is talked about at every cultural street corner: there are conservative and revisionist, revolutionary and reactionary impulses in poetry itself. What do these words mean when applied to the poetic process? If we wish to wrest them from idle talk and instill a little precision in them, we must turn not to ideological reactions but to works, not to viewpoint but to language. Many a country squire loyal to the crown will then appear as a revolutionary, many a political Jacobin as a poetic obscurantist. It seems reasonable to suppose that the revolutionary process of poetry develops in quiet, anonymous homes rather than at congresses where booming bards announce world revolutions in the language of the poetastering birdwatcher.

If we want to gain a deeper insight into what binds poetry to politics and what divorces the two from each other, we cannot hope for proof, nor can we proceed without risk; in other words, we are dependent on speculations. In conclusion, we submit three theses concerning the development of the poetic process in history and the relationship between it and the political process:

1. Poetry must be more incorrupt than ever in insisting on its birthright against all domination. What distinguishes the poetic from the political process has been growing clearer over the last hundred years. The greater the pressure to which poetry is subjected, the clearer this difference becomes. Its political mission is to refuse any political mission and to continue to speak for everyone about things of which no one speaks—a tree, a stone, that which does not exist. This is the most difficult of missions. None is easier to forget. There is no one to demand an accounting; on the contrary, the man who betrays his mission to the interests of

those in authority is rewarded. But in poetry there are no extenuating circumstances. A poem that offers itself for sale, whether in error or from baseness, is condemned to death; there is no reprieve.

2. Authority, stripped of its mythical cloak, can no longer be reconciled with poetry. What used to be called inspiration is now called criticism, which becomes the productive restlessness of the poetic process. In the eyes of authority, which can recognize no ἀρχή other than itself, poetry is anarchistic, intolerable because not at authority's disposal, subversive in its very existence. Its mere presence is an indictment of government announcements and the scream of propaganda, of manifestos and banners. Its critical function is simply that of the child in the fairy tale. No "political engagement" is necessary to see that the emperor is wearing no clothes. It is enough that a single verse breaks the speechless howl of applause.

3. Poetry transmits the future. In the face of what is currently established, it speaks what is obvious and unrealized. Francis Ponge has said that he writes his poems as if he were writing on the day following a successful revolution. This is true of all poetry. Poetry is anticipating, even when it takes the form of doubt, rejection, or negation. It is not that it speaks of the future, but that it speaks as if a future were possible, as if free speech were possible among people not free, as if there were no alienation, no inarticulateness (since inarticulateness cannot express itself and alienation cannot communicate itself). Were it not at the same time criticism, such an anticipation would prove poetry a lie; were it not in the same breath anticipation, such criticism would be impotent. The path of poetry is narrow and menaced with dangers, its chance of success modest—no less modest, even if more distinct, than our own.

Translated by Michael Roloff

3

Commonplaces on
the Newest Literature

Josephine asserts herself, a mere nothing in voice, a mere
nothing in execution, she asserts herself and gets across to us;
it does us good to think of that. A really trained singer, if
ever such a one should be found among us, we could certainly not endure at such a time and we should unanimously
turn away from the senselessness of any such performance.
May Josephine be spared from perceiving that the mere fact
of our listening to her is proof that she is not a singer. . . .
    Josephine's road, however, must go downhill. The time will
soon come when her last squeak sounds and dies into silence.
She is a small episode in the eternal history of our people,
and the people will get over the loss of her.
                    —Franz Kafka, *Josephine the Singer,*
                                    or the Mouse Folk.

1. Pompes funèbres. So now we can hear it tolling again, the
little death knell for literature. They are carefully binding tiny tin
wreaths for it. We are snowed under by invitations to the burial.
The funeral banquets, so we hear, are exceedingly well attended:
they are a hit at the book fair. The mourners don't appear overly
downcast. Rather, a manic exuberance seems to be taking hold, a
slightly heady fury. The few oddballs off in the corner don't seriously disturb the festivities. They are making their trip on their
own, perhaps with a little tea in their pipe.
    The funeral procession leaves behind a dust cloud of theories,

little of which is new. The literati are celebrating the end of literature. The poets prove to themselves and others the impossibility of making poetry. The critics extol the definitive demise of criticism. The sculptors produce plastic coffins for their plastics. The event as a whole takes for itself the appellation "cultural revolution," but it has more the look of a country fair.

2. **Period of deliberation.** Almost everyone longs for certainty, even if it were the certainty that it is all over and done with for writing. That, too, evidently would be some kind of solace. But the relief of one group is as premature as the glee and panic of the others. Old habits die hard; inveterate poets can scarcely be reformed through vociferous cold-turkey treatments; the loudness of the saw conceals how thick the branch is on which literature sits.

Also worth contemplating: the "death of literature" itself is a literary metaphor, and scarcely of recent vintage. For at least a hundred years, say since the days of Lautréamont, the victim who has been pronounced dead has in fact found itself in a permanent state of agony, and like bourgeois society itself has known how to make its own crisis the basis of its existence. Its interment is an event without a foreseeable end, during which the deceased keeps popping up with ominous freshness in better fettle each time and more highly rouged.

The mourners stay in each other's company—that is, in the minority. As regards the masses, they have other worries. They take about as much notice of the death of literature, which has never gotten as far as the newsstand, as they did of its life. Not even the book business needs be concerned; because at seven in the morning when the deceased is having her beauty rest, the world is back in kilter.

Nonetheless, despite the dumb theses, the broken-winded intermezzi, and the monotonous bleating that accompany them, a mere shrug of the shoulder by the rest of us would be too little in face of the obsequies. For the mood on which they are based and that they cannot articulate runs deep. The symptoms of the illness cannot be simply dismissed. Not only is contemporary production hit by it, making self-doubt the dominant feature of its esthetic; but discomfort, impatience, and disgust have seized writers and readers to a degree that—at least for the Second German Republic—is new and unheard-of. Both suddenly understand what has always been the case: that literature, perhaps even more than other products, is at the mercy of the laws of the marketplace. However, since production of literature is much less easily controlled through a monopolistic administration than is the production of margarine, such an insight puts the whole enterprise into question. Deliver, consume; deliver, consume: that is the imperative of the market; when writers and readers notice that those who deliver are swallowed and those who swallow are delivered up, this leads to blockages.

It is this very elitist character of our literature that makes it susceptible to such seizures. It can only operate undisturbed as long as it is unaware of its own situation. Since literature is made by the few for the few, it takes little to disturb this equilibrium. When the brightest heads between twenty and thirty are more interested in an agitation model than an "experimental text"; when they prefer to use "factographs" over picaresque novels; when they sneer at literature, both its production and consumption—these are indeed promising signs. But they must be understood.

3. Local paper. Someone from whose lips the word *epoch* slips a little too easily and who wants to pronounce statements about literature qua literature may get his tongue caught in the process. Premature globalization usually conceals the specifics of a situation, and these are what should be clarified. A few provisional pieces of information may perhaps be gained by localizing the problem.

Since World War II, West German society has assigned a peculiar role to "cultural life" and to literature in particular. A leading journal of the postwar period was called *Die Wandlung* ["Transformation"]. The mandate of German literature after 1945 has been to demonstrate to the Germans, and even more to the outside world, such a transformation. The less thought was given to real social change, to the rearrangement of power and ownership conditions, the more indispensable became for West German society an alibi in the superstructure. Very different motives came together here in unprecedented amalgamation:

the wish to compensate, at least intellectually, for the complete bankruptcy of the German Reich;

the evidently urgent need, regardless of the great collective crime, to once again be regarded as a "cultured people";

the hunger of a state, devoid of such, for prestige of any kind;

the sufficiently well-known "idealism" that wanted to assuage its bad conscience in the face of rising mass consumption with atavistic antipathies to civilization;

a form of anti-fascism, that satisfies itself with having better taste than the Nazis and that manifested its democratic mentality by buying what the former called "degenerate": pictures on which nothing can be recognized and poems with nothing in them;

the need to be at least esthetically "with it" in the world, the wish to be classy enough to make it in world cultural circles—this objective was recently achieved with *The Tin Drum*.

There's one point these factors have in common: they have heaped exonerating and surrogate functions on a literature that of course was unequipped to cope with them. Literature was supposed to take the place of a void in the Federal Republic—the absence of a genuine political life. Thus, the restoration was opposed as though it were a literary phenomenon, that is with literary means; opposition could be repressed into the book reviews; revolutions in poetry were the substitute for the nonoccurrence of revolutions in the social structure; artistic avant-garde was to conceal political regression. And the more West German society stabilized itself, the more urgently it asked for social criticism in literature; the fewer results the writer's engagement produced, the louder the clamor for it. This mechanism secured literature an uncontested place in society; but it also led to self-deceptions that seem grotesque today.

The rise of this literature was bought with an optimism that was blind to theory, with a naive presumptuousness and an increasing incompatibility of political demand with political practice. And so there was no avoiding the inevitable hangover. When the totality of imperialism became evident, when social contradictions could no longer be covered up, when politics took to the street, the cracks began to show through the cultural façade. What had "engaged" itself for twenty years now saw itself confronted by alternatives that no longer bore the initials of the parties in Bonn. Freshly baked writers of "classics" who had become accustomed to reading their position papers in front of the TV cameras with the aplomb of ministers of health suddenly found themselves—stupefied and peeved—confronted by a public that rewarded their sermons with salvos of laughter. However, if what succumbed to its own fictions was literature, it has indeed long since ceased to suffer.

4. The old questions, the old answers. However, the dilemma in which literature, like all the arts, finds itself is deeper and older than our local obsessions. In any event, at the latest by 1968, it was realized that the dilemma cannot be solved with phrases. Kafka's story of the singer Josephine dates from 1924. Six years later André Breton wrote: "In the area about whose specific expressive possibilities you are enquiring (namely the artistic and literary production) my thinking can only oscillate between the awareness of its complete autonomy and that of its strict dependence." And he develops this contradiction with the demand for a literature that is simultaneously "conditional and unconditional, utopian and realistic, which sees its purpose only in itself and wants nothing but to serve."

The surrealists made the squaring of the circle into a program. They committed themselves unreservedly to the cause of the Communist world revolution and simultaneously maintained their intellectual sovereignty, the autonomy of their literary criteria. As the foundation of this attitude, Breton invoked the laws of "poetic determinism," laws that he felt to be as inescapable as those of dialectical materialism. In today's discussion, the same matter bears a different tag. There is talk about the "objective state of the genre" and of "artistic compulsion"—categories that bear suspicious resemblance to the "material compulsion" to which the administrators of the status quo hold fast.

The surrealists' attempt to establish themselves in their dilemma as though it were a citadel had something stubbornly heroic about it; the same cannot be said of their successors, the dispersed troops of the neo-avant-garde. The declarations of revolutionary positions that one can hear from some authors of the Tel-quel group in Paris, the Gruppo 63 in Italy, and the Noigandres-Circle in Brazil have sacrificed every connection with their literary production, which shows no structural differences from the work of other authors who avoid any form of political engagement or are openly reactionary. Evidently the "material compulsion" to which this literature feels obligated succeeds in asserting itself, despite the subjective insights, as a kind of literary meta-ideology from which there is no escaping for these authors.

This ideology avoids any social content. It is technocratic. Its concept of progress aims at means of production, not at production relationships, which is why their products remain ambiguous; and it is scarcely accidental that concepts like *indeterminacy, accident,* and *gratuitousness* play such a central role in their esthetic. The manufacturers of such a literature may be subjectively honest when they mouth the word *revolution,* but of necessity they move into the proximity of industrial technocrats like Servan-Schreiber.

A literature that thinks of itself as a mere instrument of agitation is antithetical to the technocratic avant-garde. Regis Debray, in a letter from Bolivia, pleaded with great decisiveness, if also in the tone of traditional poetic noblesse, for such a literature:

> For the fight that is being fought before our eyes and within each of us, the fight between prehistory and the wish to live in accordance with our idea of what it means to be a human being, we need works that give testimony of that: we need fragments and screams, we need the sum of all actions of which such works give us news. Only when we have them, indispensable and simple reports, songs for the march, cries for help and watchwords of the day, only then do we have the right to take pleasure in beautiful literary products.

A literature that corresponds to such demands does not exist, at least not in Europe. All attempts so far to break out of the ghetto of cultural life and "to reach the masses," for example, by means of agitprop songs and street theater, have been defeated. They proved literarily irrelevant and politically ineffective. Of course this is not a question of talent. Those who are addressed, even if they cannot give articulate account of why, see effortlessly through the bad immediacy, the helpless mental short-circuiting, the self-deception of such attempts, and sense it as a form of ingratiation. On this subject too, Breton said the necessary thing forty years ago: "I don't believe in the present possibility of a literary art that can express the endeavors of the working class. I have good reason to refuse to consider something of that kind possible. For in a prerevolutionary epoch the writers or artists are necessarily rooted in the bourgeoisie and, if only for that reason, are incapable of finding the language to express the needs of the proletariat."

5. **Omnivorous.** This, half a century after the October Revolution, needs a few additions. The Soviet Union so far lacks a revolutionary literature, too. (Mayakovsky remained an exception; the literary avant-garde of the Russian twenties primarily propagated and radicalized bourgeois poetics; the spread of the "cultural heritage" that is now indeed available to a large majority of Soviet citizens may be regarded as a socialist accomplishment, however it rests on an exclusively quantitative conception of culture that derives from old social democratic traditions and on an entirely retrospective interpretation of the slogan "art for the people." A revolutionary culture cannot be founded on such premises, as the present condition of Soviet literature shows only too clearly.)

To this day the products of the bourgeois epoch in world literature set the tone, determine the operative criteria, the existing possibilities, the usual conflicts, and the increasing contradictions. Bourgeois in origin are socialist realism and abstract poetry, literature as affirmation and literature of protest, absurd and documentary theater. Culture is the sole area in which the bourgeoisie rules uncontested, and the end of this rule is not in sight.

On the other hand, the importance of literature in the class struggle has diminished since the nineteenth century. Although it was impossible to separate them neatly, it was always possible to distinguish between two elements from the very beginning. As the ruling literature was, on the one hand, also the literature of the ruling class, it had to serve the consolidation of class rule and its camouflaging. On the other hand, it is a product of a revolution and, inasmuch as it has remained loyal to this origin, it has transgressed the limits of its mandate. Its function in the class struggle therefore was a double one from the beginning: it served mystification but also enlightenment. These functions, however, on which a criticism of literature could also orient itself decisively, have obviously been atrophying, at least since the end of World War I. Since that time imperialism has developed such mighty instruments for the industrial manipulation of consciousness that it is no longer dependent on literature. Vice versa, literature's critical function has also kept shrinking. Already in the thirties Walter Benjamin could ascertain "that the bourgeois production and publication apparatus can assimilate, even propagate, an astonishing mass of revolutionary themes without putting its own existence into serious doubt." Since then the capacity of the capitalist society to reabsorb, suck up, swallow "cultural goods" of widely varying digestibility has enormously increased. Today the political harmlessness of all literary, indeed, all artistic products, is clearly evident: the very fact that they can be defined as such neutralizes them. Their claim to be enlightening, their utopian surplus, their critical potential has shriveled to mere appearance.

Precisely analogous to this wasting away of the social content is the assimilation of their formal inventions by late capitalist society. Even the most extreme esthetic contraventions no longer meet with serious resistance. A percentage of the season ticket holders of course are against them. But sooner or later, and usually sooner, by way of detours via advertising, design, and styling the inventions become part and parcel of the consumer sphere. This means the end of an equivocation that has ruled progressive literature for fifty years: the parallelism or even equation of formal and social innovation.

A critical rhetoric that transposes the concept of revolution to esthetic categories was only possible at a time when breaking with the conventions of writing (painting, composing, etc.) could still be regarded as a challenge. This time is now over. Proclamations and manifestos announcing "revolts," "revolutions" of language, syntax, metaphor, sound hollow today. It is not by accident that they meet with well-meaning understanding from the ruling institutions and are correspondingly remunerated.

> What does it take to be a . . . *revolutionary?* From our experience with thousands of applicants we know that not everyone is suited to be an independent salesman. But we also know that there are thousands of able men who don't have the opportunity to develop themselves because of the limitations of their present income.
> The world-renowned Chase Group, one of whose by no means insignificant subsidiaries is the Securities Management

Corporation, was founded in Boston in 1932. It offers a solid, even conservative, solution for long-term investments to small as well as large investors. Scientific analysts of the first rank insure a sensible aggressiveness of capital growth.

If you are revolutionary enough to work exclusively on a commission basis and work particularly hard the first few months you will create for yourself a winning existence with a winner's income.

—job offer in a German daily,
summer 1968

6. Not responsible for personal property. I summarize: a revolutionary literature does not exist unless it be in a completely vapid sense of the word. There are objective reasons for this that writers are in no position to alter. Literary works cannot be accorded an essential social function under present conditions. From this follows that one also cannot find usable criteria for judging them. Hence, a literary criticism that could more than belch forth its personal preferences and regulate the market is not possible.

These findings appear lapidary. Therefore, one should not forget that one cannot base a wholesale judgment of contemporary literature on them. The statement that one cannot attribute a cogent social function to literature, regarded logically, makes no new certainties available to us. It denies that there are such certainties. And if that is indeed the case, it points to a risk that from now on is part of the composing of poems, stories, and dramas: the risk that such works are useless and futile, regardless of their artistic success or failure. Whoever makes literature as art isn't discredited by this; but he cannot feel justified either.

If I am right, if no verdict is possible on writing, all the revolutionary haranguing, which looks for relief from its own impotence in the liquidation of literature, won't accomplish anything either. A political movement that, instead of attacking the power of the state, tangles with aging belletrists would only manifest its own cowardice in this manner. If we have a literature that exists merely on the basis of a wild guess, if basically there is no making out whether writing still contains an element, if only the slightest, of the future, that is, if irrelevance constitutes the social essence of this kind of work, then a cultural revolution can neither be made with nor against it. Instead of shouting "Hands up!" to the producers of slim volumes, the militant groups should attack the cultural apparatuses whose social function—in contrast to that of poetry and prose—is only too clearly recognizable and without whose rule ruling has become inconceivable. However, these apparatuses aren't impotent opponents against whom the Left can turn its fear, its puritanism, and its philistinism into aggression without actually risking something.

7. Writing and reading, oyez. For writers who cannot become accustomed to their irrelevance (and how many is that?) I only have modest, even paltry, suggestions. What is evidently the most difficult job, an appropriate estimate of our significance, would presumably be to our advantage. Nothing is won if we let ourselves be consumed by doubt and intimidated by the protesters' rhythmic chants and substitute for the traditional air of importance a newly practiced gesture of humility. In a society where political illiteracy celebrates triumphs, it should not be all that difficult for people who can read and write to find limited but useful occupations. That is certainly not a new task. Börne began to work at it 150 years ago in Germany, and Rosa Luxemburg has been dead for fifty years already. What we have today, measured against these models, makes a modest impression: for example, Günther Wallraff's reports from German factories, Bahman Nirumand's book on Persia, Ulrike Meinhoff's columns, Georg Alsheimer's Vietnam report. I consider the usefulness of such works uncontestable. The discrepancy between the task they set themselves and the results they have achieved cannot be reduced to a question of talent. It is to be traced back to the production relationship of the mind industry, which the inculcators of literacy have been incapable of outplaying to date. The authors hold fast to the traditional means: the book, individual authorship, the distribution limits of the market, the separation of theoretical and practical work. A counter example is the work of Fritz Teufel.[1] Other possibilities that are less personality-bound have to be thought up and tested.

The effort to render Germany politically literate is an immense project. Like any such undertaking, it of course must begin with the achievement of literacy by the would-be inculcators of literacy. This itself is a protracted and tortuous process. Furthermore, every such enterprise depends on the principle of mutuality. Only those are suited for it who continually learn from those who learn from them. That, incidentally, is one of the most pleasant aspects of this project. The writer who lets himself get involved in this suddenly feels critical reciprocity, a feedback between reader and writer of which he could not have dreamed as a belletrist. Instead of moronic reviews that certify that he has developed promisingly from his second to third book but that his fourth has been a bitter disappointment, he now finds corrections, resistance, curses, counterproof—in a word, *consequences.* What he says and what is said to him is usable, can become practice, even mutual practice. These consequences are fragmentary and temporary. They are isolated. But there is no real reason for their remaining so. Perhaps the inculcator of literacy will one day achieve what was denied him while he sought to make art: that the utilitarian value of his work outgrows its market value.

8. **Almanac saying.** "There are no worms in the door hinges."

Translated by Michael Roloff

4

Constituents of a
Theory of the Media

> If you should think this is Utopian, then I would ask you
> to consider why it is Utopian.
>
> Brecht, *Theory of Radio*

With the development of the electronic media, the industry that shapes consciousness has become the pacesetter for the social and economic development of societies in the late industrial age. It infiltrates into all other sectors of production, takes over more and more directional and control functions, and determines the standard of the prevailing technology.

In lieu of normative definitions, here is an incomplete list of new developments that have emerged in the last twenty years: news satellites, color television, cable-relay television, cassettes, videotape, videotape recorders, videophones, stereophony, laser techniques, electrostatic reproduction processes, electronic high-speed printing, composing and learning machines, microfiches with electronic access, printing by radio, time-sharing computers, data banks. All these new forms of media are constantly forming new connections both with each other and with older media such as printing, radio, film, television, telephone, teletype, radar, and so on. They are clearly coming together to form a universal system.

1. The general contradiction between productive forces and productive relationships emerges most sharply, however, when they

46

are most advanced. By contrast, protracted structural crises, as in coal mining, can be solved merely by updating and modernizing, that is to say, essentially they can be solved within the terms of their own system, and a revolutionary strategy that relied on them would be shortsighted.

Monopoly capitalism develops the consciousness-shaping industry more quickly and more extensively than other sectors of production; it must at the same time fetter it. A socialist media theory has to work at this contradiction, demonstrate that it cannot be solved within the given productive relationships—rapidly increasing discrepancies, potential explosive forces. "Certain demands of a prognostic nature must be made" of any such theory (Benjamin).

> A "critical" inventory of the status quo is not enough. There is danger of underestimating the growing conflicts in the media field, of neutralizing them, of interpreting them merely in terms of trade unionism or liberalism, on the lines of traditional labor struggles or as the clash of special interests (program heads/executive producers, publishers/authors, monopolies/medium sized businesses, public corporations/private companies, etc.). An appreciation of this kind does not go far enough and remains bogged down in tactical arguments.

So far there is no Marxist theory of the media. There is therefore no strategy one can apply in this area. Uncertainty, alternations between fear and surrender, mark the attitude of the socialist Left to the new productive forces of the media industry. The ambivalence of this attitude merely mirrors the ambivalence of the media themselves without mastering it. It could only be overcome by releasing the emancipatory potential that is inherent in the new productive forces—a potential that capitalism must sabotage just as surely as Soviet revisionism, because it would endanger the rule of both systems.

2.   The open secret of the electronic media, the decisive political factor, which has been waiting, suppressed or crippled, for its moment to come, is their mobilizing power.

> When I say *mobilize* I mean *mobilize*. In a country that has had direct experience of fascism (and Stalinism), it is perhaps still necessary to explain, or to explain again, what that

means—namely, to make men more mobile than they are. As free as dancers, as aware as football players, as surprising as guerrillas. Anyone who thinks of the masses only as the object of politics cannot mobilize them. He wants to push them around. A parcel is not mobile; it can only be pushed to and fro. Marches, columns, parades, immobilize people. Propaganda, which does not release self-reliance but limits it, fits into the same pattern. It leads to depoliticization.

For the first time in history, the media are making possible mass participation in a social and socialized productive process, the practical means of which are in the hands of the masses themselves. Such a use of them would bring the communications media, which up to now have not deserved the name, into their own. In its present form, equipment like television or film does not serve communication but prevents it. It allows no reciprocal action between transmitter and receiver; technically speaking, it reduces feedback to the lowest point compatible with the system.

This state of affairs, however, cannot be justified technically. On the contrary. Electronic techniques recognize no contradiction in principle between transmitter and receiver. Every transistor radio is, by the nature of its construction, at the same time a potential transmitter; it can interact with other receivers by circuit reversal. The development from a mere distribution medium to a communications medium is technically not a problem. It is consciously prevented for understandable political reasons. The technical distinction between receivers and transmitters reflects the social division of labor into producers and consumers, which in the consciousness industry becomes of particular political importance. It is based, in the last analysis, on the basic contradiction between the ruling class and the ruled class—that is to say, between monopoly capital or monopolistic bureaucracy on the one hand and the dependent masses on the other.

> This structural analogy can be worked out in detail. To the programs offered by the broadcasting cartels there correspond the politics offered by a power cartel consisting of parties constituted along authoritarian lines. In both cases marginal differences in their platforms reflect a competitive relationship that, on essential questions, is nonexistent. Minimal independent activity on the part of the voter/viewer is

desired. As is the case with parliamentary elections under the two-party system, the feedback is reduced to indices. "Training in decision making" is reduced to the response to a single, three-point switching process: Program 1; Program 2; Switch off (abstention).

"Radio must be changed from a means of distribution to a means of communication. Radio would be the most wonderful means of communication imaginable in public life, a huge linked system— that is to say, it would be such if it were capable not only of transmitting but of receiving, of allowing the listener not only to hear but to speak, and did not isolate him but brought him into contact. Unrealizable in this social system, realizable in another, these proposals, which are, after all, only the natural consequences of technical development, help towards the propagation and shaping of that *other* system." [1]

3.   George Orwell's bogey of a monolithic consciousness industry derives from a view of the media that is undialectical and obsolete. The possibility of total control of such a system at a central point belongs not to the future but to the past. With the aid of systems theory, a discipline that is part of bourgeois science—using, that is to say, categories that are immanent in the system—it can be demonstrated that a linked series of communications or, to use the technical term, a switchable network, to the degree that it exceeds a certain critical size, can no longer be centrally controlled but only dealt with statistically. This basic "leakiness" of stochastic systems admittedly allows the calculation of probabilities based on sampling and extrapolations; but blanket supervision would demand a monitor bigger than the system itself. The monitoring of all telephone conversations, for instance, postulates an apparatus that would need to be n times more extensive and more complicated than that of the present telephone system. A censor's office, which carried out its work extensively, would of necessity become the largest branch of industry in its society.

But supervision on the basis of approximation can only offer inadequate instruments for the self-regulation of the whole system in accordance with the concepts of those who govern it. It postulates a high degree of internal stability. If this precarious balance is upset, then crisis measures based on statistical methods of control are useless. Interference can penetrate the leaky nexus of the media, spreading and multiplying there with the utmost speed, by resonance. The regime so threatened will in such cases, insofar as it is still capable of action, use force and adopt police or military methods.

A state of emergency is therefore the only alternative to leakage in the consciousness industry; but it cannot be maintained in the long run. Societies in the late industrial age rely on the free exchange of information; the "objective pressures" to which their controllers constantly appeal are thus turned against them. Every attempt to suppress the random factors, each diminution of the average flow and each distortion of the information structure must, in the long run, lead to an embolism.

The electronic media have not only built up the information network intensively, they have also spread it extensively. The radio wars of the fifties demonstrated that, in the realm of communications, national sovereignty is condemned to wither away. The further development of satellites will deal it the *coup de grâce*. Quarantine regulations for information, such as were promulgated by fascism and Stalinism, are only possible today at the cost of deliberate industrial regression.

> Example. The Soviet bureaucracy, that is to say the most widespread and complicated bureaucracy in the world, has to deny itself almost entirely an elementary piece of organizational equipment, the duplicating machine, because this instrument potentially makes everyone a printer. The political risk involved, the possibility of a leakage in the information network, is accepted only at the highest levels, at exposed switchpoints in political, military, and scientific areas. It is clear that Soviet society has to pay an immense price for the suppression of its own productive resources—clumsy procedures, misinformation, *faux frais*. The phenomenon incidentally has its analogue in the capitalist West, if in a diluted form. The technically most advanced electrostatic copying machine, which operates with ordinary paper—which cannot, that is to say, be supervised and is independent of suppliers—is the property of a monopoly (Xerox), on principle it is not sold but rented. The rates themselves ensure that it does not get into the wrong hands. The equipment crops up as if by magic where economic and political power are concentrated. Political control of the equipment goes hand in hand

with maximization of profits for the manufacturer. Admittedly, this control, as opposed to Soviet methods, is by no means "watertight" for the reasons indicated.

The problem of censorship thus enters a new historical stage. The struggle for the freedom of the press and freedom of ideas has, up till now, been mainly an argument within the bourgeoisie itself; for the masses, freedom to express opinions was a fiction since they were, from the beginning, barred from the means of production—above all from the press—and thus were unable to join in freedom of expression from the start. Today censorship is threatened by the productive forces of the consciousness industry which are already, to some extent, gaining the upper hand over the prevailing relations of production. Long before the latter are overthrown, the contradiction between what is possible and what actually exists will become acute.

4.   The New Left of the sixties has reduced the development of the media to a single concept—that of manipulation. This concept was originally extremely useful for heuristic purposes and has made possible a great many individual analytical investigations; but it now threatens to degenerate into a mere slogan that conceals more than it is able to illuminate, and therefore itself requires analysis.

The current theory of manipulation on the Left is essentially defensive; its effects can lead the movement into defeatism. Subjectively speaking, behind the tendency to go on the defensive lies a sense of impotence. Objectively, it corresponds to the absolutely correct view that the decisive means of production are in enemy hands. But to react to this state of affairs with moral indignation is naive. There is in general an undertone of lamentation when people speak of manipulation that points to idealistic expectations—as if the class enemy had ever stuck to the promises of fair play it occasionally utters. The liberal superstition that in political and social questions there is such a thing as pure, unmanipulated truth seems to enjoy remarkable currency among the socialist Left. It is the unspoken basic premise of the manipulation thesis.

This thesis provides no incentive to push ahead. A socialist perspective that does not go beyond attacking existing property relationships is limited. The expropriation of Springer is a desirable goal, but it would be good to know to whom the media should be handed over. The party? To judge by all experience of that solution, it is not a possible alternative. It is perhaps no accident that the Left has not yet produced an analysis of the pattern of manipulation in countries with socialist regimes.

The manipulation thesis also serves to exculpate oneself. To cast the enemy in the role of the devil is to conceal the weakness and lack of perspective in one's own agitation. If the latter leads to self-isolation instead of a mobilization of the masses, then its failure is attributed holus-bolus to the overwhelming power of the media.

The theory of repressive tolerance has also permeated discussion of the media by the Left. This concept, which was formulated by its author with the utmost care, has also, when whittled away in an undialectical manner, become a vehicle for resignation. Admittedly, when an office-equipment firm can attempt to recruit sales staff with the picture of Che Guevara and the slogan "We would have hired him," the temptation to withdraw is great. But fear of handling shit is a luxury a sewerman cannot necessarily afford.

The electronic media do away with cleanliness; they are by their nature "dirty." That is part of their productive power. In terms of structure, they are antisectarian—a further reason why the Left, insofar as it is not prepared to reexamine its traditions, has little idea what to do with them. The desire for a cleanly defined "line" and for the suppression of "deviations" is anachronistic and now serves only one's own need for security. It weakens one's own position by irrational purges, exclusions, and fragmentation, instead of strengthening it by rational discussion.

These resistances and fears are strengthened by a series of cultural factors that, for the most part, operate unconsciously, and that are to be explained by the social history of the participants in today's leftist movement—namely their bourgeois class background. It often seems as if it were precisely because of their progressive potential that the media are felt to be an immense threatening power; because for the first time they present a basic challenge to bourgeois culture and thereby to the privileges of the bourgeois intelligentsia—a challenge far more radical than any self-doubt this social group can display. In the New Left's opposition to the media, old bourgeois fears such as the fear of "the masses" seem to be reappearing along with equally old bourgeois longings for preindustrial times dressed up in progressive clothing.

> At the very beginning of the student revolt, during the Free Speech Movement at Berkeley, the computer was a favorite target for aggression. Interest in the Third World is not always free from motives based on antagonism toward civilization which has its source in conservative culture critique. During the May events in Paris the reversion to archaic forms of production was particularly characteristic. Instead of carrying out agitation among the workers with a modern offset press, the students printed their posters on the hand presses of the École des Beaux Arts. The political slogans were hand-painted; stencils would certainly have made it possible to produce them en masse, but it would have offended the creative imagination of the authors. The ability to make proper strategic use of the most advanced media was lacking. It was not the radio headquarters that were seized by the rebels, but the Odéon Theatre, steeped in tradition.

The obverse of this fear of contact with the media is the fascination they exert on left-wing movements in the great cities. On the one hand, the comrades take refuge in outdated forms of communication and esoteric arts and crafts instead of occupying themselves with the contradiction between the present constitution of the media and their revolutionary potential; on the other hand, they cannot escape from the consciousness industry's program or from its esthetic. This leads, subjectively, to a split between a puritanical view of political action and the area of private "leisure"; objectively, it leads to a split between politically active groups and subcultural groups.

In Western Europe the socialist movement mainly addresses itself to a public of converts through newspapers and journals that are exclusive in terms of language, content, and form. These news sheets presuppose a structure of party members and sympathizers and a situation, where the media are concerned, that roughly corresponds to the historical situation in 1900; they are obviously fixated on the *Iskra* model. Presumably, the people who produce them listen to the Rolling Stones, watch occupations and strikes on television, and go to the cinema to see a Western or a Godard movie; only in their capacity as producers do they make an exception, and, in their analyses, the whole media sector is reduced to the slogan of "manipulation." Every foray into this territory is regarded from the start with suspicion as a step toward integration. This suspicion is not unjustified; it can, however, also mark one's own ambivalence and insecurity. Fear of being swallowed up by the system is a sign of weakness; it presupposes that capitalism could overcome any contradiction—a conviction that can easily be refuted historically and is theoretically untenable.

If the socialist movement writes off the new productive forces of the consciousness industry and relegates work on the media to a subculture, then we have a vicious circle. For the underground may be increasingly aware of the technical and esthetic possibilities of the disc, of videotape, of the electronic camera, and so on, and systematically exploring the terrain; but it has no political viewpoint of its own and therefore mostly falls a helpless victim to commercialism. The politically active groups then point to such cases with smug maliciousness. A process of unlearning is the result and both sides are the losers. Capitalism alone benefits from the Left's antagonism to the media, as it does from the depoliticization of the counterculture.

5. Manipulation—etymologically, "handling"—means technical treatment of a given material with a particular goal in mind. When the technical intervention is of immediate social relevance, then manipulation is a political act. In the case of the media industry, that is by definition the case.

Thus, every use of the media presupposes manipulation. The most elementary processes in media production, from the choice of the medium itself to shooting, cutting, synchronization, dubbing, right up to distribution, are all operations carried out on the raw material. There is no such thing as unmanipulated writing, filming, or broadcasting. The question is therefore not whether the media are manipulated, but who manipulates them. A revolutionary plan should not require the manipulators to disappear; on the contrary, it must make everyone a manipulator.

All technical manipulations are potentially dangerous; the manipulation of the media cannot be countered, however, by old or new forms of censorship, but only by direct social control, that is to say, by the mass of the people, who will have become productive. To this end, the elimination of capitalistic property relationships is a necessary but by no means sufficient condition. There have been no historical examples up until now of the mass, self-regulating learning process that is made possible by the electronic media. The Communists' fear of releasing this potential, of the mobilizing capabilities of the media, of the interaction of free producers, is one of the main reasons why even in the socialist countries the old bourgeois culture, greatly disguised and distorted but structurally intact, continues to hold sway.

> As a historical explanation, it may be pointed out that the consciousness industry in Russia at the time of the October Revolution was extraordinarily backward; their productive capacity has grown enormously since then, but the productive relationships have been artificially preserved, often by force. Then, as now, a primitively edited press, books, and theater were the key media in the Soviet Union. The development of radio, film, and television is politically arrested. Foreign stations like the BBC, the Voice of America, and the *Deutsche Welle*, therefore, not only find listeners, but are received with almost boundless faith. Archaic media like the handwritten pamphlet and poems orally transmitted play an important role.

6. The new media are egalitarian in structure. Anyone can take part in them by a simple switching process. The programs themselves are not material things and can be reproduced at will. In this sense the electronic media are entirely different from the older media like the book or easel painting, the exclusive class character of which is obvious. Television programs for privileged groups are certainly technically conceivable—closed-circuit television—but run counter to the structure. Potentially, the new media do away with all educational privileges and thereby with the cultural monopoly of the bourgeois intelligentsia. This is one of the reasons for the intelligentsia's resentment against the new industry. As for the "spirit" that they are endeavoring to defend against "depersonalization" and "mass culture," the sooner they abandon it the better.

7. The new media are oriented toward action, not contemplation; toward the present, not tradition. Their attitude toward time is completely opposed to that of bourgeois culture, which aspires

to possession, that is to extension in time, best of all, to eternity. The media produce no objects that can be hoarded and auctioned. They do away completely with "intellectual property" and liquidate the "heritage," that is to say, the class-specific handing-on of nonmaterial capital.

That does not mean to say that they have no history or that they contribute to the loss of historical consciousness. On the contrary, they make it possible for the first time to record historical material so that it can be reproduced at will. By making this material available for present-day purposes, they make it obvious to anyone using it that the writing of history is always manipulation. But the memory they hold in readiness is not the preserve of a scholarly caste. It is social. The banked information is accessible to anyone, and this accessibility is as instantaneous as its recording. It suffices to compare the model of a private library with that of a socialized data bank to recognize the structural difference between the two systems.

8. It is wrong to regard media equipment as mere means of consumption. It is always, in principle, also means of production and, indeed, since it is in the hands of the masses, socialized means of production. The contradiction between producers and consumers is not inherent in the electronic media; on the contrary, it has to be artificially reinforced by economic and administrative measures.

An early example of this is provided by the difference between telegraph and telephone. Whereas the former, to this day, has remained in the hands of a bureaucratic institution that can scan and file every text transmitted, the telephone is directly accessible to all users. With the aid of conference circuits, it can even make possible collective intervention in a discussion by physically remote groups.

On the other hand, those auditory and visual means of communication that rely on "wireless" are still subject to state control (legislation on wireless installations). In the face of technical developments, which long ago made local and international radio-telephony possible, and which constantly opened up new wave bands for television—in the UHF band alone, the dissemination of numerous programs in one locality is possible without interference, not to mention the possibilities offered by wired and satellite television—the prevailing laws for control of the air are anachronistic. They recall the time when the operation of a printing press was dependent on an imperial license. The socialist movements will take up the struggle for their own wavelengths and must, within the foreseeable future, build their own transmitters and relay stations.

9.   One immediate consequence of the structural nature of the new media is that none of the regimes at present in power can release their potential. Only a free socialist society will be able to make them fully productive. A further characteristic of the most advanced media—probably the decisive one—confirms this thesis: their collective structure.

For the prospect that in the future, with the aid of the media, anyone can become a producer, would remain apolitical and limited were this productive effort to find an outlet in individual tinkering. Work on the media is possible for an individual only insofar as it remains socially and therefore esthetically irrelevant. The collection of transparencies from the last holiday trip provides a model of this.

That is naturally what the prevailing market mechanisms have aimed at. It has long been clear from apparatus like miniature and 8-mm. movie cameras, as well as the tape recorder, which are in actual fact already in the hands of the masses, that the individual, so long as he remains isolated, can become with their help at best an amateur but not a producer. Even so potent a means of production as the shortwave transmitter has been tamed in this way and reduced to a harmless and inconsequential hobby in the hands of scattered radio hams. The programs that the isolated amateur mounts are always only bad, outdated copies of what he in any case receives.

> Private production for the media is no more than licensed cottage industry. Even when it is made public it remains pure compromise. To this end, the men who own the media have developed special programs that are usually called "Democratic Forum" or something of the kind. There, tucked away in the corner, "the reader (listener, viewer) has his say," which can naturally be cut short at any time. As in the case of public-opinion polling, he is only asked questions so that he may

have a chance to confirm his own dependence. It is a control circuit where what is fed in has already made complete allowance for the feedback.

The concept of a license can also be used in another sense—in an economic one: the system attempts to make each participant into a concessionaire of the monopoly that develops his films or plays back his cassettes. The aim is to nip in the bud in this way that independence that video equipment, for instance, makes possible. Naturally, such tendencies go against the grain of the structure, and the new productive forces not only permit but indeed demand their reversal.

The poor, feeble, and frequently humiliating results of this licensed activity are often referred to with contempt by the professional media producers. On top of the damage suffered by the masses comes triumphant mockery because they clearly do not know how to use the media properly. The sort of thing that goes on in certain popular television shows is taken as proof that they are completely incapable of articulating on their own.

Not only does this run counter to the results of the latest psychological and pedagogical research, but it can easily be seen to be a reactionary protective formulation; the "gifted" people are quite simply defending their territories. Here we have a cultural analogue to the familiar political judgments concerning a working class that is presumed to be "stultified" and incapable of any kind of self-determination. Curiously, one may hear the view that the masses could never govern themselves out of the mouths of people who consider themselves socialists. In the best of cases, these are economists who cannot conceive of socialism as anything other than nationalization.

10. Any socialist strategy for the media must, on the contrary, strive to end the isolation of the individual participants from the social learning and production process. This is impossible unless those concerned organize themselves. This is the political core of the question of the media. It is over this point that socialist concepts part company with the neoliberal and technocratic ones. Anyone who expects to be emancipated by technological hardware, or by a system of hardware however structured, is the victim of an obscure belief in progress. Anyone who imagines that freedom for the media will be established if only everyone is busy transmitting and receiving is the dupe of a liberalism that, decked

out in contemporary colors, merely peddles the faded concepts of a preordained harmony of social interests.

In the face of such illusions, what must be firmly held on to is that the proper use of the media demands organization and makes it possible. Every production that deals with the interests of the producers postulates a collective method of production. It is itself already a form of self-organization of social needs. Tape recorders, ordinary cameras, and movie cameras are already extensively owned by wage earners. The question is why these means of production do not turn up at factories, in schools, in the offices of the bureaucracy, in short, everywhere where there is social conflict. By producing aggressive forms of publicity that were their own, the masses could secure evidence of their daily experiences and draw effective lessons from them.

Naturally, bourgeois society defends itself against such prospects with a battery of legal measures. It bases itself on the law of trespass, on commercial and official secrecy. While its secret services penetrate everywhere and plug in to the most intimate conversations, it pleads a touching concern for confidentiality and makes a sensitive display of worrying about the question of privacy when all that is private is the interest of the exploiters. Only a collective, organized effort can tear down these paper walls.

Communication networks that are constructed for such purposes can, over and above their primary function, provide politically interesting organizational models. In the socialist movements the dialectic of discipline and spontaneity, centralism and decentralization, authoritarian leadership and antiauthoritarian disintegration has long ago reached deadlock. Networklike communications models built on the principle of reversibility of circuits might give indications of how to overcome this situation: a mass newspaper, written and distributed by its readers, a video network of politically active groups.

More radically than any good intention, more lastingly than existential flight from one's own class, the media, once they have come into their own, destroy the private production methods of bourgeois intellectuals. Only in productive work and learning processes can their individualism be broken down in such a way that it is transformed from morally based (that is to say, as individual as ever) self-sacrifice to a new kind of political self-understanding and behavior.

11. An all-too-widely-disseminated thesis maintains that present-day capitalism lives by the exploitation of unreal needs. That is at best a half-truth. The results obtained by popular American sociologists such as Vance Packard are not unuseful but limited. What they have to say about the stimulation of needs through advertising and artificial obsolescence can in any case not be adequately explained by the hypnotic pull exerted on the wage earners by mass consumption. The hypothesis of "consumer terror" corresponds to the prejudices of a middle class, which considers itself politically enlightened, against the allegedly integrated proletariat, which has become petty bourgeois and corrupt. The attractive power of mass consumption is based not on the dictates of false needs, but on the falsification and exploitation of quite real and legitimate ones without which the parasitic process of advertising would be ineffective. A socialist movement ought not to denounce these needs, but take them seriously, investigate them, and make them politically productive.

That is also valid for the consciousness industry. The electronic media do not owe their irresistible power to any sleight-of-hand but to the elemental power of deep social needs that come through even in the present depraved form of these media.

Precisely because no one bothers about them, the interests of the masses have remained a relatively unknown field, at least insofar as they are historically new. They certainly extend far beyond those goals that the traditional working class movement represented. Just as in the field of production, the industry that produces goods and the consciousness industry merge more and more, so too, subjectively, where needs are concerned, material and nonmaterial factors are closely interwoven. In the process old psychosocial themes are firmly embedded—social prestige, identification patterns—but powerful new themes emerge that are utopian in nature. From a materialistic point of view, neither the one nor the other must be suppressed.

Henri Lefèbvre has proposed the concept of the *spectacle*—the exhibition, the show—to fit the present form of mass consumption. Goods and shop windows, traffic and advertisements, stores and the world of communications, news and packaging, architecture and media production come together to form a totality, a permanent theater, which dominates not only the public city centers but also private interiors. The expression "beautiful living" makes the most commonplace objects of general use into props for this universal festival, in which the fetishistic nature of the commodities triumphs completely over their use value. The swindle these festivals perpetrate is, and remains, a swindle within the present social structure. But it is the harbinger of something else. Consumption as spectacle contains the promise that want will disappear. The deceptive, brutal, and obscene features of this festival derive from the fact that there can be no question of a real fulfillment of its promise. But so long as scarcity holds sway, use value remains a decisive category that can only be abolished by trickery. Yet trickery on such a scale is only conceivable if it is based on mass need. This need—it is a utopian one—is there. It is the desire for a new ecology, for a breaking down of environmental barriers, for an esthetic not limited to the sphere of "the artistic." These desires are not—or are not primarily—internalized rules of the game as played by the capitalist system. They have physiological roots and can no longer be suppressed. Consumption as spectacle is—in parody form—the anticipation of a utopian situation.

The promises of the media demonstrate the same ambivalence. They are an answer to the mass need for nonmaterial variety and mobility—which at present finds its material realization in private-car ownership and tourism—and they exploit it. Other collective wishes, which capitalism often recognizes more quickly and evaluates more correctly than its opponents, but naturally only so as to trap them and rob them of their explosive force, are just as powerful, just as unequivocally emancipatory: the need to take part in the social process on a local, national, and international scale; the need for new forms of interaction, for release from ignorance and tutelage; the need for self-determination. "Be everywhere!" is one of the most successful slogans of the media industry. The readers' parliament of *Bild-Zeitung* * was direct democracy used against the interests of the *demos*. "Open spaces" and "free time" are concepts that corral and neutralize the urgent wishes of the masses.

> There is corresponding acceptance by the media of utopian
> stories: e.g., the story of the young Italo-American who hi-

* The Springer Verlag tabloid.

62 · *Hans Magnus Enzensberger*

jacked a passenger plane to get home from California to Rome
was taken up without protest even by the reactionary mass
press and undoubtedly correctly understood by its readers.
The identification is based on what has become a general need.
Nobody can understand why such journeys should be reserved for politicians, functionaries, and businessmen. The role
of the pop star could be analyzed from a similar angle; in it
the authoritarian and emancipatory factors are mingled in an
extraordinary way. It is perhaps not unimportant that beat
music offers groups, not individuals, as identification models.
In the productions of the Rolling Stones (and in the manner
of their production) the utopian content is apparent. Events
like the Woodstock Festival, the concerts in Hyde Park, on
the Isle of Wight, and at Altamont, California, develop a mobilizing power that the political Left can only envy.

It is absolutely clear that, within the present social forms, the
consciousness industry can satisfy none of the needs on which it
lives and which it must fan, except in the illusory form of games.
The point, however, is not to demolish its promises but to take
them literally and to show that they can be met only through a
cultural revolution. Socialists and socialist regimes which multiply
the frustration of the masses by declaring their needs to be false,
become the accomplices of the system they have undertaken to
fight.

12. Summary.

Repressive use of media	Emancipatory use of media
Centrally controlled program	Decentralized program
One transmitter, many receivers	Each receiver a potential transmitter
Immobilization of isolated individuals	Mobilization of the masses
Passive consumer behavior	Interaction of those involved, feedback
Depoliticization	A political learning process
Production by specialists	Collective production
Control by property owners or bureaucracy	Social control by self-organization

13. As far as the objectively subversive potentialities of the
electronic media are concerned, both sides in the international class

struggle—except for the fatalistic adherents of the thesis of manipulation in the metropoles—are of one mind. Frantz Fanon was the
first to draw attention to the fact that the transistor receiver was
one of the most important weapons in the Third World's fight for
freedom. Albert Hertzog, ex-Minister of the South African Republic and the mouthpiece of the right wing of the ruling party, is of
the opinion that "television will lead to the ruin of the white man
in South Africa."[2] American imperialism has recognized the situation. It attempts to meet the "revolution of rising expectations"
in Latin America—that is what its ideologues call it—by scattering
its own transmitters all over the continent and into the remotest
regions of the Amazon basin, and by distributing single-frequency
transistors to the native population. The attacks of the Nixon administration on the capitalist media in the United States reveal its
understanding that their reporting, however one-sided and distorted, had become a decisive factor in mobilizing people against
the war in Vietnam. Whereas only twenty-five years ago the French
massacres in Madagascar, with almost one hundred thousand dead,
became known only to the readers of *Le Monde* under the heading
of "Other News" and therefore remained unnoticed and without
follow-up in the capital city, today the media drag colonial wars
into the centers of imperialism.

The direct mobilizing potentialities of the media become still
clearer when they are consciously used for subversive ends. Their
presence is a factor that immensely increases the demonstrative
nature of any political act. The student movements in the United
States, in Japan, and in Western Europe soon recognized this and,
to begin with, achieved considerable momentary success with the
aid of the media. These effects have worn off. Naive trust in the
magical power of reproduction cannot replace organizational work;
only active and coherent groups can force the media to comply
with the logic of their actions. That can be demonstrated from the
example of the Tupamaros in Uruguay, whose revolutionary practice has implicit in it publicity for their actions. Thus the actors
become authors. The abduction of the American ambassador in
Rio de Janeiro was planned with a view to its impact on the media. It was a television production. The Arab guerrillas proceed in
the same way. The first to experiment with these techniques inter-
nationally were the Cubans. Fidel appreciated the revolutionary

potential of the media correctly from the first (Moncada, 1953). Today, illegal political action demands at one and the same time maximum secrecy and maximum publicity.

14. Revolutionary situations always bring with them discontinuous, spontaneous changes brought about by the masses in the existing aggregate of the media. How far the changes thus brought about take root and how permanent they are demonstrates the extent to which a cultural revolution is successful. The situation in the media is the most accurate and sensitive barometer for the rise of bureaucratic or Bonapartist anticyclones. So long as the cultural revolution has the initiative, the social imagination of the masses overcomes even technical backwardness and transforms the function of the old media so that their structures are exploded.

> With our work the Revolution has achieved a colossal labor of propaganda and enlightenment. We ripped up the traditional book into single pages, magnified these a hundred times, printed them in color and stuck them up as posters in the streets. . . . Our lack of printing equipment and the necessity for speed meant that, though the best work was hand-printed, the most rewarding was standardized, lapidary and adapted to the simplest mechanical form of reproduction. Thus State Decrees were printed as rolled-up illustrated leaflets, and Army Orders as illustrated pamphlets.[3]

In the twenties, the Russian film reached a standard that was far in advance of the available productive forces. Pudovkin's *Kinoglas* and Dziga Vertov's *Kinopravda* were no "newsreels" but political television-magazine programs *avant l'écran*. The campaign against illiteracy in Cuba broke through the linear, exclusive, and isolating structure of the medium of the book. In the China of the Cultural Revolution, wall newspapers functioned like an electronic mass medium—at least in the big towns. The resistance of the Czechoslovak population to the Soviet invasion gave rise to spontaneous productivity on the part of the masses, who ignored the institutional barriers of the media. (To be developed in detail.) Such situations are exceptional. It is precisely their utopian nature, which reaches out beyond the existing productive forces (it follows that the productive relationships are not to be permanently overthrown), that makes them precarious, leads to reversals and defeats. They demonstrate all the more clearly what enormous political and cultural energies are hidden in the enchained masses and with what imagination they are able, at the moment of liberation, to realize all the opportunities offered by the new media.

15.   That the Marxist Left should argue theoretically and act practically from the standpoint of the most advanced productive forces in their society, that they should develop in depth all the liberating factors immanent in these forces and use them strategically, is no academic expectation but a political necessity. However, with a single great exception, that of Walter Benjamin (and in his footsteps, Brecht), Marxists have not understood the consciousness industry and have been aware only of its bourgeois-capitalist dark side and not of its socialist possibilities. An author such as Georg Lukács is a perfect example of this theoretical and practical backwardness. Nor are the works of Horkheimer and Adorno free of a nostalgia that clings to early bourgeois media.

> Their view of the cultural industry cannot be discussed here. Much more typical of Marxism between the two wars is the position of Lukács, which can be seen very clearly from an early essay on "Old Culture and New Culture."[4] "Anything that culture produces" can, according to Lukács, "have real cultural value only *if it is in itself* valuable, if the creation of each individual product is from the standpoint of its maker a single, finite process. It must, moreover, be a process conditioned by the *human* potentialities and capabilities of the creator. The most typical example of such a process is the work of art, where the entire genesis of the work is exclusively the result of the artist's labor and each detail of the work that emerges is determined by the individual qualities of the artist. In highly developed mechanical industry, on the other hand, any connection between the product and the creator is abolished. *The human being serves the machine, he adapts to it.* Production becomes completely independent of the human potentialities and capabilities of the worker." These "forces which destroy culture" impair the work's "truth to the material," its "level," and deal the final blow to the "work as an end in itself." There is no more question of "the organic unity of the products of culture, its harmonious, joy-giving being." Capitalist culture must lack "the simple and natural

harmony and beauty of the old culture—culture in the true,
literal sense of the word." Fortunately things need not remain
so. The "culture of proletarian society," although "in the
context of such scientific research as is possible at this time"
nothing more can be said about it, will certainly remedy these
ills. Lukács asks himself "which are the cultural values which,
in accordance with the nature of this context, *can be taken
over from the old society* by the new *and further developed.*"
Answer: Not the inhuman machines but "the idea of mankind as an end in itself, the basic idea of the new culture,"
for it is "the inheritance of the classical idealism of the nineteenth century." Quite right. "This is where the philistine
concept of *art* turns up with all its deadly obtuseness—an
idea to which all technical considerations are foreign and
which feels that with the provocative appearance of the new
technology its end has come."[5]

These nostalgic backward glances at the landscape of the
last century, these reactionary ideals, are already the forerunners of socialist realism, which mercilessly galvanized and then
buried those very "cultural values" that Lukács rode out to
rescue. Unfortunately, in the process, the Soviet cultural revolution was thrown to the wolves; but this esthete can in any
case hardly have thought any more highly of it than did J. V.
Stalin.

The inadequate understanding Marxists have shown of the media and the questionable use they have made of them has produced a vacuum in Western industrialized countries into which a
stream of non-Marxist hypotheses and practices has consequently
flowed. From the Cabaret Voltaire of the Dadaists to Andy Warhol's Factory, from the silent film comedians to the Beatles, from
the first comic-strip artists to the present managers of the underground, the apolitical have made much more radical progress in
dealing with the media than any grouping of the Left (exception:
Münzenberg). Innocents have put themselves in the forefront of
the new productive forces on the basis of mere intuitions with
which communism—to its detriment—has not wished to concern
itself. Today this apolitical avant-garde has found its ventriloquist
and prophet in Marshall McLuhan, an author who admittedly lacks
any analytical categories for the understanding of social processes,
but whose confused books serve as a quarry of undigested observations for the media industry. Certainly his little finger has experienced more of the productive power of the new media than all

the ideological commissions of the CPSU and their endless resolutions and directives put together.

Incapable of any theoretical construction, McLuhan does not present his material as a concept but as the common denominator of a reactionary doctrine of salvation. He admittedly did not invent but was the first to formulate explicitly a mystique of the media that dissolves all political problems in smoke—the same smoke that gets in the eyes of his followers. It promises the salvation of man through the technology of television and indeed of television as it is practiced today. Now McLuhan's attempt to stand Marx on his head is not exactly new. He shares with his numerous predecessors the determination to suppress all problems of the economic base, their idealistic tendencies, and their belittling of the class struggle in the naive terms of a vague humanism. A new Rousseau—like all copies, only a pale version of the old—he preaches the gospel of the new primitive man who, naturally on a higher level, must return to prehistoric tribal existence in the "global village."

It is scarcely worthwhile to deal with such concepts. This charlatan's most famous saying—"the medium is the message"—perhaps deserves more attention. In spite of its provocative idiocy, it betrays more than its author knows. It reveals in the most accurate way the tautological nature of the mystique of the media. The one remarkable thing about the television set, according to him, is that it moves—a thesis that in view of the nature of American programs has, admittedly, something attractive about it.

> The complementary mistake consists in the widespread illusion that media are neutral instruments by which any "messages" one pleases can be transmitted without regard for their structure or for the structure of the medium. In the East European countries the television newsreaders read fifteen-minute-long conference communiques and Central Committee resolutions that are not even suitable for printing in a newspaper, clearly under the delusion that they might fascinate a public of millions.

The sentence "the medium is the message" transmits yet another message, however, and a much more important one. It tells us that the bourgeoisie does indeed have all possible means at its disposal to communicate something to us, but that it has nothing more to say. It is ideologically sterile. Its intention to hold on to the control of the means of production at any price, while being incapable of making the socially necessary use of them, is here expressed with complete frankness in the superstructure. It wants the media *as such* and *to no purpose.*

This wish has been shared for decades and given symbolic expression by an artistic avant-garde whose program logically admits only the alternative of negative signals and amorphous noise. Example: the already outdated "literature of silence," Warhol's films in which everything can happen at once or nothing at all, and John Cage's forty-five-minute-long *Lecture on Nothing* (1959).

16. The revolution in the conditions of production in the superstructure has made the traditional esthetic theory unusable, completely unhinging its fundamental categories and destroying its "standards." The theory of knowledge on which it was based is outmoded. In the electronic media, a radically altered relationship between subject and object emerges with which the old critical concepts cannot deal. The idea of the self-sufficient work of art collapsed long ago. The long-drawn discussion over the death of art proceeds in a circle so long as it does not examine critically the esthetic concept on which it is based, so long as it employs criteria that no longer correspond to the state of the productive forces. When constructing an esthetic adapted to the changed situation, one must take as a starting point the work of the only Marxist theoretician who recognized the liberating potential of the new media. Thirty-five years ago, that is to say, at a time when the consciousness industry was relatively undeveloped, Walter Benjamin subjected this phenomenon to a penetrating dialectical-materialist analysis. His approach has not been matched by any theory since then, much less further developed.

> One might generalize by saying: the technique of reproduction detaches the reproduced object from the domain of tradition. By making many reproductions it substitutes a plurality of copies for a unique existence and in permitting the reproduction to meet the beholder or listener in his own particular situation, it reactivates the object reproduced. These two processes lead to a tremendous shattering of tradition

which is the obverse of the contemporary crisis and renewal of mankind. Both processes are intimately connected with the contemporary mass movements. Their most powerful agent is the film. Its social significance, particularly in its most positive form, is inconceivable without its destructive, cathartic aspect, that is, the liquidation of the traditional value of the cultural heritage.

For the first time in world history, mechanical reproduction emancipates the work of art from its parasitical dependence on ritual. To an ever greater degree the work of art reproduced becomes the work of art designed for reproducibility. . . . But the instant the criterion of authenticity ceases to be applicable to artistic production, the total function of art is reversed. Instead of being based on ritual, it begins to be based on another practice—politics. . . . Today, by the absolute emphasis on its exhibition value, the work of art becomes a creation with entirely new functions, among which the one we are conscious of, the artistic function, later may be recognized as incidental.[6]

The trends that Benjamin recognized in his day in the film, and the true import of which he grasped theoretically, have become patent today with the rapid development of the consciousness industry. What used to be called art has now, in the strict Hegelian sense, been dialectically surpassed by and in the media. The quarrel about the end of art is otiose so long as this end is not understood dialectically. Artistic productivity reveals itself to be the extreme marginal case of a much more widespread productivity, and it is socially important only insofar as it surrenders all pretensions to autonomy and recognizes itself to be a marginal case. Wherever the professional producers make a virtue out of the necessity of their specialist skills and even derive a privileged status from them, their experience and knowledge have become useless. This means that as far as an esthetic theory is concerned, a radical change in perspectives is needed. Instead of looking at the productions of the new media from the point of view of the older modes of production we must, on the contrary, analyze the products of the traditional "artistic" media from the standpoint of modern conditions of production.

Earlier much futile thought had been devoted to the question of whether photography is an art. The primary question—

whether the very invention of photography had not transformed the entire nature of art—was not raised. Soon the film theoreticians asked the same ill-considered question with regard to the film. But the difficulties which photography caused traditional esthetics were mere child's play as compared to those raised by the film.[7]

The panic aroused by such a shift in perspectives is understandable. The process not only changes the old, carefully guarded craft secrets in the superstructure into white elephants, it also conceals a genuinely destructive element. It is, in a word, risky. But the only chance for the esthetic tradition lies in its dialectical supersession. In the same way, classical physics has survived as a marginal special case within the framework of a much more comprehensive theory.

This state of affairs can be identified in individual cases in all the traditional artistic disciplines. Their present-day developments remain incomprehensible so long as one attempts to deduce them from their own prehistory. On the other hand, their usefulness or uselessness can be judged as soon as one regards them as special cases in a general esthetic of the media. Some indications of the possible critical approaches that stem from this will be made below, taking literature as an example.

17.   Written literature has, historically speaking, played a dominant role for only a few centuries. Even today, the predominance of the book has an episodic air. An incomparably longer time preceded it in which literature was oral. Now it is being succeeded by the age of the electronic media, which tend once more to make people speak. At its period of fullest development, the book to some extent usurped the place of the more primitive but generally more accessible methods of production of the past; on the other hand, it was a stand-in for future methods that make it possible for everyone to become a producer.

The revolutionary role of the printed book has been described often enough and it would be absurd to deny it. From the point of view of its structure as a medium, written literature, like the bourgeoisie who produced it and whom it served, was progressive (see the *Communist Manifesto*). On the analogy of the economic development of capitalism, which was indispensable for the development of the industrial revolution, the nonmaterial productive forces could not have developed without their own capital accumulation. (We also owe the accumulation of *Das Kapital* and its teachings to the medium of the book.)

Nevertheless, almost everybody speaks better than he writes. (This also applies to authors.) Writing is a highly formalized technique that, in purely physiological terms, demands a peculiarly rigid bodily posture. To this there corresponds the high degree of social specialization that it demands. Professional writers have always tended to think in caste terms. The class character of their work is unquestionable, even in the age of universal compulsory education. The whole process is extraordinarily beset with taboos. Spelling mistakes, which are completely immaterial in terms of communication, are punished by the social disqualification of the writer. The rules that govern this technique have a normative power attributed to them for which there is no rational basis. Intimidation through the written word has remained a widespread and class-specific phenomenon even in advanced industrial societies.

These alienating factors cannot be eradicated from written literature. They are reinforced by the methods by which society transmits its writing techniques. While people learn to speak very early, and mostly in psychologically favorable conditions, learning to write forms an important part of authoritarian socialization by the school ("good writing" as a kind of breaking-in). This sets its stamp forever on written communication—on its tone, its syntax, and its whole style. (This also applies to the text on this page.)

The formalization of written language permits and encourages the repression of opposition. In speech, unresolved contradictions betray themselves by pauses, hesitations, slips of the tongue, repetitions, anacoluthons, quite apart from phrasing, mimicry, gesticulation, pace, and volume. The esthetic of written literature scorns such involuntary factors as "mistakes." It demands, explicitly or implicitly, the smoothing out of contradictions, rationalization, regularization of the spoken form irrespective of content. Even as a child, the writer is urged to hide his unsolved problems behind a protective screen of correctness.

Structurally, the printed book is a medium that operates as a monologue, isolating producer and reader. Feedback and interaction are extremely limited, demand elaborate procedures, and only in the rarest cases lead to corrections. Once an edition has been printed it cannot be corrected; at best it can be pulped. The control circuit in the case of literary criticism is extremely cumbersome and elitist. It excludes the public on principle.

None of the characteristics that distinguish written and printed literature apply to the electronic media. Microphone and camera abolish the class character of the mode of production (not of the production itself). The normative rules become unimportant. Oral interviews, arguments, demonstrations, neither demand nor allow orthography or "good writing." The television screen exposes the esthetic smoothing-out of contradictions as camouflage. Admittedly, swarms of liars appear on it; but anyone can see from a long way off that they are peddling something. As at present constituted, radio, film, and television are burdened to excess with authoritarian characteristics, the characteristics of the monologue, which they have inherited from older methods of production—and that is no accident. These outworn elements in today's media esthetics are demanded by the social relations. They do not follow from the structure of the media. On the contrary, they go against it, for the structure demands interaction.

It is extremely improbable, however, that writing as a special technique will disappear in the foreseeable future. That goes for the book as well, the practical advantages of which for many purposes remain obvious. It is admittedly less handy and takes up more room than other storage systems, but up to now it offers simpler methods of access than, for example, the microfilm or the tape bank. It ought to be integrated into the system as a marginal case and thereby forfeit its aura of cult and ritual.

> This can be deduced from technological developments. Electronics are noticeably taking over writing: teleprinters, reading machines, high-speed transmissions, automatic photographic and electronic composition, automatic writing devices, typesetters, electrostatic processes, ampex libraries, cassette encyclopedias, photocopiers and magnetic copiers, speedprinters.
>
> The outstanding Russian media expert El Lissitsky, incidentally, demanded an "electro-library" as far back as 1923—a request that, given the technical conditions of the time, must have seemed ridiculous or at least incomprehensible. This is how far this man's imagination reached into the future:

"I draw the following analogy:

Inventions in the Field of Verbal Traffic	*Inventions in the Field of General Traffic*
Articulated language	Upright gait
Writing	The wheel
Gutenberg's printing press	Carts drawn by animal power
?	The automobile
?	The airplane

"I have produced this analogy to prove that so long as the book remains a palpable object, i.e. so long as it is not replaced by auto-vocalizing and kino-vocalizing representations, we must look to the field of the manufacture of books for basic innovations in the near future.

"There are signs at hand suggesting that this basic innovation is likely to come from the neighborhood of the collotype."[8]

Today, writing has in many cases already become a secondary technique, a means of transcribing orally recorded speech: tape-recorded proceedings, attempts at speech-pattern recognition, and the conversion of speech into writing.

18. The ineffectiveness of literary criticism when faced with so-called documentary literature is an indication of how far the critics' thinking has lagged behind the stage of the productive forces. It stems from the fact that the media have eliminated one of the most fundamental categories of esthetics up to now—fiction. The fiction/nonfiction argument has been laid to rest just as was the nineteenth century's favorite dialectic of "art" and "life." In his day, Benjamin demonstrated that the "apparatus" (the concept of the medium was not yet available to him) abolishes authenticity. In the productions of the consciousness industry, the difference between the "genuine" original and the reproduction disappears—"that aspect of reality which is not dependent on the apparatus has now become its most artificial aspect." The process of reproduction reacts on the object reproduced and alters it fundamentally. The effects of this have not yet been adequately explained epistemologically. The categorical uncertainties to which it gives rise also affect the concept of the documentary. Strictly speaking, it has shrunk to its legal dimensions. A document is

something the "forging"—i.e., the reproduction—of which is punishable by imprisonment. This definition naturally has no theoretical meaning. The reason is that a reproduction, to the extent that its technical quality is good enough, cannot be distinguished in any way from the original, irrespective of whether it is a painting, a passport, or a bank note. The legal concept of the documentary record is only pragmatically useful; it serves only to protect economic interests.

The productions of the electronic media, by their nature, evade such distinctions as those between documentary and feature films. They are in every case explicitly determined by the given situation. The producer can never pretend, like the traditional novelist, "to stand above things." He is therefore partisan from the start. This fact finds formal expression in his techniques. Cutting, editing, dubbing—these are techniques for conscious manipulation without which the use of the new media is inconceivable. It is precisely in these work processes that their productive power reveals itself—and here it is completely immaterial whether one is dealing with the production of a reportage or a play. The material, whether "documentary" or "fiction," is in each case only a prototype, a half-finished article, and the more closely one examines its origins, the more blurred the difference becomes. (Develop more precisely. The reality in which a camera turns up is always "posed," e.g., the moon landing.)

19. The media also do away with the old category of works of art that can only be considered as separate objects, not as independent of their material infrastructure. The media do not produce such objects. They create programs. Their production is in the nature of a process. That does not mean only (or not primarily) that there is no foreseeable end to the program—a fact that, in view of what we are now presented with, admittedly makes a certain hostility to the media understandable. It means, above all, that the media program is open to its own consequences without structural limitations. (This is not an empirical description but a demand, a demand that admittedly is not made of the medium from without; it is a consequence of its nature, from which the much-vaunted open form can be derived—and not as a modifica-

tion of it—from an old esthetic.) The programs of the consciousness industry must subsume into themselves their own results, the
reactions and the corrections that they call forth, otherwise they
are already out-of-date. They are therefore to be thought of not
as means of consumption but as means of their own production.

20. It is characteristic of artistic avant-gardes that they have,
so to speak, a presentiment of the potentiality of media that still
lie in the future.

> It has always been one of the most important tasks of art to
> give rise to a demand, the time for the complete satisfaction
> of which has not yet come. The history of every art form has
> critical periods when that form strives towards effects which
> can only be easily achieved if the technical norm is changed,
> that is to say, in a new art form. The artistic extravagances
> and crudities which arise in this way, for instance in the so-
> called decadent period, really stem from art's richest histori-
> cal source of power. Dadaism in the end teemed with such
> barbarisms. We can only now recognize the nature of its
> striving. Dadaism was attempting to achieve those effects
> which the public today seeks in film with the means of paint-
> ing (or of literature).[9]

This is where the prognostic value of otherwise inessential productions, such as happenings, flux, and mixed-media shows, is to
be found. There are writers who in their work show an awareness
of the fact that media with the characteristics of the monologue
today have only a residual use value. Many of them admittedly
draw fairly shortsighted conclusions from this glimpse of the truth.
For example, they offer the user the opportunity to arrange the
material provided by arbitrary permutations. Every reader, as it
were, should write his own book. When carried to extremes, such
attempts to produce interaction, even when it goes against the
structure of the medium employed, are nothing more than invitations to freewheel. Mere noise permits of no articulated interac-
tions. Short cuts, of the kind that Concept Art peddles, are based
on the banal and false conclusion that the development of the productive forces renders all work superfluous. With the same justification, one could leave a computer to its own devices on the as-

sumption that a random generator will organize material production by itself. Fortunately, cybernetics experts are not given to such childish games.

21. For the old-fashioned "artist"—let us call him the author—it follows from these reflections that he must see it as his goal to make himself redundant as a specialist in much the same way as a teacher of literacy only fulfills his task when he is no longer necessary. Like every learning process, this process, too, is reciprocal. The specialist will learn as much or more from the nonspecialists as the other way round. Only then can he contrive to make himself dispensable.

Meanwhile, his social usefulness can best be measured by the degree to which he is capable of using the liberating factors in the media and bringing them to fruition. The tactical contradictions in which he must become involved in the process can neither be denied nor covered up in any way. But strategically his role is clear. The author has to work as the agent of the masses. He can lose himself in them only when they themselves become authors, the authors of history.

22. "Pessimism of the intelligence, optimism of the will" (Antonio Gramsci).

Translated by Stuart Hood

Part Two

POLITICS
AND
HISTORY

1

Toward a Theory of Treason

> Our laws are not widely known. They are the secret of the small group of nobles that rules us. . . . It is a tradition that the laws exist and are entrusted to the nobility as a secret, but it is no more and cannot be more than an ancient tradition which has become credible through its very age, for the character of these laws also requires that their content be kept secret.
>
> —Franz Kafka,
> *On the Question of the Law*

1. Traitors—those are the others. No one wants to be considered a traitor. No matter who their legislator is, no matter under what social arrangements they live, most everyone is firmly convinced that he does not deserve that label—but just as firmly convinced, however, that there are traitors and that they should be punished as harshly as possible, preferably by the death penalty, but in any case with the strongest penalty the law knows.

2. Everyone as traitor. These convictions are puzzling to the point of stupefaction. They evidently stand in stark contrast to the historical experiences everyone could, and can still, have during his lifetime. If, for the time being, one places in abeyance the question of what actually constitutes treason—scarcely one of those who believe in it can give a definition—that is, if one orients one-

79

80 · Hans Magnus Enzensberger

self for the present by the legal systems that have been in effect for the past thirty years, at least on the European continent, then there is no doubt whatever that almost every inhabitant of this continent has been at some point in his life a traitor in the eyes of the state. However, not all these treasonable acts were discovered, prosecuted, and punished; that would only have been possible at the price of the depopulation of our part of the earth.

3. Inevitability of treason. It seems superfluous to offer proof of a fact that is so well known. However, to establish the fact that everyone *can* become a traitor is insufficient. To argue the point decisively it must be shown that under certain historical conditions everyone *must* become a traitor. For example, the entire populations of Norway, Holland, France, Greece, and Yugoslavia consisted of traitors (always in the technical-legal sense of the word) during the German occupation of these countries. No matter which government each individual considered to be his, there existed always another in whose eyes he was committing treason. Similar mirrorlike compulsory situations come about in all partitioned countries, such as, for example, Germany since 1948.

4. Dialectic of treason. Each radical change in sovereignty turns millions of people into traitors vis-à-vis the valid laws, and this event is as simple as the flip of a coin. Those who weren't, previously, become potential traitors now, and vice versa. The only thing that can protect one from this reversal is the immediate relinquishment of the previously maintained position and lightning-quick adaptation to the new principles that now obtain. Whoever doesn't want to be considered a traitor has to betray without delay what he was previously attached to.

On March 8, 1943, the seventy-five-year-old pensioner Wilhelm Lehmann was condemned to death in Berlin for instigating high treason because he had written on the wall of a public toilet: "Hitler, you mass murderer, must be murdered."[1] Ten years later it would have approximated a treasonable act to express the opposite view. A reversal in the other direction has taken place in Spain. Margaret Boveri reports that the word *loyalist* described the republicans between 1936 and 1945, whereas today, in the United States, it is generally used to designate the followers of Franco.[2]

The concept of treason of course undergoes a corresponding reversal. One can produce any number of analogous examples. The different phases of the Algerian conflict made every Frenchman between 1954 and 1962 into a traitor at one point or another. The same holds true for the inhabitants of all African and Asian countries who liberated themselves by force from colonialism, not to speak of the history of the Soviet Union under Stalinism.

5. **Antiquatedness.** Under these circumstances it is a wonder that treason has been able to maintain itself at all as a consistent concept in legal practice. What it means scarcely anyone knows, least of all those who defend themselves most vehemently against it or most eagerly call for its persecution. Even professional jurists aren't capable of rational clarification of the matter. They confine themselves to a purely formal interpretation of whatever legal text happens to fit. In striking contrast to this general puzzlement stands the consistent outrage over the traitor and the general agreement to use the sharpest sanctions against him. The conception of treason is so firm that no historical experience can shake it and so irrational that it seems above and beyond every scrutiny, every doubt, both of which point to its old age, its antiquity. In fact, the oldest European code of law, the Roman twelve-table law, already names a crime of treason (*perduellio*), and the oldest permanent court of law of Roman history was a special court that only acted in cases of treason (the *duumvire perduellionis*).

6. **Treason as Laesa Maiestas.** The archaic kernel of the crime is obscured in the twelve-table law, as under all republican, not to speak of democratic, constitutions. In Roman law it steps out of its obscurity again at the time of the emperors. Treason from now on is called *crimen maiestatis* or *laesa maiestas,* a term that has survived through the history of European law. The English *Treason Act* of 1351, which is still valid today, designates as high treason "to compass or imagine the death of the king, the queen, or their eldest son and heir." The law books of all European monarchies begin with similar definitions; for example, paragraphs eighty and eighty-one of the first German penal code, which invokes the death penalty for murder or attempted murder of the emperor or head of the country. The *laesa maiestas* lives on in

nineteenth-century laws in the form of prohibiting insult to majesties. In contemporary republican legislation the murder of the head of state has apparently been edged to the periphery of the concept of treason; but not a single law book is without it. It is not possible to omit it, because it points to the secret, basic thought behind treason. The German word *verraten*, to betray, etymologically has the root meaning "to reach a decision to undo someone." This someone is no other than the one who holds power.

7. **The ruler taboo and its double meaning.** The archaic and irrational kernel of treason is a magic prohibition whose source has to be sought beyond all written laws in the ruler taboo. The "violation" of this taboo finds very clear expression in the Roman word for treason: *laesa*.[3]

Taboo is, as we know, a prohibition against touching. The person to whom it is attached may not be touched and is therefore protected against all aggression. The actual accomplishment of the taboo, however, lies in its double meaning. The ruler taboo not only protects the ruler from the ruled, but also the ruled from the ruler. "He must not only be guarded, he must also be guarded against."[4] This twin purpose is achieved by means of a highly complicated system of rules. What is admirable in these limitations is their complete symmetry and mutuality.

This taboo constitutes the prerequisite of the possibility of ruling per se, which is proved by the extreme sanctions that go with it. They alone guarantee the security of the ruler, as well as of his subjects, and neutralize the deadly threat in their fear of each other.

The ruler's *mana*, a magic "charge" that is the raison d'être for the taboo and supposedly makes touching dangerous, is to be regarded as the actual substance of his power. This *mana*, like an electric potential, allows of gradations and therefore of intermediaries between the ruler and the ruled. Thus a subchief or lesser adviser with lesser *mana* can touch the ruler without danger to himself and can himself afford to be touched by underlings. This conception allows the creation of hierarchies. One characteristic of a taboo is its transferability: it is, so to speak, infectious. What the ruler has touched becomes itself taboo. What counts is the principle of contiguity, something that, in any case, is a primary trait of magical thought. Freud has pointed out its close resemblance to association. This has remained the determining principle of treason to this day. We encounter it in the principle of *guilt by association* and invariably in the laws that deal with treason.

8. Treason as sacrilege. The relationship between the ruler and his subjects changes with the birth of the high religions. There exists a particular relationship between gods and kings of which the ruled do not partake. *Mana* is replaced by consecration; might becomes sacred; violating it verges on sacrilege. In Roman imperial law treason and sacrilege were already two aspects of one and the same phenomenon; they are called *laesa maiestas* and *laesa maiestas divina.* The automatic sanction accompanying the taboo, which revenges its violation, is replaced by persecution through the worldly organs. The identification of sovereignty with divinity, which goes far and beyond the "by God's grace" of absolutism, leads to the point where treason and blasphemy become one and the same thing: in classic Roman law the profession of faith in Christianity was regarded as *crimen maiestatis,* that is, as treason.

In other words, the wrong opinion is enough to violate the ruling majesty. The importance of this development is self-evident. Simultaneously, the religious consecration of power endangers the greatest achievement of the ruler taboo, which lies in its double meaning. A remnant of it is retained in the concept of loyalty, still deemed to be a reciprocal relationship. Institutionally, it finds expression in the oath that only makes sense as long as it is kept by both parties. The double sense of the taboo is maintained under conditions as they obtained for a long time in the feudal system: the feudal lord was just as capable of treason as his vassal, and if he broke the oath he was, in principle, threatened with the same sanctions as his vassal. However, the more the sacredness of a sacred rule is consolidated, the less reciprocity appears necessary. Its erosion becomes progressively greater, a process that can be observed down to the smallest detail in the laws. The subjects of treason now are the people, its object the ruler. A reversal of this relationship has become almost legally unthinkable; it can only be theoretically imagined. The archaic taboo that imbues treason has turned into a pure implement of sovereign rule.

9. Uncertainty and infection. "A government only needs to leave uncertain what treason is and it becomes despotic."[5] If one takes this Montesquieu observation at its word, one will scarcely find a government devoid of despotic traits. The concept of treason contained the tendency toward rank proliferation from its very beginning, that is, in its very taboo character that constituted the effectiveness of the prohibition. Simultaneously, it allows the arbitrary spread of the indicated crime through transference and infection. Its indeterminacy is not accidental. Rather, it represents the treason taboo's usefulness in the hands of rulers. Roman law already contains its core—the prohibition against killing the ruler—which is overgrown to such an extent by secondary and tertiary considerations that it has become nearly invisible. At the time of Justinian treason not only included all acts against the honor and security of the Roman people, but also desertion, criticism of the succession, the occupation of public places, the freeing of prisoners, the falsification of public documents, and the acceptance of illegal oaths. Intention was sufficient for a guilty verdict; traitors were beheaded. The oilspotlike spreading of the definition of treason finally led jurists to codify what did *not* constitute treason. Someone was *not* a traitor who restored an emperor's weatherbeaten statue, who melted down an unconsecrated metal statue, who unintentionally tossed a stone at such a statue.

Holding reasonable convictions was an even graver crime. It spread over all of Europe and led to monstrous results in the late Middle Ages and in the Renaissance. Henry VIII of England, for example, had two daughters who had claims to the throne. Englishmen became guilty of high treason, according to the law of 1534, by doubting Mary's claim or considering Elizabeth's justified; according to a law of 1536, to support either of these claims was treason; and finally, according to the law of 1543, to doubt either one of these claims.

The treason taboo is treated in a completely modern manner in the above instance: the ruler defines arbitrarily and one-sidedly who is to be considered a traitor. This method corresponds precisely to the procedure of our present-day rulers, who just as arbitrarily determine what deviations from official doctrine are to be regarded as treasonable. Treason is, as it were, imposed on the traitor without any act on his part; the victim becomes an "objective opponent," in the language of Stalinism.[6] The circle of these "objective traitors" can not only be immeasurably enlarged by means of new definitions of the crime; it also enlarges itself of its own accord through the taboo principle of infection. Not only relatives and acquaintances of the traitor are considered "inadmissible," "security risks," potential traitors, but also everyone who has knowledge of the treasonable crime or suspects it or fails to denounce the culprit. The magic, "infectious" character of the crime becomes clearly apparent in the term *contact person*. The advantage of the taboo as an instrument for ruling, and not just as an avoidable side effect or symptom of degeneration, consists of its capacity to make everyone a potential traitor and every action potentially traitorous.

10. **Paranoid structure.** The indiscriminate growth of treason crimes and the bestial sanctions—from disembowelment of living persons and drawing and quartering customary during the Christian Middle Ages to the "special treatment" in modern concentration camps—indicate the degree to which rulers regard their domain as threatened. As the reciprocity of the old taboo falls into disuse, so does their sense of security become undermined. Because every act of their subjects seems a threat, they reply with a counterthreat to punish each act, no matter what, and every possible belief as treason. Loyalty cannot be presumed among his subjects when it is alien to the ruler himself. The ruler considers himself constantly pursued, which lends him the justification to pursue all others at all times: the consequence is a vicious circle.

This pattern of treason and the war against it manifests a conformation we recognize from psychiatry, the structure of paranoia. A classic example of this structure is provided by the report of the Arab scholar Ibn Batuta from his stay at the court of the sultan of Dehli, Mohammed Tughlak. He recounts the following arguments by the ruler:

> Today there are far more evil and unruly people than there used to be. I punish them as soon as I have the slightest suspicion or presumption of their rebellious and traitorous intention, and the slightest act of disobedience I punish by death. I will continue to do this until the people start to behave decently and give up rebellion and disobedience. . . . I punish the people because they all suddenly became my enemies and opponents.[7]

By the logic of paranoia no one is innocent; there are only those who haven't yet been convicted of treason—that is, masked traitors. Paranoia senses conspiracies everywhere: it becomes only a question of exposing them, "of tearing the masks off their faces." That is the language of Hitler's *Völkischer Beobachter,* of today's Chinese press, and the language of fanatic anticommunism.

What is required to fight the "world conspiracies" of the paranoid delusionary system are counterconspiracies. Wherever the treason taboo is employed as a means for ruling, an organized system of informers makes its appearance. The profession of the informer, the *delator,* came into existence in Rome at the time of Tiberius. The corresponding modern version is the secret police, which becomes *the* central political organ as the number of treasonable acts and therefore the number of potential traitors increases.

11. Projection. Such an interpretation of treason meets with the objection that it neglects the role of the enemy. Indeed, the enemy appears very early, in the legal codes that refer to treason, as the interested third party who benefits from the crime; yes, one can say that the reference to the outside enemy is indispensable for these laws. Moreover, the term is ascribed without regard for what is probable: thus, in the Union of South Africa every act directed against the government's apartheid policy is considered high treason; this interdiction is justified by reference to the Soviet Union, for whose benefit—yes, in whose service—this treasonable act is being committed. On the other hand, Stalin's regime interpreted every oppositional act as treason for the benefit and in the service of the capitalist powers. The German "stab in the back" legend after World War I, which was the psychological prerequisite for many treason trials during the Weimar Republic, had a similar function. Of course, there is nothing easier to find than some third party to cheer any internal criticism and each opposition move, and therefore every country always has a plethora of "enemies" from all sorts of other countries. That is the logic of paranoia.

The psyche mechanism at work here is called *projection.* The unresolved conflict between the ruler and his subject is shifted to the outside opponent; the threat to the rule from inside is transposed outside. The role that projection plays during the start of wars is well known, and without projection the treason taboo would collapse. As soon as one has seen through this projection, it turns out that the enemy whom it conjures up is none other than the internal one. The only thing that is feared and called treason is the threat to the rule that emanates from the subjects themselves. High treason is nothing but the juristic name for revolution.

12. Revolution and treason. The magic, infectious power of the treason taboo also extends to those who break it. Everywhere the history of revolutionary conspiracy shows the traces of this infection. The oath by means of which the ruler seeks to protect himself against treason corresponds to the oath the conspirators swear. The revolutionaries fight a traitor in their own ranks more relentlessly than their actual enemy. Thus, the paranoid structure of the old order is transposed onto the new one even before it has been erected. The conspiracies of Netchajev and the Fighting Organization of the Social Revolutionaries offer an excellent illustration of this. Their structural similarities to their opponent, the secret police, are striking; they are what makes possible a double game like that of Asev, who remained unrecognized as a traitor for the very reason that the habits of revolutionary activity resembled those of the counterrevolution to the point where both became practically indistinguishable from one another.

13. New treason taboos. After the revolution is victorious its achievements are secured against the *ancien régime* in the same manner as the *ancien régime* initially secured itself against the revolution. The treason taboo thus is not removed, but only reversed, a process during which, however, the central figure to whom one could be traitorous vanishes. The *mana* of the sovereign ruler is transferred to abstract "values," "goods," doctrines and their administrators, the anonymous state apparatus. The result is an enormous extension of potential treason crimes. Aspects of the taboo that were of secondary importance until now move into the foreground: the sovereignty and the territorial integrity of the national state, for example. Completely new touch prohibitions are added. The private ownership of the means of production, the party "line," the socialist achievement, the interests of a "race" or a class are now considered untouchable. The treason taboo serves in each instance whatever rule has been established.

Bourgeois democracy, with its rules about betraying the constitution, made an attempt to reestablish the original reciprocity of the treason taboo. These regulations (paragraph eighty-nine of the penal code of the Federal Republic of Germany) count on the possibility that a state apparatus itself can become traitorous and place a taboo on certain constitutional guarantees against intrusion by the rulers themselves. Meanwhile, scarcely half a dozen of the more than 150,000 investigations launched by the public prosecutor of the Federal Republic for crimes against the state and treasonable acts have been against government politicians.[8] For a guilty verdict of high treason, it suffices if a worker distributes Communist leaflets; but when an office-holding minister of the interior declares before parliament that the government is moving outside the bounds of legality, that does not constitute sufficient grounds. Someone who asks *Bundeswehr* soldiers to refuse to service atomic weapons can be prosecuted for "treasonable subversion of the constitution." Four Adenauer government ministers, on the other hand, became trustees of an organization (the Occidental Academy) that openly supported the removal of parliamentary democracy; no one took them to task. The reciprocity of the taboo therefore remains fictitious, at least in West Germany. In fact, the interdiction of treason continues to serve as the one-sided instrument of the rulers.

14. The state secret. The prohibition against delivering secrets to a foreign power is not part of the old core of the law against treason. This very aspect, which stands official propaganda in such useful stead, is completely peripheral and is based on a much later extension of the concept of treason. It plays no role in the older laws. In Anglo-Saxon law the betrayal of state secrets isn't called treason at all; the crime does not fall under the Treason Act but under the Official Secrets Act of 1889. *State secret* and *espionage,* as legal concepts, are inventions of the late nineteenth century. They were born out of the spirit of imperialism. Their victorious march begins in 1894 with the Dreyfus affair.

Since that time the state secret has been raised to an instrument for ruling of the first rank. Its productivity is nearly unlimited. Its success and its arbitrariness derive from the fact that the magic conceptions that have always been part and parcel of the treason taboo are joined in a single complex. The old *mana* of the chiefs and priest-kings objectifies itself once more in the state secret—palpable and immaterial at the same time; this is the secret of power per se. Its presence evokes shudders of respect, its exposure hysterical outrage. No longer is there need of aggression for violation of the taboo; a question suffices. That is a degree of remoteness the likes of which no ruler has ever enjoyed before. The *mana* of the state secret communicates itself to its bearers and immunizes them, each according to the degree of his initiation, against the question; therefore, they are free not to answer and, in the real sense of the word, are irresponsible. How many state secrets someone knows becomes the measure of his rank and his privilege in a finely articulated hierarchy. The mass of the governed is without secrets; that is, it has no right to partake of power, to criticize it and watch over it.

15. Uncertainty and infectiousness of the secret taboo. Part of the state secret's magic character is that it allows of no definition. This uncertainty, indeterminability, which was always peculiar to the treason taboo, is not merely an external feature; it constitutes its essence. At first, a simple rubber stamp will do to declare something secret. But even this is not absolutely necessary and by no means binding. German law, for example, is being quite consistent in assuming that the official designation does not completely guarantee the character of the secret; something that lacks it can at any time, even retroactively, be made secret by means of a simple and unilateral government act. Nor is the taboo limited to state organs such as the government apparatus or the military: according to German law, a party's foreign-policy program can also be considered secret, even its "mood." According to the so-called mosaic theory, such a secret can, moreover, be created in a certain sense through spontaneous generation by means of the simple compilation of information, none of which is secret by itself.

The infectiousness of the secret taboo is unlimited. It is transferred onto each and every thing that comes into contact with it. The one who betrays the secret infects his "contact persons" with it. The court action against him itself becomes secret in turn. Organizations that protect secret matters go underground themselves. Someone who carries secrets can be considered secret, as can someone who doesn't. *But what is primarily secret is what is a secret and what isn't; that is perhaps the actual state secret.* In German law it is guarded by means of a particular protective rule that one may regard as the culmination of the entire system. It threatens to penalize whoever "intentionally publicizes as true or genuine or lets get into unauthorized hands facts, objects, or news about them that are false, falsified, or untrue but that if they were genuine and true *would* be state secrets."

In other words, what is liable to be punished here is the betrayal of state secrets that are nothing of the kind; it suffices that they might be. The taboo infects its negation. With this step the system is letter-perfect. If something (p) is the case, not only is giving out information about it treason (q), but also giving out its negation (q̄) is treason. If something isn't the case (p̄), the situation is the same: (q̄) as well as (q) are considered treason. With the logical precision of the calculus of propositions, every imaginable utterance about arbitrarily determined cases is prohibited.

16. Projection, once again. The logic of paranoia is manifested with clinical purity in the delusionary system that is developed out of the secret taboo. The "tapping of thoughts," the aura of secretiveness by which the patient feels surrounded, the feeling of being watched and overheard, are classic features of the physiognomy of this illness. Therefore, the state secret is more useful than any personal taboo as a crystallizing agent for a delusionary system. This system owes its enormous success to a mechanism with which we have already become familiar, namely projection.

In every instance the secret taboo is based on and justified by the existence of an external enemy. This enemy is portrayed as boundlessly ignorant and craving for knowledge; he is opposed by an appeal to national solidarity. The model situation that lies in back of this is war. Only in the military secret does the state secret come into full flower. Since war is posited a priori as a permanent and total condition, any matter at all may be subsumed under military categories: vis-à-vis the enemy, everything has to be considered secret and every citizen a potential traitor.

What this principle accomplishes in internal politics is obvious: it renders taboo the military as an instrument of the rulers and removes it from control by the subjects. Since modern war reaches into every aspect of life and can no longer be isolated from social existence, all imaginable secrets also have military character, no matter whether it is a question of weapons or food supplies, the economic conditions or the civilian population's "frame of mind."

Those who establish the secret and treason taboos doubtless do so with a clear conscience and the best of intentions. Not only those for whom it is intended, but its authors too, fall victim to the delusionary system. What constitutes the achievement of the system is that those who employ this form of projection cannot see through it. One cannot expect an administrator to have greater insight into the delusionary aspect of the taboo than a paranoid into his illness. Each attempt to enlighten him must fail for this very reason; no insight, no matter how lucid, into the unreality of their convictions can convince them. The perception that the secret taboo is by no means meant for the external but invariably for the internal population can therefore expect to meet with violent objections. For this there is no lack of evidence.

First of all, informing the public is usually made commensurate with betrayal to the external enemy. In any event, according to German law it is irrelevant whether the secret was known to the enemy at time of publication or not. Yes, even the highest court of the Weimar Republic punished the reprinting of foreign newspaper comments about internal German conditions. And with that it merely expressed the actual sense of the taboo: the keeping secret of political matters not from the external but from the internal enemy, namely the public. The trials of Dreyfus, Ebert, and Ossietzky, as well as the espionage trials in Stalinist Russia and the treason trials of the German resistance in the Third Reich, were exclusively directed against internal political enemies.

17. The mythology of espionage. During World War II Goebbels began a propaganda campaign in Germany that stood under the motto: "Watch out! The enemy is listening!" On all walls and wherever else one could post bills there appeared a black man on a yellow background. This figure is the phantom of espionage. Like other taboo-protected phantoms, such as sovereignty, the less reality it possesses, the more zealously is it conjured up. In not a single modern war has espionage or the betrayal of secrets played a decisive role of any kind. Hitler's defeat is not due to ransacked wastepaper baskets or notes written with invisible ink. Mata Hari and the secret courier on the Orient Express belong to the realm of political yellow journalism. The traditional spy legends flesh out the delusions of the official taboo, popularize them, and make them acceptable.

Espionage, in this sense, has an exclusively mythological function: it helps preserve the internal political taboo of the state secret. If it ever contained a trace of reality, it has long since become an anachronism. It has nothing whatever in common with the kind of work the information services of the superpowers are capable of. This work is part of regular military routine, is so to speak a fourth branch of the service. Significantly, it is handled in an atmosphere of extreme sobriety. The opponents maintain certain rules of the game, so that one can almost speak of teamwork between the warring services, which of course maintain constant contact with each other. For example, if one takes a prisoner, one exchanges him at the first opportune moment. Hysterical and paranoid features are entirely absent. Men who perform this kind of work have perfectly normal, respected jobs. The leading heads of these information, defense, and planning staffs are usually firmly convinced that their mutual efforts serve solely the keeping of the peace.

The primary data that these services process derive almost exclusively from two sources: first, from the normal internal flow of information of a modern, industrial society that cannot be suppressed without doing grave harm to the society itself; and second, as a result of technological observation of the opponent by means of airplanes and satellites. Compared to this, bedtime secrets and hidden microphones no longer provide much worthwhile information. Coinciding with this is the appearance of the expert, who has replaced the spy with dark glasses: they are mostly mathematicians, statisticians, game theorists, and other data-processing experts. The concept of the secret has no room in their methodical work; each side not only knows precisely what the other side is doing, it also knows that this knowledge is based on reciprocity.

Besides, the strategy of deterrence that applies undisputed throughout the world today leads to a situation where the newest state of armament (that is, *the* military secret par excellence) has to be ostentatiously demonstrated to the opponent so as to be effective. In this respect this strategy finds itself in complete agreement with extreme pacifist theories: their effectiveness is based on the elimination of the secret.

18. Treason as circumstantial evidence. One can therefore draw two opposite conclusions from the threat of total war: either that everything is a state secret or that state secrets no longer exist. In a certain sense both sentences mean the same thing; the first changes into the second, but with the following result: the betrayal of such secrets is prosecuted ever more ruthlessly the more eagerly statesmen proclaim them. The absurdity of this situation is apparent; but the very delusionary character of the taboo prevents its dissolution. It cannot be combined with genuine democracy. Politics has to be conducted out in the open. If the political freedoms as they are guaranteed in the constitutions have any meaning, that meaning lies here.

The projections the great taboo invokes implode before everyone's eyes. The kind of treatment accorded those who dare touch it becomes a telling verdict on the internal conditions of the respective country. The more state secrets a government guards, the more it has to hide from those it pretends to represent. The more treason taboos it erects, the more it despises and fears the citizens of its own country, and the more it stinks.

Translated by Michael Roloff

2

Reflections
before a Glass Cage

1. Definitions. We know what a crime is, and yet we don't. The
Encyclopedia Britannica defines it in the following way:

> (lat. *crimen,* accusation), the general term for offences against
> the criminal law (q.v.). Crime has been defined as "a failure
> or refusal to live up to the standard of conduct deemed bind-
> ing by the rest of the community." Sir James Stephen de-
> scribed it as "some act of omission in respect of which legal
> punishment may be inflicted on the person who is in default
> whether by acting or omitting to act."[1]

Thomas Hobbes wrote in a similar vein three hundred years
ago: "A crime is a sin, consisting in the committing, by deed or
word, of that which the law forbiddeth, or the omission of what
it has commanded."[2]

The tautological structure of these sentences is manifest, and
like all tautologies they are reversible: what is punished is a crime,
what is a crime is punished; everything deserving of punishment
is punishable and vice versa. The linguistic model of such definitions can be found in the biblical sentence "I am the one I am."
Such sentences place the legislator above reason and above argument, and the codified law acquires this syntactical attitude for
itself. The German penal code simply says: "An act threatened
with imprisonment of five or more years is a crime."

Defining concepts in such a way as to eliminate all discussion has definite advantages, because it relieves legal practice once and for all of the problem of what constitutes a crime, relegating it forthwith to the realm of theory as an amusement for particularly esoteric minds. A good deal of thought has been given, in seminars, to "the material concept of crime," but little of any validity has been discovered. No wonder then that the penal codes aren't a consistent system but at best a heterogeneous, frequently bizarre assemblage of historically deposited orders to protect the most varied kinds of legal prerogatives and interests, codified concepts of taboos and morality, and rules of the game that are value-free only from a purely pragmatic viewpoint.

Besides, legal scholars find themselves in a perfectly common bind: the more general and more fundamental something is, the less distinct its concept tends to be. No one (or everyone) can say what a nation is (but everyone in his way). Everyone knows what money is, and some people know how to handle it; the economists, however, can't agree on what it is. What is health? Medicine makes educated guesses. What is death? Biologists are full of suggestions.

In confusing cases such as these, it is perhaps best to go on the street and ask the first ten persons what they think. The most frequent reply will not be a definition but an example that, moreover, is strikingly often the same: "A crime, for example, is a murder." The frequency of this reply bears no relationship to criminal statistics, where entirely different infractions play the chief role. Although comparatively rare, murder plays a key role in the general public consciousness. It is due to the power of its example that one begins to understand the very nature of crime.

Crime novel and crime film, as reflections of this general consciousness, confirm that murder occupies a central role in it—yes, becomes synonymous with crime as such.

From its punishment, according to the *lex talionis*, one also gathers that murder is the actual and the oldest capital crime per se: certainly, the oldest and most severe penalty—and until deep into the Middle Ages also the chief penalty—is the death penalty, which reflects what it wants to revenge, and that is murder.

2. **Natural history of crime.** We have no certain knowledge of the ethnological origin of crime. Even the most primitive societies

that are open to observation have "lawbreakers," even, that is, when they lack codified rules. Murder plays a significant role in the oldest documents of human society. Since the primordial condition of society is nowhere ascertainable, every attempt to discover its natural history must remain hypothetical. However, we have a number of aids available: biological behavior studies (which, however, only allow limited inferences for human behavior), ethnology, the study of myths, as well as psychoanalysis.

Sigmund Freud provides us with the classical description of the "original crime." It begins with "Darwin's primal horde": "a violent, jealous father who keeps all women for himself and drives out the growing sons." The crime itself is described in the following way:

> One day the brothers who had been driven out banded together, killed and devoured the father, and thus put an end to the horde. United they dared and accomplished what had been impossible for them alone. . . . The violent original father had certainly been the envied and feared model of each member of the tribe of brothers. Their act of devouring completed their identification with him; each of them acquired a piece of his strength. The totem meal, perhaps humanity's first feast, would be the repetition and the memorial celebration of this memorable criminal act which was the beginning of so many things: the social organizations, the ethical limitations, and religion.[3]

This description is met with the facile objection that one can't speak of a crime where there is no law; but such a consideration is legalistic, not philosophical, and misses the point. Such a pseudo-objection resembles the question: "Which came first, the chicken or the egg?" Law can only be defined by injustice, at its limit, to be recognized as law; the "ethical limitations" can only be taught as a reply to a challenge. And in that sense the original crime is undoubtedly a creative act. (Walter Benjamin treats its legislative power in *Zur Kritik der Gewalt*.)

This hypothesis, which Freud established in his essay "The Infantile Return to Totemism," is both famous and unknown—and for a good reason. Freud had few illusions about the resistance that would meet his attempt "to trace back our cultural heritage, of which we are justly proud, to a horrible crime that is an insult to all our feelings." Aside from a number of specialists, people did not so much oppose his "scientific myth" as simply ignore it.[4] It is no longer the sexual taboos that block reception of Freud's theses, as in the thirties, but their social and political consequences. The more manifest these become in history, the more thoroughly they are repressed.

3. Politics and murder. If we are to give credence to Freud, the original political act thus coincides with the original crime. An ancient, intimate, and dark connection exists between murder and politics, and it is retained in the basic structure of all sovereignty to date. For power is exercised by those who can have their underlings killed. The ruler is the "survivor." This definition is Elias Canetti's, who has provided us with an excellent phenomenology of sovereignty.[5]

To this day the language of politics reflects the criminal act of its origin. Even in the most harmless and civilized election campaign, one candidate "beats" the other (which actually means beats him to death); a government is "toppled" (which means to fall down and die); a minister is "shot down." The action that such expressions symbolically retain unfolds and realizes itself in extreme social situations. No revolution can do without killing the previous ruler. It has to break the taboo that forbids the underlings to touch him; for "only someone who has proved capable of transgressing such a prohibition has acquired the character of the forbidden."[6] The *mana* of the killed ruler is transferred to his murderers. All revolutions to date have infected themselves with the prerevolutionary conditions and have inherited the basic structure against which they fought.

4. Contradiction. Even the more "progressive," "civilized" constitutions allow for the killing of people, and permit it—but only in "extreme" cases, such as war or revolutionary situations. In other respects the basic structure of the government remains concealed. Any command is still a "suspended death sentence," now as then (Canetti). But this verdict is expressed only as an infinitely mediated threat; it only exists virtually;[7] and throughout history we find this limitation institutionally anchored in the body of laws.

Every philosophy of law to date has sought to resolve the contradiction at the root of this law, which is that this law, like every social order, is based on the original crime; that it was created by means of injustice. For every body of laws to date simultaneously protects against the ruler and is his instrument. Perhaps the entire history of law can be interpreted as its removal from the political sphere. This immense process can only be unraveled by someone with the calling for it; yet it seems as though it has been unable to resolve the inner contradictions at its root. The separation of the executive from the legislative and judiciary powers, the independence and permanence of the judge, the separation of the public prosecutor's office from the court and its institutionalization as a "party," the multifarious procedural safeguards during a trial—all of these mediations are invaluable, but nonetheless the ruler always remains the supreme judge; and the judge, the impartial arbitrator, always stands in the service of the state.

The ambiguous nature of the legal order is most clearly discernible from the problematic nature of punishment. If every command is a "suspended death sentence," then punishment constitutes its execution, no matter in how attenuated a form. Death is the oldest, most powerful, the actual punishment. If the death penalty is taken away, the duty and right of the state to mete out punishment moves from the magic darkness of religious conceptions into the field of rational reflection. Once the death penalty is questioned, punishment as such becomes questionable; and that is why opinions and constitutions diverge at this point, and this alone explains the passion with which the question of the death penalty is argued. What nourishes this quarrel is neither the possibility of a miscarriage of justice nor simple pity for the condemned, not to mention the intention to protect society from the criminal. No matter what the argument of those who call for the death penalty, a hysterical undertone gives evidence of their longing for an all-powerful authority with which they can identify. What is forbidden to the individual—that is, to kill—is permitted to him as a member of the collective, through the execution. Therefore its characteristic mystique: that of a ritual. It is completely consistent with this mystique that the death penalty used to be performed in public: killing in the name of everyone can only occur in public, because then everyone partakes in it; the hangman is only our deputy.

If thought through to its ultimate consequence, the removal of the death penalty would change the nature of the state; it would be the anticipation of a social order from which we are far removed, because it deprives the state of the permission to decide the death or life of the individual. This power, however, constitutes the actual heart of sovereignty.

5. **Sovereignty.** "Sovereignty in the judicial sense," wrote the German historian Heinrich von Treitschke, "the complete independence of the state from any other power on earth, constitutes the state's nature to such an extent that one can say that it represents the very criterion of the state."[8] The power of this concept remains unbroken, although it is obvious that sovereignty of this kind has never existed. It follows from this conception of the state that it is above and beyond any legal order, and anyone who maintains this idea can never believe in the existence of international law. National sovereignty and international law are mutually exclusive.

A reference work published in 1959 maintains quite appropriately that "it is very doubtful whether such a thing as international law actually exists . . . the so-called 'international law' has limited itself to date essentially to the development of diplomatic rules for the exchange of declarations and rules for the eventuality of war. . . . There exists no binding social norm between states as yet."[9]

The purest way in which a state expresses its sovereignty, as Treitschke understands this word, is in its internal politics, in the intercourse with its individual antagonist, by means of the death penalty; in foreign politics, in its relationship with other states, this sovereignty is expressed by means of war. If the state, as the overlord of the legal order, is permitted to kill one individual, it is also permitted to kill many or if necessary everyone, in its and its people's name, and to make the execution of this sovereign act a duty to its citizens.

Sigmund Freud wrote of World War I:

> In this war the individual member of a state can notice with horror what had perhaps occurred to him already in peace-time: that the state has forbidden all acts of injustice to him not because it wants to eliminate injustice but because it wants

to monopolize it like salt and tobacco. The war-making state allows itself every injustice, every act of violence which would dishonor the individual. . . . One should not interject that the state cannot do without committing injustice because this would put it at a disadvantage. The obedience to ethical norms and the relinquishment of the use of brute power is usually very disadvantageous to the individual too.[10]

What surprises us even more than the violence the states unleashed during World War I is the astonishment of the bourgeois world in face of its accomplishments and its catastrophe. The simplest reflection shows that private murder throughout history has never been comparable to public murder. All individual acts of violence, from Cain to Landru, do not add up to the injustice caused by the Wars of Succession in eighteenth-century Europe alone or the sovereign actions of a colonial power during a single decade.

Such reflections, of course, are considered amateurish. At least, influential statesmen and influential jurists have never paid particular attention to them, and this reluctance is understandable. However, the connection between crime and politics has never been entirely forgotten. The nineteenth century, too, retained a sense of it. Pushed to the edge of consciousness, and therefore to the edge of society, the problem became the domain of outsiders. Anyone who, like Freud, paid attention to it found himself in motley company, among the disadvantaged and exploited, among iconoclasts and oddballs, among peculiar holy men and sectarians of every ilk. The more self-confident a society feels of its foundations, the more it allows these outsiders to call them into question. The bourgeois nineteenth century throttled every armed attack on its form of society, but it allowed the most radical examination of its basic structure . . . as a pastime for world-improvers. It is not for nothing that, to this day, it is regarded as the ultimate folly to want to improve the world, whereas the contrary effort can always depend on meeting with a certain respect. Anyone who wants to take the lessons of World War II seriously is met with especial ridicule, which serves as repression: however, ridicule no longer kills, not by itself, as the rubber truncheons and police files, which are meant to assist it, go to prove.

6. Epoch. Anyone wanting to know in what age he lives only needs to open the nearest newspaper. There he will find out that he lives in the age of synthetic fiber, tourism, professional sports, or the theater of the absurd. The information industry has also reduced to this level the knowledge that we live in the age of Hiroshima and Auschwitz. Twenty years after our baptism with this phrase, it already sounds like a cliché. Valid sentences today become threadbare before they have had an opportunity to take full effect and are treated like consumer articles that can be discarded at will and replaced by newer models. Everything that is said appears to be at the mercy of an artificial aging process; people believe they are done with a sentence once it has been scrapped. But it is easier to get rid of a consumer article than of a truth.

What happened in the 1940s does not age; instead of becoming more remote, it inches up on us and forces us to revise all human forms of thinking and of relating to each other; only at the price of continual mortal danger to us and all future generations can we maintain our conceptions of justice and injustice, of crime and of state.

Although it is scarcely a recent discovery that the modern nation state and its adherents are capable of everything—the spokesmen of imperialism already announced this proudly in the nineteenth century—we now know that it is also technically capable of everything. The age-old connection between crime and politics, the internal contradictions of law, the delusionary conceptions of sovereignty must as a consequence become more and more prominent and become, literally, explosive.

Nothing can remain as it was and is. However, the revision that, as everyone knows, we are forced to make if we are to avoid suicide has, as everyone knows, hardly begun and already is about to be choked off by the highly specialized propaganda about "overcoming guilt." The reality of the name Auschwitz is to be exorcised as though it belonged only to the past, and even an exclusively national one at that—not a collective present and future. What assists in this development is a complicated ritual of inconsequential self-accusation, which wants to have done with an event that laid bare the roots of all politics to date (and that finally means: wants to forget) without drawing the consequences to which it forces the participants (and there are no nonparticipants). It is obvious that such an "overcoming" must remain sterile, that it cannot even heed the most superficial and most proximate consequences; not to speak of being able to eliminate the prerequisites that made the event possible in the first place.

The compulsive notion of sovereignty has undergone practically no revision at all. The "nature of the state" continues to consist of its "inability to endure a power higher than itself" (Treitschke); now as then, sovereignty of this kind continues to be "the criterion for the existence of the state," except that, fifteen years after the German defeat and the destruction of Hiroshima the criterion for this criterion has become—in the eyes of leading German politicians and military men—the power to dispose over nuclear weapons.

But this implement is the present and future of Auschwitz. How can one condemn the genocide of yesterday, or even try to "overcome" it, while carefully preparing with all scientific and industrial means at one's command the genocide of tomorrow? Every rationalization with which the parties have armed themselves from the arsenal of their respective ideologies is struck out of its masters' (servants') hands by the implement. It cannot serve as the defense of freedom and rights; rather, the very existence of the implement suspends all human rights—from the right to go for a walk, the right to found parties, to the right to work or eat. They all exist under its protection—that is, under its threat; exist only upon recall and become a mere exercise in mercy that can be revoked at any moment. Simultaneously the implement rescinds all political freedoms and only permits democracy under a proviso that steadily erodes it. As the Cuban missile crisis demonstrated to the blindest, the bomb withdraws the genuine decisions once and for all from parliament and places it in the hands of a few individuals, each of whom is more powerful and is able and is forced to make lonelier and more irrevocable decisions than any despot in history.

Every invocation of the strategy of deterrence is impotent. The Nazis, too, had their analogy. (Hannah Arendt, among others, has described it with all imaginable precision.) No less paranoid than the delusionary notion of the "Jewish world conspiracy" is the principle of an armaments race whose objective is too well known for anyone even to bother to inquire after it. The implement is not a weapon in class warfare; it is neither a capitalist nor a Communist weapon; it is no weapon at all, just as little as the gas chamber.

Someone who wants to legislate or adjudicate finds himself in an odd position under conditions as they have prevailed for the past twenty years. This situation can be easily illustrated. There is no lack of examples.

7. **First example: animal protection.** Statute about the killing and keeping of live fish and other cold-blooded animals, of January 14, 1936:

> # 2(1) Crabs, lobsters, and other crustaceans whose meat is designed for human consumption are to be killed, if possible, by being tossed singly into strongly boiling water. It is prohibited to put the animals into cold or lukewarm water and bring the water to a boil afterwards.

Telex Berlin Nr. 234 404 of November 9, 1938, to all Gestapo offices and headquarters:

> 1. VERY SHORTLY ACTIONS AGAINST JEWS, PARTICULARLY AGAINST SYNAGOGUES, WILL OCCUR IN ALL OF GERMANY. THESE ACTIONS ARE NOT TO BE INTERFERED WITH. . . . 3. PREPARATIONS ARE TO BE MADE FOR THE ARREST OF ROUGHLY 20 TO 30 THOUSAND JEWS IN THE REICH. PARTICULARLY WEALTHY JEWS ARE TO BE SELECTED. FURTHER INSTRUCTIONS WILL FOLLOW THIS NIGHT. . . .
> GESTAPO II. SIGNED: MÜLLER"[11]

Statute for the protection of wild plants and nonhuntable animals, of March 18, 1936:

> # 16. (1) Property owners, those permitted the use of property, or their representatives are permitted to catch cats and take them into custody during the period of March 15 to August 15 and as long as snow covers the ground if the cats are found in gardens, orchards, cemeteries, parks and similar grounds. Cats taken into custody are to be properly cared for. . . .

Telex Warsaw Nr. 663/43 of May 24, 1943, to the SS and Police Chief/East:

RE NUMBER 1. OF THE 56,065 JEWS SEIZED SO FAR, ROUGHLY 7000 HAVE BEEN DESTROYED IN WAKE OF THE ACTION IN THE FORMER JEWISH QUARTER. 6929 JEWS WERE DESTROYED BY MEANS OF TRANSPORT TO T. II, SO THAT A TOTAL OF 13,929 JEWS HAVE BEEN DESTROYED. ABOVE AND BEYOND THE FIGURE OF 56,065, ROUGHLY FIVE TO SIX THOUSAND JEWS WERE DESTROYED THROUGH DETONATION AND FIRE. . . .
THE SS AND POLICE CHIEF IN THE WARSAW DISTRICT. SIGNED: STROOP.[12]

From Heinrich Himmler's conversation with his masseur:

"Herr Kersten, how can you possibly shoot from an ambush at the poor animals which are grazing so innocently, defenselessly and unawares at the edge of the woods? If you take the right view of your action, it is murder pure and simple. Nature is very beautiful, and after all, every animal has a right to live. It is this point of view which I admire so much in our ancestors. Respect for animals is something you find in all Indo-Germanic people. It interested me terribly to hear the other day that Buddhist monks still wear little bells when they walk through the forest, so that the animals on whom they might step have a chance to get out of the way. But here everyone steps on worms and snails without giving it a second thought."[13]

Speech by Heinrich Himmler to the SS Group Leaders in Posen, on October 3, 1943:

". . . most of you will know what it means when you see one hundred corpses lying in one spot, three hundred, or a thousand. To have seen this through to the end and—aside from exceptions of human weakness—to have remained decent, that is what has made us hard. This is an unwritten and never to be written page of honor in the annals of our history."[14]

Statute for the protection of wild plants and nonhuntable animals:

No. 23 (I) For the protection of the remaining nonhuntable animals it is prohibited:
    1. To catch them en masse without a reasonable or justified purpose or to kill them en masse.

8. Second example: game plan. In April, 1961, the trial of the former Obersturmbannführer A. Eichmann opened at a court in Jerusalem. The indictment did not say that the accused had personally operated the gas chambers, but that Eichmann conscientiously and in detail *planned* the murder of six million people.

Also in the year 1961, in Princeton, New Jersey, there appeared a work by the mathematician, physicist, and military theoretician Herman Kahn, *On Thermonuclear War*. This work contains the following table:

Tragic but distinguishable postwar statistics.

DEAD:	ECONOMIC RECUPERATION
2,000,000	1 year
5,000,000	2 years
10,000,000	5 years
20,000,000	10 years
40,000,000	20 years
80,000,000	50 years
160,000,000	100 years

Will the survivors envy the dead?[15]

Objective investigations show that the sum of human tragedy (sic) would rise considerably in the postwar period, but this rise would not exclude the possibility of a normal happy existence for the majority of survivors and their progeny.[16]

But will the survivors be in a position to lead the kind of life Americans are used to living? That is with cars, country homes, iceboxes, etc.? No one can say for sure, but I believe that even if we make no preparation for our recovery—disregarding the acquisition of radiation detection equipment, the distribution of handbooks and the practice of certain counter measures—the country would get back on its feet fairly quickly.

[The death of embryos] is of limited significance. . . . Presumably there will be five million such cases during the first generation, and 100 million in the course of subsequent generations. I regard the last-named figure as not all that serious, disregarding that minority of cases of obvious abortions or stillbirths. However that may be, humanity is so fertile that a slight decrease of this fertility does not need to be taken that seriously, not even by the individuals affected.

[What price] should the Russians be made to pay as punishment for their aggression? I have discussed this question with many Americans, and after talking for about a quarter of an hour they usually arrive at an acceptable price of between ten and sixty million. Usually one agrees on a figure somewhat closer to the higher of the two figures. . . . The ways and means how the upper limit seems to be reached is rather interesting. Namely, one mentions a third of the total population of a country, in other words something less than half.

A. Eichmann was condemned to death in December, 1961, and was hanged.

H. Kahn is advisory member of the Scientific Advisory Committee of the U.S. Air Force, of the technical committee of the Atomic Energy Commission, evaluator for the office of Civil Defense, and head of the Hudson Institute in White Plains, New York, which provides expert opinions for U.S. military planning. Kahn is married, has two children, and is known as a gourmet.

A question: can one compare K. and E.? Is there such a thing as the "objective investigation" of "the sum of human tragedy"? What moral cogency has a language that can call sixty million killed "an acceptable price"? Can genocide be the object of "impartial observation and calculation"? Where lies the difference between observation and planning, between calculation and preparation? Do such differences exist? Can one prevent genocide by planning it? Can prevention and planning be entrusted to "experts"? To whom do these experts offer their services? Does their advice have any consequences? Do their predispositions play a role? Who gave them their orders, who judges them?

9. Third example: understandable excitement. How many people are prepared to obey, unconditionally and of their own accord, even when they know that the execution of an order will put another person to considerable pain?

Setup for an experiment: two rooms, with a control panel in one and an electric chair in the other. It is explained to subject A that an experiment is being conducted to find out to what degree an adult's capacity to memorize can be increased by administering corporal punishment. A is asked to take over the role of the tester while someone else assumes the role of the learner. The leader of the experiment places a memory test in front of B and fastens him onto the electric chair in front of A's eyes. A goes to the adjacent room with the switchboard, where he turns a lever whenever B makes a mistake. The shocks are graded according to a scale attached to the implement administering the punishment. The chastisement begins with a 15-volt shock and is increased with each memorization mistake that B makes. At the twentieth shock, which has a power of 300 volts, B drums against the wall. At 375 volts a warning lights up on the switchboard: "Danger. Heavy shocks." The last lever, for 435 and 450 volts, merely has the designation XXX. The arrangement of the experiment is fictitious. There is no connection between the switchboard and the electric chair; the electrodes are not activated. The person in the chair only simulates his reactions, something the person administering the test cannot know: he finds himself in the role of a genuine torturer.

A series of experiments of this kind were conducted in 1963 at Yale University under the guidance of the psychologist Dr. Stanley Milgram. The subjects were volunteers, all of them citizens in good standing; 65 percent of the guinea pigs performed all the orders the leader of the experiment gave them and worked all levers according to instructions.[17]

In 1964 in Kempten in the Allgäu (Bavaria) the former Feldwebel L. Scherer was put on trial. He was accused of having captured fifteen men, women, and children whom he encountered while searching a forest in the Brjansk region during World War II, locking them in a wooden shed, setting fire to the shed, and throwing hand grenades into it. Professor Maurach of the University of Munich presented the court with expert testimony to the effect that the verdict would have to take into account the defendant's "boiling excitement" while he committed these acts. Maurach did not regard the killing of fifteen men, women, and children "illegal." The court delivered a not-guilty verdict; the accused, it said, had been placed in an acute state of distress by his orders.

At the same time, however, the German legal code still punished people

> who drive a sled in the cities without a firm shaft or without a bell or ringing mechanism (#366, section 4);
> whoever tears off public notices, orders or advertisements posted by officials or official bodies (#134);

whoever intentionally and illegally damages objects which serve the beautification of public thoroughfares (#304, section I);

whoever advertises means for birth control or for the prevention of venereal diseases in a manner injurious to public mores and good behavior (#184, section 3a);

whoever defaces officially affixed signs of the sovereignty of the Federal Republic of Germany (#96, section 2).

10. Artificial figure. The criminal in the traditional sense of the word, as one still finds him at court trials, belongs to the mythological substratum of the present age. He has long since assumed the traits of an artistic creation, for he claims a place in our imagination incommensurable with his real significance, his deeds, and the actuality of his existence. It remains extraordinary and puzzling how much passionate interest we bring to bear on him and what an enormous apparatus we keep up to fight him off. He enjoys an irrational publicity. It can be gleaned from our headlines that a simple murder interests us more than a war that is taking place far enough away—and much more than a war that hasn't started yet but is just being prepared. One is tempted to think the reason for this zealousness has something to do with the tenacity of our legal institutions. Undoubtedly, justice holds on more tenaciously than any other social institution—not excepting churches—to old ideas and forms, even when they no longer correspond to anything in reality (the worse for reality). Even the newest reasons for the so-called reform of the penal code reflect the cultural lag that dominates the whole legal sphere. The language of our law books is rife with turns of phrase so old-fashioned it requires recourse to philosophy to understand them. *Breach of peace, ringleader, workhouse, torts, armed rabble,* and the like are linguistic fossils that preserve historical conditions long since passed. In a certain sense it is almost admirable how the legal code has maintained itself unchanged in an alien world.

The role of the criminal in our world, however, is not to be explained solely by means of institutions. Taking a closer look, one finds that an entire system of roles that makes him indispensable and raises him to the rank of a mythological figure has been entrusted to him.

11. Palliative. The primary function of the "ordinary criminal" is to pacify. Although his appearance in society evokes fear, this fear is of an extraordinarily harmless kind. Moreover, in contrast to the far more real political and military threats to society, it is readily identifiable. The perpetrator of the cause for this fear appears on *Wanted* posters on every wall. His behavior, in contrast to that of the ruling powers, is comprehensible and overseeable. His act can be morally categorized without the slightest difficulty. The law books tell us what we are to think of the act. The murderer's fate makes it apparent to us that there "are still judges," and to his figure there is attached the wished-for illusion that killing is indeed prohibited. By punishing the criminal, society supports its conviction that its legal order is intact. All of this has a pacifying effect.

12. Scapegoat. For the individual, each condemnation of another—and the criminal is regarded as the Other, per se—constitutes an acquittal of himself. Whoever is guilty is punished; therefore, anyone who is not punished isn't guilty. It is instructive to observe the glee with which the collective citizenry participates in the pursuit of an escaped convict. The vocabulary from the hunting world is employed at once: the criminal is "fair game" and is allowed to be "shot down." The police practice of shooting at criminals, which is appalling in any event, can be encouraged at any given moment by means of a referendum. The demand for the death penalty also enjoys extreme popularity; especially after the discovery of so-called sex crimes, which always enjoy incredible publicity, does this call break out in hysterical waves. The role of the criminal as scapegoat for society is age-old; however, it is becoming particularly distinct under present conditions.

13. Deputy. The criminal not only receives his punishment in everyone's stead—he also acts in everyone's name, if not on their instruction. For he only does what everyone would like to do, and he does it on his own without a concession from the state. The outrage over the fact that he takes upon himself to do what everyone else forbids himself as long as it is prohibited and not ordered—this outrage expresses itself by demanding an eye for an eye and by revisiting the criminal's act upon himself. However, this repetition occurs at the hands of the state, therefore is again performed through deputies. What the individual foregoes, in reality he partakes of twice symbolically, through vicarious participation in the criminal's act and through participation in his punishment. Murderer and hangman relieve us of what we wish and yet don't wish to do, thus providing us not only with moral alibis, but also with a sense of moral superiority. Perhaps this helps explain that undercurrent of gratitude the public occasionally manifests toward some criminal, particularly toward the "successes" in their field. They are respected, as experts. Evil is their specialty, and the criminal practices it; thus, the society that practices division of labor delegates this area to him.

14. Competition. The criminal is not only the deputy for the individual, but for society as a whole, which he confronts by assuming its prerogatives: that is, he regards himself, in the words of Paule Ackermann, the lumberjack from Alaska, as a man who "has permission to permit himself everything." With this claim he puts himself in the same position as, and consequently against, the state, and becomes its competitor; he questions the state's monopoly on violence. This is an old role, too. The robbers and pirates of times past have given the purest performances of it, and every rebel assumes their features, if not of his own accord then by default; they are attributed to him by the world either through its disgust or admiration.[18]

Although the state's superior power vis-à-vis the criminal is never in doubt, although the criminal's means of exercising force stands in no relationship whatsoever to the state's capacity, the latter considers itself directly threatened by the individual's or the gang's actions. The state loves to claim that its "foundations are endangered." And it does not take a holdup murder to "shake" them—the simple picking of a pocket or the writing of an article can be quite sufficient. However, what seems to irritate modern legislators more than anything else is "resistance to the power of the state." Wherever this crime is mentioned, the text gladly abandons its anachronistic equanimity. Foam begins to form at the guardians' mouths, harmless hubbub becomes a "dangerous mob," the passerby, a criminal. The fury with which his crime is punished shows the other side of the coin of overwhelming power: the insecurity of our public order. Not even a diamond or oil monopoly will appear so strong yet so susceptible, so hypersensitive yet so brutal; and scarcely a one of them will go to battle against an outsider with such resounding righteousness.

15. Parody. As soon as criminals organize themselves they tend to form a state within the state, and the structure of such criminal societies gives a fairly faithful reflection of the rules of government employed by their rivals and competitors. The robber bands of the late Middle Ages imitated the feudal constitution, and a form of vassalage has been maintained by gangs to this day. The forms of military organizations were frequently copied, too. The *Carbonari* of the nineteenth century counted royalist bandits among them. Other secret societies, such as the Camorra, had something of a republican organization; but Salvatore Giuliano considered himself the liberator of Sicily "by the grace of God." The Sicilian Mafia imitated the structure of the patriarchal government down to its smallest detail and actually replaced the government in large areas of the country: it possessed an intricate administration, collected duties and taxes, and had its own court system.

Similar symmetries can be observed between the secret police of Czarist Russia, the Ochrana, and the conspiratorial groups it had been designed to combat. Rival organizations always tend to resemble each other. It is difficult to distinguish between the physical behavior and physiognomy of the bodyguards of gangsters and the guards of statesmen.

Specific capitalist organizational forms have found their criminal correspondence, too. Modern American gangster organizations are called "crime syndicates" or "Murder, Inc." They are constructed on the pattern of the large corporations, have their own tax advisers, accounting and legal departments, and they afford their employees the same social benefits as a legal company. Fascism as a "racket"—from Peachum's "middle class" center for harboring criminals to the Cauliflower Trust—has been described by Brecht. Thus the criminal societies appear as parodies of the general social and political arrangements, and vice versa. However, the criminals usually lag behind the development of the country as a whole, and that lends them a romantic aura. Fascism soon surpassed Brecht's description of it, which was perhaps accurate of a traditional basher-of-heads such as Röhm, even Göring possibly, but looks quite anachronistic when confronted with figures such as Heydrich, Bormann, or Höss, who manifest a far more abstract structure of the social "order."

The criminals already lagged far behind fascism. Today, when fascism itself is superannuated, since the nuclear implement makes even the accomplishments of an Eichmann look paltry by comparison, the most advanced criminal gang looks like an heirloom of former times, and it is unjust when the scholasticists of atomic strategy, authors such as Morgenstern, Brodie, Kahn, and their Soviet counterparts, speak of a "two-gangster situation" during their dry runs: their calculations far exceed the imagination of a criminal. After all, the ambition of two antagonistic gangsters is to kill each other off, whereas the above-mentioned scholars have their eye trained on the millions who are left out of their dry runs.

16. Phraseology. The delinquent in our world therefore cuts a comparatively harmless, almost sympathetic and humane figure. His motives are comprehensible. As a victim and accomplice of the now-illusory moral division of labor, he is fitted out by society in a mythological costume. The gangster has been unable to follow the inexorable progress of society; the technological development liquidated his artisan's methods of liquidation and replaced them by industrial methods. Even figures like Trujillo and many "benefactors" of his kind, who are still holding power in dozens of countries, testify—no matter how actual their rule—to the historical lag of the countries they govern rather than to the future of their metier. The old-time gangster, as well as the criminal traitor, is superannuated.

This explains the semantic difficulties one encounters as soon as one tries to apply traditional legal concepts to the misdeeds of the middle of the twentieth century. *Instigator, culprit, aiding and abetting, accomplice, accessory to the crime*—useful terms all when used to describe a robbery—have become vague and senseless. As it says in the Jerusalem verdict:

> With a huge and complicated crime of the kind with which we are dealing here, a crime in which many people participated on many different levels and through different acts—as

planners, as organizers and as executors, depending on their individual rank—with a crime such as this the normal concepts of instigation and conspiracy make little sense. For these crimes were committed massively, not only with respect to the number of victims but also with respect to the number of perpetrators; and the remove of a particular perpetrator from the one who actually killed the victim, or his proximity to him, is not a significant yardstick of his responsibility. Quite on the contrary, this responsibility generally increases the further we get away from the one who actually wielded the deadly instrument with his own hands.

But it is not only the concept of justice and its classifications, but even the concept of crime itself, which becomes self-defeating when applied to figures such as those who stand before our courts today or who man the planning staffs for the crimes of tomorrow. Whoever calls Hitler a common criminal belittles him and transfigures him into the realm of the comprehensible. (Brecht's Arturo Ui is nothing but *understatement*: the playwright vainly seeks to make the figure commensurable with the gangster.) Similarly, all the talk about "war criminals" amounts to prettification, as unintentional as that may be—as though modern war could be given the same denominator as petty crime. Crime, having become total, explodes its concept.

This too is just one more example of the impotence of our habits of mind and speech in the face of the atomic situation. It was a well-intentioned but absurd attempt that some American citizens made some years ago when they brought suit against the continuation of atomic tests to the Supreme Court. The Court declared itself incompetent. Our concepts, too, have become incompetent. Günter Anders was the one who showed most clearly that our military implementation can no longer be understood as a weapon. A political decision that would eliminate all further political decisions no longer deserves that label. There can be no responsibility—in the traditional sense of that word—for an act that would not leave anyone to ask any questions.

17. Final solution.

"I can build a device—I think I know how to do it today, I doubt that it would take me ten years to do and I doubt that it would cost me 10 billion dollars—and this device which I could bury, say, 2000 feet underground and, if detonated, it would destroy everybody in the world—at least all unprotected life. It can be done, I believe. In fact, I know it can be done."—*Herman Kahn at the Centenary Celebration of M.I.T., 1961.* [19]

With quantum mechanics, mathematics has brought forth a discipline that permits the scientist to calculate with the modification of the infinitely small and infinitely large. A moral quantum mechanics does not exist. Whoever seeks to make distinctions within the unspeakably evil is not just dealing with semantic difficulties. The failure of language only manifests the failure of our moral capacities in the face of our own capabilities.

Legal casuistry is as incapable of handling the situation as political practice has been to date. Posterity attempts to judge those responsible for Hitler's "Final Solution" even while busying itself with the preparation of its own. This is its inconsistency. This inconsistency is our only hope—a tiny one. No future misdeed can be equal to those of the past; misdeeds do not allow of subtraction, only of summation. (Doubtlessly there exists a form of moral impotence that believes Auschwitz can be diminished. It is particularly prevalent in Germany, where some persons seriously use the word *Wiedergutmachung*—indemnification—even in official documents.) "Final Solutions" cannot be made good again and weighed, not even on the scale of justice. That is one further reason why the world must hold court over them; and one further reason why this court does not suffice.

There are differences between the "Final Solution" of yesterday and the "Final Solution" of tomorrow—that is, between two unimaginable acts:

1. The Final Solution of yesterday was accomplished. The Final Solution of tomorrow is only being prepared. But it is a feature of the unconcept of this act that it can only be judged as long as it has not been accomplished, for it will leave no judges, no defendants, and no witnesses behind.

2. The Final Solution of yesterday was not prevented. The Final Solution of tomorrow can be prevented, although society seeks to delegate its prevention, as well as its preparation, usually to one and the same specialist. The prevention of the Final Solution can be delegated no more than the Solution itself can be delegated.

Neither one nor the other will be the work of a single individual, but the work of everyone; or it will not be at all. The mighty are impotent without the impotent ones.

3.   The Final Solution of yesterday was the work of a single nation, the German one. Four nations have possession of the implement for the Final Solution of tomorrow. The governments of many other nations are trying to obtain the implement. Some are not.

4.   The planning and realization of the Final Solution of yesterday was accomplished in secret. The planning of the Final Solution of tomorrow occurs in public. In 1943 there lived persons who were not accessories to the act. In 1964 there are only accessories.

5.   The perpetrators of the Final Solution of yesterday were recognizable. They wore uniforms; their victims wore a star. The perpetrators of the Final Solution of tomorrow can no longer be distinguished from their victims.

The Israeli psychiatrist who examined Eichmann called him "a completely normal man: he seems more normal to me than I do to myself after having examined him." Another expert considered him an exemplary family man and father. Eichmann busied himself primarily with statistics, traffic schedules, and paperwork; still, he saw his victims with his own eyes. The planner of the final world war will be spared this sight.

For example, is Edward Teller guilty? Is the journalist guilty who writes an article supporting the demand of German politicians to have the implement? Is the unknown mechanic from Oklahoma or Magnitogorsk guilty? Is Mao Zedong guilty? Are those guilty who believe in the chimera of "the relaxation of tension" while candidates like Franz Josef Strauss and Barry Goldwater can campaign for the power over life and death? Is the construction firm owner guilty who builds a control bunker? Are there still guilty parties in the future? Are there still innocent ones? Or are there only family men and fathers, nature lovers, normal persons? The glass cage in Jerusalem stands empty.

Translated by Michael Roloff

3

Las Casas,
or A Look Back
into the Future

The Indies [that is: the West Indian Islands and the coasts of Central and South America] were discovered in the year one thousand four hundred and ninety-two. In the following year a great many Spaniards went there with the intention of settling the land. Thus, forty-nine years have passed since the first settlers penetrated the land, the first so-claimed being the large and most happy isle called Hispaniola, which is six hundred leagues in circumference. Around it in all directions are many other islands, some very big, others very small, and all of them were, as we saw with our own eyes, densely populated with native peoples called Indians. This large island was perhaps the most densely populated place in the world. . . . And all the land so far discovered is a beehive of people; it is as though God had crowded into these lands the great majority of mankind.

"And of all the infinite universe of humanity, these people are the most guileless, the most devoid of wickedness and duplicity, the most obedient and faithful to their native masters and to the Spanish Christians whom they serve. They are by nature the most humble, patient, and peaceable, holding no grudges, free from embroilments, neither excitable nor quarrelsome. These people are

116

the most devoid of rancors, hatreds, or desire for vengeance of any people in the world. And because they are so weak and complaisant, they are less able to endure heavy labor and soon die of no matter what malady. . . .

"Yet into this sheepfold, into this land of meek outcasts there came some Spaniards who immediately behaved like ravening beasts, wolves, tigers or lions that had been starved for many days. And Spaniards have behaved in no other way during the past forty years, down to the present time, for they are still acting like ravening beasts, killing, terrorizing, afflicting, torturing, and destroying the native peoples, doing all this with the strangest and most varied new methods of cruelty, never seen or heard of before. . . .

"We can estimate very surely and truthfully that in the forty years that have passed, with the infernal actions of the Christians, there have been unjustly slain more than twelve million men, women and children. In truth, I believe without trying to deceive myself that the number of the slain is more like fifteen million. . . .

"Their reason for killing and destroying such an infinite number of souls is that the Christians have an ultimate aim, which is to acquire gold, and to swell themselves with riches in a very brief time and thus rise to a high estate disproportionate to their merits. It should be kept in mind that their insatiable greed and ambition, the greatest ever seen in the world, is the cause of their villainies. And also, those lands are so rich and felicitous, the native peoples so meek and patient, so easy to subject, and that our Spaniards have no more consideration for them than beasts. And I say this from my own knowledge of the acts I witnessed. But I should not say 'than beasts' for, thanks be to God, they have treated beasts with some respect; I should say instead like excrement on the public squares."

So begins the *Brief Account of the Devastation of the Indies,* which Fray Bartolomé de Las Casas wrote in 1542.

II

Whether what this book says is true, whether its author should be believed—this question has produced a quarrel that has been smoldering, burning, and flaming up for four hundred years. This quarrel has been waged by scholars, and their tracts and dissertations, their investigations and commentaries could fill an entire library. Even in our day a generation of specialists in Spain, Mexico, South America, and the United States is poring over the faded prints, letters, and manuscripts from the pen of the Dominican monk from Seville. Yet the quarrel about Las Casas is not an academic one: what is under dispute is genocide, committed on twenty million people.

Since such a state of affairs does not sit well with the preferred contemplative stance of historical writing without anger and prejudice, it is scarcely surprising that the colleagues from the monk's fraternity, the theologians, historians, and legal scholars have dropped all niceties in their choice of weapons. Where they lacked arguments they reached for rusty knives. They are, as we shall see, in use even today. The *Brief Account* had scarcely been published when the Court historian of Charles V, the famous Dr. Juan Ginés de Sepúlveda, produced a pamphlet *Against the premature, scandalous and heretical assertions which Fray Bartolomé de las Casas has made in his book about the conquest of the Indies, which he has had printed without permission of the authorities.* The very title heavy-handedly alludes to the censor and the Inquisition. Later Las Casas was called a traitor and a Lutheran. In 1562 the Council of the City of México petitioned the King that Las Casas's writings had caused such an uproar that they had had to convene a commission of legal scholars and theologians to draw up an expert opinion against this "impudent frater and his teachings"; the king ought to reprimand Las Casas publically and prohibit his books. A few years later the viceroy of Perú wrote: "The books of this fanatic and malicious bishop endanger the Spanish rule in America." He too demanded a royal prohibition; he too commissioned a refutation: for the official historians the fight against Las Casas turned into a flourishing business. The assessor, a man by the name of Pedro Sarmiento de Gamboa, had the following to say: "The devil has made a cunning chess move by making this deluded churchman his tool." In 1659 the censor of the Inquisition office in Aragón ruled that "this book reports of very horrifying and cruel actions, incomparable in the history of other nations, and ascribes them to Spanish soldiers and colonizers whom the Spanish King sent forth. In my opinion such reports are an insult to Spain. They must therefore be suppressed." Thereupon the Holy Tribunal of Saragossa finally issued a prohibition of the book in 1660. Yet new editions kept appearing: in 1748 the Seville chamber of commerce had a Latin translation confiscated, and even in 1784 the Spanish ambassador to France demanded a confiscation of a reprint.

Since the seventeenth century Las Casas's opponents have developed an even more elegant method to extirpate him. The historian Juán Meléndez, a Dominican, simply declared at that time that the *Brief Account* was a forgery; "noted authorities," whom he asked, had informed him that the book was written by a Frenchman and had been translated into Spanish with a forged title, something which should surprise no one: as the Spanish enjoyed the greatest fame as proclaimers of truth, the forgers had no choice but to camouflage their lies in this manner. Even in 1910 a Spanish historian seriously maintained that the *Brief Account,* to the best of human judgment, was not by Las Casas.

The reputation of the accused was not notably improved by this astonishing acquittal. Recent historians who write in Spanish have characterized him in the following words: "mentally ill" (1927); "a pig-headed anarchist" (1930); "a preacher of Marxism" (1937); "a dangerous demagogue" (1944); "a leveler possessed by the devil" (1946); "delusionary in his conceptions, boundless and inopportune in his expression" (1947); and the most respected Spanish historian of the twentieth century, Ramón Menéndez Pidal, in 1963 in Madrid, at age ninety-three, published an extensive book, in which he sought to exorcise the spirit of Las Casas once and for all. An American, Lewis Hanke, who has devoted his life to the study of the *Conquista,* remarks about this work of exorcism:

> Don Ramón passionately denies that Las Casas was an honorable man. He calls him a megalomaniac paranoid. In his retrospective look at the conquista Don Ramón scarcely detects a single dead Indian through his colored glasses: instead he sees a scene of well-being and of cultural progress for which America has to thank the Spaniards.

Only the unparalleled success that the *Brief Account* has had makes these tenacious and furious polemics comprehensible. Las Casas wrote a great deal: large-scale chronicles, theological and legal disputations, petitions and tractates. To this day there is no complete edition of his works. The ones with the greatest scholarly significance were first published in 1877 and 1909. There are obvious reasons for their long submersion in darkness. The *Brief Account*, true to its title, is nothing but a concise synopsis of the investigations and experiences that Las Casas elaborates in greater detail elsewhere. It was meant for a single reader: his Catholic Majesty, Charles I of Spain, as Charles V, Emperor of the Holy Roman Empire. Yet the *Brief Account's* appearance in book form, at a time when printing was just beginning to flourish, acquainted all of Europe with it. Its original publication in 1552 in Seville was followed by translations into all the important languages of the time: Paris (1579), London (1583), Amsterdam (1607), and Venice (1630) were the first foreign places of publication, followed by Barcelona, Brussels, Lyon, Frankfort, and later by Philadelphia, New York, Havana, Buenos Aires, Lima, São Paula, México, and Santiago de Chile.

The book's sensational effect provides an early example of the power of the press. The *Brief Account* reached one of its climaxes during the rivalry between Spain and England at the turn of the sixteenth century. A second wave of translations was brought on by the French Enlightenment. The third flood of reprints occurred between 1810 and 1830 in Latin America; at that time the *Brief Account* won direct influence on the leaders of the wars of independence against the Spanish colonial power. Simón Bolívar valued Las Casas, and the fact that he himself was a descendant of the conquistadors did not prevent him from making the book serve his revolutionary intentions. Las Casas had to serve as the chief witness against the Spanish even during the Spanish American War in 1899, which secured control over the Caribbean area and rule over the Philippines for the United States.

The *Brief Account* was not spared by the tumult of power-political interests. Time and again Spain's opponents used Las Casas, often in a pharisaical manner, and so it is not surprising that the Hispanic world to this day discusses the book from a perspective that seems foolish to us: namely, whether or not it "sullies" the honor of Spain. Las Casas has become the exponent of the so-called Black Legend, *leyenda negra,* as the Spanish historians with a terminological trick call every conception of the conquest of South

America that does not sing the official song of praise: as though what disparages the "honor of Spain" had been seized, willy-nilly, out of the blue.

This whole polemic is antiquated and superfluous. Spain's honor does not interest us. The French enlightener Jean François Marmontel, in his work on the destruction of the Inca empire, referring to Las Casas, already stated in 1777 what there is to be said on this subject: "All nations have their robbers and fanatics, their times of barbarousness, their attacks of rabies." The question of national character is not on the agenda. The extermination of the European Jews by the Germans, the Stalinist purges, the destruction of Dresden and Nagasaki, the French terror in Algeria, the Americans in Southeast Asia have demonstrated even to the most obtuse that all peoples are capable of everything; and as the *Brief Account of the Devastation of the Indies* is published once more, in a new English translation, the last of the Indians in Brazil are being inexorably exterminated.

The historians of the nineteenth century tried tenaciously, at times desperately, to invalidate Las Casas, and not only out of chauvinism or cowardice, but because the events he describes would have destroyed their historical picture. They believed in the mission of Christianity or in the "values" of European civilization, and what transpired during their own time in the Congo, in Indonesia, in India and China they would have considered as impossible as the genocide Las Casas described.

We have no such doubts. The news we receive on TV each day would suffice to disabuse us of them. The actuality of the book is monstrous, has a penetratingly contemporaneous smell to it. Of course our way of reading it is not devoid of an element of deception. Every historical analogy is ambiguous: for whoever rejects this analogy, history becomes a pile of meaningless facts; for whoever accepts it at face value, leveling the specific differences, it becomes aimless repetition, and he draws the false conclusion that it has always been this way and the tacit consequence that, therefore, it will always remain so too. No, Las Casas was not our contemporary. His report treats colonialism in its earliest stage; that is, the stage of robbery pure and simple, of unconcealed plundering. The complicated system of exploitation of international raw materials was as yet unknown at his time. Trade relations did not play a role during the Spanish *Conquista,* nor the spread of a superior material civilization; no "development policy" of whatever kind served it as justification—only a veneer of Christianity that proposed to convert the heathen, inasmuch as they survived the Christians' arrival. In its primal state colonialism could do without the fiction of partnership, of bilateral trade. It did not offer anything; it took what it found: slaves, gold, anything it pleased. Its investments were confined to the indispensable essentials of every colonial exploitation: to armed power, administration, and the fleet. For these reasons the Spanish conquerors could also ignore the dialectic of enslavement that Sartre describes in a few sentences:

> That is what is so annoying about slavery: if you tame a member of our species, you diminish his or her profitability; and as little as you provide him or her with, a human being as a workhorse is always going to cost more than he or she earns. That is why the colonial masters are forced to stop their breaking-in process halfway. The result: neither human being nor animal, but native. . . . Poor colonial masters: that constitutes his dilemma. He should really kill those whom he robs. But that is just what he cannot do, because he also has to exploit them. He cannot transform the massacre into genocide or the enslavement to the point of brutalization, and that is why he must necessarily lose control.

Such a dilemma only occurs when the colonialists set themselves long-term objectives, when they begin to calculate the profitability of their venture. Such a rational procedure of exploitation was unknown in the sixteenth century. The conquistadors did not know double-entry bookkeeping, not even the tally of the simplest statistics; the continent's depopulation did not trouble them.

Las Casas's opponents did not hesitate to make him responsible, as it were, for the irrationality of the genocide. There is no trusting his figures, it was and still is said; they betray a medieval relationship to arithmetic. South and Central America never held twelve, fifteen or twenty million inhabitants during the time of the conquest; as in the reports of the crusaders the word *million* simply means many people. Such an approach has something repulsive about it from the very outset. It would like to prove Las Casas a liar but let the murderers go scot-free because they only killed eight, five or three million Indians instead of twenty million. That is the way the *National Zeitung* protects the German fascists, claiming that not six million Jews were killed but at most five.

Aside from the moral insanity manifested by such sophistry, it is also factually wrong. Two American scholars who have investigated the demographic conditions in old Mexico in recent years reached the conclusion that in the thirty years between Cortez's landing and the writing of the *Brief Account* the population of Central Mexico dwindled from twenty-five to roughly six million. That means that the *Conquista* must have had nineteen million victims in Mexico alone; Las Casas names only four. Even if one takes into account viral illnesses, malaria, famine, and forced labor—that is, the indirect causes of the depopulation—one reaches the conclusion that Las Casas was probably rather too careful with his figures.

Let us leave these arithmetic examples aside. Las Casas spent more than forty years in the American colonies. What he reports are, in large part, observations and firsthand experiences. The witness's life testifies to their authenticity. Where his observations contradict the reports of other witnesses the historical investigator must engage in lengthy comparisons. We are not engaged in anything of the kind. What is decisive for today's reader of the *Brief Account* are two criteria that academic investigators usually ignore; that is, first of all, the inner cohesiveness of the book, its eye for detail, its care in sketching the episode. Las Casas rarely spends much time with abstract theses, and he not only decribes the most horrible cruelties, but also shows the grinding everyday life; he shows us, if the abbreviation be permitted, not only the torture instrument, but also the fight for the daily crust of bread.

A second, external criterion of Las Casas's credibility is the precision of his view of the structure of colonial rule. Since these structures still exist today his statements are verifiable. For this, one does not need to be a Hispanic scholar; a visit to South Africa will suffice.

If one tests the *Brief Account* from this perspective one notices, first of all, its author's economic acuity. The cleric Las Casas did not confine himself to theological observations; he analyzed the basic structure and exposed the technique of colonial exploitation, whose first step is the recruitment of forced labor. For this purpose there existed the so-called *encomienda* system. *Encomienda* means as much as recommendation. A random number of Indians were distributed by the local commanders to the individual Spanish landowners and "recommended" to them for the reason that they required this protection for their prompt conversion. In reality, the status of these protégés was that of serfs: they were totally at the mercy of their new masters and received no wages or upkeep for the work that their protector (*encomendero*) asked them to do.

The economy of the colonializers concentrated on two forms of business that dominate the economy of many South American nations to this day: mining and plantations. But whereas the North America concerns now extract tin, copper, lead, and vanadium, the conquistadors were interested in one metal only: gold.

Contact with the motherland during the time of the *Conquista* was expensive, time-consuming, and dangerous; exploitation of the overseas possessions thus had to confine itself to the most valuable commodities. That explains a further specialty of the colonializers: the pearl fishing in the Caribbean of which Las Casas provides an unforgettable description:

> The pearl fishers dive into the sea at a depth of five fathoms, and do this from sunrise to sunset, and remain for many minutes without breathing, tearing the oysters out of their rocky beds where the pearls are formed. . . . It is impossible to continue for long diving into the cold water and holding the breath for minutes at a time, repeating this hour after hour, day after day; the continual cold penetrates them, constricts the chest, and they die spitting blood, or weakened by diarrhea. The hair of these pearl divers, naturally black, is as if burnished by the saltpeter in the water, and hangs down their back making them look like sea wolves or monsters of another species.

That is not a hearsay report; only someone who has seen the burnished hair and the encrusted shoulders with his own eyes speaks like that. This description by Las Casas led, incidentally, to a royal prohibition of pearl fishing—one of the few, albeit short-lived, victories that fell the valiant bishop's way.

Another enterprise that Las Casas deals with could only develop when one region after the other had been depopulated: the slave trade. After the Indians had been cut down by the millions and tormented to death, the colonializers noted with astonishment and even with a certain regret that they were running out of labor power. At this moment the savage became a commodity and the deportations became a profitable business in which the military and officials, who formed primitive corporations, engaged on their own account.

> The colonized world is a divided world. The dividing line, the border is marked by barracks and police stations. The rightful and institutional interlocutor of the colonized, the spokesman of the colonial masters and the repressive regime is the cop or the soldier. . . . The agent of power employs the language of pure power. He does not conceal his sovereignty, he exhibits it. . . . The colonial master is an exhibitionist. His need for security makes him remind the colonized, with a loud voice: "I am master."

These sentences are from a modern phenomenology of colonial rule. Frantz Fanon developed it in the first chapter of his book *The Wretched of the Earth* (1961). Las Casas's observations, made four hundred years earlier, agree with them exactly. Even the manifestly senseless cruelties, even the conquistadors' terroristic arbitrariness had its psychological function in that it demonstratively cut the New World in two. Proof of the fact that the Indians were not human beings was provided by the Spaniards anew every day when they acted as if they were not dealing with human beings: "But I should not say 'than beasts' for, thanks be to God, they have treated beasts with some respect; I should say instead like excrement on the public squares."

(Referring to the concentration camps of the twentieth century, Hannah Arendt has written that, if one appealed to the healthy human understanding of those in power by pointing out to them the superfluousness of the gigantic apparatus of terror, directed against completely pliable human beings, they might answer if they wanted to state the truth: this apparatus only seems superfluous to you because it serves to make human beings superfluous.)

But the blind terror with which the colonial masters demonstrate who they are and that the colonized are nothing leads to a new dilemma. It assures the colonizers of their identity while simultaneously endangering their ideology. Once they become afraid of the colonized their terror robs them of their justification, which they would not like to relinquish. For the colonial master not only wants to have power, he also wants to be in the right: he keeps asserting ad nauseam that he has a mission, that he serves God and the King, that he is spreading the Christian teachings and the values of civilization—in a word, that he basically has something higher in mind. He cannot do so without a good conscience. But this means that he must hide the terror that he practices so ostentatiously and must deny his own demonstration. Something peculiarly schizophrenic, an insane formalism, thus is attached to all colonial undertakings. Of this, too, the *Brief Account* provides an excellent example:

> And because of the pernicious blindness that has always afflicted those who have ruled in the Indies, nothing was done to *incline* the Indians to embrace the one true Faith, they were rounded up and in large numbers *forced* to do so. Inasmuch as the conversion of the Indians to Christianity was stated to be the principal aim of the Spanish conquerors, they have dissimulated the fact that only with blood and fire have the Indians been brought to embrace the Faith and to swear obedience to the kings of Castile or by threats of being slain or taken into captivity. As if the Son of God who died for each one of them would have countenanced such a thing! For He commanded His Apostles: "Go ye to all the people" (*Euntes docete omnes gentes*). Christ Jesus would have made no such demands of these peaceable infidels who cultivate the soil of their native lands. Yet they are told they must embrace the Christian Faith immediately, without hearing any sermon preached and without any indoctrination. They are told to subject themselves to a King they have never heard of nor seen and are told this by the King's messengers who are such despicable and cruel tyrants that deprive them of their liberty, their possessions, their wives and children. This is not only absurd but worthy of scorn.
> This wretch of a Governor thus gave such instructions in order to justify his and their presence in the Indies, they themselves being absurd, irrational, and unjust when he sent the thieves under his command to attack and rob a settlement of Indians where he had heard there was a store of gold, telling them to go at night when the inhabitants were securely in their houses and that, when half a league away from the

settlement, they should read in a loud voice his order: "Caciques and Indians of this land, hark ye! We notify you that there is but one God and one Pope and one King of Castile who is the lord of these lands. Give heed and show obedience!" Etc., etc. "And if not, be warned that we will wage war against you and will slay you or take you into captivity." Etc., etc.

The sentence that not the murderer but the victim is guilty becomes the dominant maxim under colonial rule. The "native" is the potential criminal per se who must be held in check, a traitor who threatens the order of the state: "Those who did not rush forth at once," Las Casas says, "to entrust themselves into the hands of such ruthless, gruesome and beastial men were called rebels and insurgents who wanted to escape the service of His Majesty."

But this guilty verdict is the very thing that helps the colonized to perceive their situation. For it leads to its own fulfillment: fiction becomes reality, the raped resort to violence. Las Casas describes several instances where it came to armed actions of resistance, even to small guerrilla wars. He calls the Indian attacks, where "a considerable number of Christians" lost their lives, a "just and holy war" whose "justifiable causes will be acknowledged by every man who loves justice and reason." Without hesitating, in three sweeping sentences that have been left unscarred by the centuries, Las Casas thinks his thoughts to their conclusion:

And those wretches, those Spaniards, blinded by greed, think they have the God-given right to perpetrate all these cruelties and cannot see that the Indians have cause, have abundant causes, to attack them and by force of arms if they had weapons, to throw them out of their lands, this under all the laws, natural, human, and divine. And they cannot see the injustice of their acts, the iniquity of the injuries and inexpiable sins they have committed against the Indians, and they renew their wars, thinking and saying that the victories they have had against the Indians, laying waste the lands, have all been approved by God and they praise Him, like the thieves of whom the prophet Zechariah speaks: "Feed the flock of the slaughter; whose possessors slay them, and hold themselves not guilty: and they that sell them say, Blessed be the Lord; for I am rich."

The book that Las Casas left behind is a scandal. In its original sense the word *scandal* means "trap." The scholars who warn us of him have entangled themselves in that old *skandalon*. They do not sense that their quarrel is only a distant echo of a huge conflict. The tempest in the teapot of their profession points to other tempests. The ruffle in the historical consciousness indicates enormous tremors in historical reality. The process that began with the *Conquista* is not yet over. It continues in South America, Africa, and Asia. It does not behoove us to speak the verdict about the monk from Seville. Perhaps he has spoken ours.

III

Don Bartolomé de Las Casas was born in 1474 as the son of an aristocrat. The family came from the Limousin region and achieved respected and prosperous status in Andalusia. In 1492, when Columbus was venturing on his first trip to the West, Las Casas was taking up theological and legal studies at the University of Salamanca. His father, Don Francisco, was one of the first Europeans to see the new continent. The name Las Casas appears in the register of the *Santa Maria*. But we have little information about the father's activities. Not even his arrival in America is certain; some historians even claim that he only took part in Columbus' second journey. In any event, Don Francisco had already returned to Seville in 1497. He left no permanent traces in the history of the *Conquista*. His son must have followed him in the last years of the fifteenth century. His presence in Hispaniola is confirmed as of 1502. In 1511 he was elected to the priesthood in Santo Domingo. Evidently Don Bartolomé began to take interest in the Indian culture almost at once. There is testimony that he was a much-sought-after interpreter. During his life he learned more than a dozen Indian dialects. Besides, for fifteen years he behaved no differently than the other colonizers. He made the acquaintance of the leading people of the *Conquista*: Cortez, Pizarro, Alvarado, Pedrarias, and Columbus the Younger. In 1512 he went with Diego Velásquez and Pánfilo de Narváez to Cuba. The intention of this expedition was to "pacify," that is to subjugate, the island completely. As Las Casas himself reports in his *History of the Indies,* he cared "more about his possessions and his mines than about the Christian teachings; for he was just as blind as the secular settlers."

It is possible to give the precise date on which he began his life-work. At Pentecost 1514, aged forty, Las Casas was to give a sermon at the newly founded Ciudad de Espíritu Santo.

> While preparing for this sermon I began to think about several principles of Holy Scripture. I came upon a place in the book Sirach, chapter 34, where it says: "The poor man has nothing but a little bread; whoever deprives him of it is a murderer. Whoever does not give the worker his wages is a bloodhound. . . ." I thought about the misery and slavery in which the native people are living here. . . . And the more I thought about it the more convinced I was that everything we had done to the Indians so far was nothing but tyranny and barbarism. . . . And as much as I studied in every book I read, no matter whether it was in Spanish or in Latin, I came on more and new reasons and authentic teachings which spoke for the right of those Indian people and against the robberies, misdeeds and injustices we had committed.

This discovery, the second discovery of the New World, a world that has not been surveyed to this day, occupied Las Casas to the end of his life. This has nothing to do with religious enlightenment. Las Casas carefully insisted that this insight was accessible to everyone; he insisted on its rationality and with shining intelligence drew from it all theoretical and practical consequences.

First of all he renounced all the possessions and slaves that had been assigned to him and proceeded to interfere in the administrative practice of the *Conquista*. The first objective of his attack was the terrorist methods of its justice. Soon occurred the first conflict between the frater and the commanders of the "pacification" of Cuba. Las Casas intervened with the Governor, appealed for mercy and wrote petitions, frequently in vain. The conflict developed a logic of its own. The monk reached the conclusion that the executions could not be fought separately from the system as a whole, which depends on the executions to maintain itself. In spring 1515 he therefore looked up the royal *general repartidor* for the Indian lands, the person who represented the system of forced labor, and revealed to him that his activity "was derisive of all Godly and human laws." Simultaneously, Las Casas turned with petitions, assessments, and complaints to the Spanish court.

The official is supposed to have listened to the unknown cleric without moving a muscle in his face; yet with this audience there began the unpleasantness that was to accompany Las Casas for the rest of his life. His letters got lost, his income did not arrive, and his attempts to get ship's passage met with the greatest difficulties. For Las Casas had decided to go to Madrid, to reach the King and effect the enactment of laws that would eliminate the whole system of slavery. This project is characteristic of Las Casas. His contemporaries thought him mad. Yet the mixture of boldness and naiveté with which he went to work was perhaps one of his greatest assets. Time and again it protected Las Casas and took his opponents by surprise. Besides, his strategy was entirely consistent. There was no authority in the colonies on whose support he could count: clerics and laymen, officials and private persons—all were participants in that firm whose earnings were threatened by Don Bartolomé's ideas.

In the summer of 1515 Las Casas began the first of fourteen journeys he undertook to protect the inhabitants of the West Indies from being exterminated. He reached King Ferdinand V, via his confessor, and before him made a thorough report of the conditions in America. There is no account of this audience, but the King was apparently sufficiently moved to convene a commission to investigate the "Indian question." Las Casas was asked to appear in Seville; his testimony made the commission recommend to the King that he should settle the matter legally. It is questionable whether Don Bartolomé at that time already knew the rules of the game that he had entered and that, always with new subterfuges, was to be protracted over a period of fifty years. He presumably did not know that the members, two bishops and one official, had a material interest in the exploitation of the West Indies: they received considerable income from that source. When the King died a few months after the audience, the commission dissolved itself. There was no further mention of the new laws. An intervention with the new monarch looked hopeless—Charles V, who was sixteen at the time, did not live in Spain. Las Casas now turned to the Grand Inquisitor, who was the King's representative. Ximenes made the Dominican *"Defensor universal de los Indios,"* the adviser to all royal authorities on the Indian question and reporter to a new commission that was to accompany him to the Indies. There were new maneuvers, bribery attempts, denunciations, and intrigues; new trips, subpoenas, reports, delays, obstacles, open and concealed sabotage. In 1520 Las Casas finally achieved an audience with Charles V.

There occurred a lively interchange about which we are informed in detail. In the conversation, which formally resembled the "hearing" of our days, there participated the chancellor of the Spanish crown, several members of the Indian council, a representative of the commission of 1516, as well as the general notary of the Indian territories, a certain Conchillos, who represented the interests of the slave trade. The vehement dispute ended with the general notary offering his resignation to the King, which was accepted. Las Casas left with the title of court chaplain. The King reached the following decision: the procedure of the conquistadors in the Indian lands had been illegal; the Indian council should work out a plan by which the American possessions could be governed "without the force of weapons."

The man who accomplished all this at the imperial court was no longer a newcomer but an experienced politician familiar with the way in which those who governed thought. Las Casas had not lost his uninhibitedness and he was less than ever prepared for compromises; yet surprisingly quickly he had developed into a tactician of great style. A few places in the *Brief Account* allow us to reconstruct his line of argument toward the King. He proceeded in every respect from the assumption that the King knew nothing of the crimes being committed in his name.

> Your Majesty will find out that there are no Christians in these lands; instead, there are demons. There are neither servants of God nor of the King. Because, in truth, the great obstacle to my being able to bring the Indians from war-making to a peaceful way of life, and to bringing the knowledge of God to those Indians who are peaceful is the harsh and cruel treatment of these Indians by the Spanish Christians. For which scabrous and bitter reason no word can be more hateful to those Indians than the word Christian which they render in their language as *Yares,* meaning Demons. And without a doubt they are right, because the actions of these

> Governors are neither Christian nor humane but are actions
> of the devil.

Such sentences acquit the King of all complicity; but they are
that much more dangerous for his representatives. Their ambiguity appears as soon as Las Casas turns to the question of how the
booty is to be divided.

> Our King and Master has been deceived by certain highly
> pernicious and deceitful machinations; just as there have been
> continual efforts to hide the truth from Him that the Spaniards in the Indies are transgressing in the most terrible manner against God and Man and against His Majesty's royal
> honor.

Of course Las Casas was completely aware that the Spanish
crown was totally dependent on the income from the colonies.
One year before the audience the Augsburg business firm Welser
had financed the election of Charles V, and his dependency on the
banks was notorious everywhere in Europe. Las Casas also turned
this situation to his advantage. He charged that the conquistadors'
violent behavior had cost the King hundreds of thousands of crowns
year after year; their conduct deprived the state treasury and only
enriched the local governors. This line of argument finally amounts
to a demand for centralization and refinement of colonial exploitation, yet it certainly must have made more of an impression on
Charles V than all the theological and legal arguments that Las
Casas brought to bear.

Besides, Las Casas himself fell victim to the tactical ingenuity
that he manifested in his 1520 audience. At that time he is supposed to have pointed out the delicate constitution of the Indians
and have said that the inhabitants of Africa were far better suited
for the toil of the mine and plantation work. This suggestion was
taken up, and in the course of the following 350 years between
fifteen and twenty million people were dragged off and sold as
slaves to America. The slave trade, one of the biggest business
deals in the history of the world, invoked the words Las Casas
had uttered in 1520 and called him its patron. He did not defend himself, but in his *Historia general de las Indias* one finds the
lapidary sentence:

The priest Las Casas was the first to suggest that one should introduce Africans to the West Indies. He did not know what he was doing. When he heard that the Portuguese were catching people in Africa against all laws and made them into slaves he bitterly regretted his words . . . the right of the Blacks is the same as that of the Indians.

Las Casas had found the support of the King. But the King was remote. The laws got stuck. Little changed in the practice of American colonialization. In 1523 Don Bartolomé entered a Dominican monastery in Hispaniola where he remained for nearly ten years. During this time he laid the theoretical foundation for his future actions. His major scholarly works were begun and conceived at that time: first the *Apologetic History of the Indies,* then the source book, the *Historia general de las Indias.* Though they may find some fault with Las Casas's methods, these works are invaluable for the modern historian of the *Conquista.* Their author was gifted with the instinct and sagacity of the true historian. He systematically collected manuscripts, letters, and official documents that referred to the conquest of America. The world is indebted to him, for example, for the knowledge of Columbus's ships' diaries—a transcript in his archives preserved them. However, Las Casas did not confine himself to the role of a chronicler. His understanding of the Indian cultures helped him to gain anthropological insights that were completely alien to his contemporaries. He supported the opinion that the American cultures could not be measured by European standards, one should understand them out of their own prerequisites. He was probably the first to compare the Mayan temples in Yucatán to the pyramids. He felt that the Spanish had no reason whatsoever to feel superior to the Indians; he preferred them in many respects to his own countrymen. Such insights announce, two hundred years before Vico, the dawning of a historical consciousness. Las Casas understood human culture as an evolutionary process and he understood that civilization is not a singular but a plural: he discovered the discontemporaneity of historical developments and the relativity of the European position. With such a historical understanding he stands, as far as I can tell, quite alone in the sixteenth century. To the governments of the West, judging by their actions, such an understanding has remained alien to this day.

In the 1530s Las Casas resumed the political fight. He first visited Venezuela, Perú, New Granada, Darién, and Guatemala. There was another fracas in Nicaragua in 1539. One of the Dominican's sermons provoked the soldiers of a Spanish expeditionary corps to desert. The expedition ended with a defeat of the depleted troops whose commander denounced Las Casas in Madrid for treason. Again he had to make the trip to Spain, which at that time took from eight to sixteen weeks, so as to defend himself. It was at this time that he wrote the *Brief Account,* had himself consecrated bishop, and finally effected a comprehensive legal regulation of the Indian question. The new laws—*Las Nuevas Leyes de las Indias*—were announced in Seville in 1542. They prohibited the viceroys and governors, all royal officials and soldiers, the clerics and monasteries, and all public institutions from taking Indians into their service by way of the *encomienda.* All Indians who were subject to this law or those who had been "recommended" without royal decree were considered free. The law awarded every native worker an appropriate wage. Pearl fishing was prohibited. The new laws end with the sentence: "The inhabitants of the Indian Lands are to be treated in every respect as free subjects of the crown of Castile: for there exists no difference between the latter and the former."

The new laws immediately encountered bitter and organized resistance in the Spanish colonies in America. The entrepreneurs openly declared that they were dependent on the slave economy. The judges for the most part sided with the local interests; but even when they were not bribed it proved impossible for them to assert the new laws against the will of the military and civil administration. After four years the attempt by the "protector of all the Indians" to secure their rights legislatively broke down once and for all. Under pressure from the American interests, Charles V revoked the laws on November 20, 1545.

Las Casas, already an old man, must have realized that his fight could not be won politically. However, he did not think of resigning. He withdrew to a terrain where the pressure group of plantation owners could not attack him. This was the area of everyday theological practice. As bishop of Chiapas in Mexico, he issued a text with the following title: *Confessional: that is, Aid to all confessors who have to give the sacrament to the Spanish gentlemen in the Indian lands.* This penitential sets forth the condition under which a conquistador, a plantation or mine owner, a slave or weapon dealer can receive absolution. Las Casas demanded as prerequisite a notarized protocol in which the penitent had to obligate himself to complete indemnification—in legally binding form. Since such documents were usually drawn up at the deathbed, this amounted to a creation of testaments in favor of the Indians. The *Aid* determined down to the smallest detail how the dying person's possessions were to be disposed of and how the inheritance was to be legally handled. The effect of the text was sensational. Las Casas had found a stronger ally than the King: the Spaniard's fear of hell. The advice he gave to the confessors meant that everyone who refused to fulfill the conditions would be excommunicated. Of course Las Casas's penitential was effective in only a few dioceses. After a few years the horror of the faithful subsided and the penitential fell into disuse. Still, it earned its author a new denunciation for high treason and insult to the crown; the penitential could have the effect, so the accusation claimed, of undermining royal sovereignty in the West Indies. Once again Las Casas had to follow a subpoena to Madrid. He left America in the summer of 1547, never to return.

Las Casas was almost eighty years old. The proceeding against him petered out. He had himself divested of his bishop's office. In the decade left in his life he continued his anthropological and legal research and published the first edition of his works. Everything he thought and wrote focused on the problem of colonialism. He was to have one last great public appearance before the political and academic world in 1550. This was the famous disputation of Valladolid. The man whom Las Casas confronted there was the leading ideologist of the *Conquista:* Juan Ginés de Sepúlveda. The conflict was conducted very sharply by both sides. There exists a record of this conversation, whose florid title points to the heart of the dispute: *Disputation or controversy between the bishop Fray Don Bartolomé de Las Casas, formerly head pastor of the royal city of Chiapas, which lies in the Indies and belongs to New Spain; and Dr. Ginés de Sepúlveda, the court chronicler of our imperial majesty; about whether, as the Doctor claims, the conquest of the Indian lands and the war against the Indians is justified; or whether, as the Bishop counters and proclaims, the war is tyrannical, unjust and illegal; which question was probed in the presence of many theological and legal scholars at an assembly which was convened by the wish and will of his majesty in Valladolid in 1550.*

The disputation ended with a complete defeat for Sepúlveda, who withdrew from his courtly office and whose book *About the Just War Against the Indians* fell victim to the Inquisition. Like all of Las Casas's victories, this, too, was a Pyrrhic one. The theory of the *Conquista* had been heavily damaged, but nothing changed in the condition of the Indians.

Las Casas died in the summer of 1566 in Madrid. On his desk was found his last manuscript: *About the Sixteen Remedies against the Plague which has Exterminated the Indians.* "The death candle in his hand," it says in a contemporary report, "and prepared to depart this world, he begged his friends to continue the defense of the Indians. He was sad that he had been able to achieve so little for them, yet was convinced that in everything he had done he had done right."

There is no monument in Spain to remind you of Las Casas, and no one knows where he is buried.

Bartolomé de las Casas was not a radical. He did not preach revolution. His loyalty to the church and to the crown are undisputed. He fought for the equal rights of the Indians as subjects of an authority he acknowledged. A radical transformation of the social order was as unthinkable for him as for his contemporaries; he wanted to bring the one that existed to the point where it would live up to its own ideology. Every social order contains a utopia with which it decorates itself and that it simultaneously distorts. Las Casas did not guess that this promise, which was also contrary to the idea of the state of his time, can only be fulfilled at the price of revolution, partially, occasionally, as long and insofar as a new form of domination does not encapsulate and negate it again.

Yet utopian thoughts were not alien to Las Casas. He was the contemporary of Thomas More and of Machiavelli, of Rabelais and of Giovanni Botero. In 1521 he tried nothing less than the founding of his own Nova Atlantis. The undertaking shows the unity of theory and practice that characterizes all his work. It ended catastrophically.

At his audience with Charles V, Las Casas suggested to the Emperor, as proof that his principles withstood the test of practice, to found a model colony of "the plough and the word." The Emperor decreed the district of Cumaná in Venezuela to him with the proviso that "no Spanish subject may enter this territory with arms." Las Casas recruited a group of farmers, outfitted an unarmed expedition, and started to build his colony. Attacks by Spanish soldiers and by slave dealers on the peaceful territory, uprisings by embittered Indians, whiskey smuggling, and acts of violence destroyed the colony in a short time. None of the defeats he suffered hurt Las Casas more deeply than this loss.

The proof of the experiment has not been exhausted to this day. There is no peaceful colonialism. Colonial rule cannot be founded on the plough and the word, but only on the sword and the fire. Every "alliance for progress" needs its "gorillas," every "peaceful penetration" is dependent on its bomber commando, and every "reasonable reformer" such as General Lansdale finds his Marshal Ky.

Bartolomé de Las Casas was not a reformer. The new colonialism that today rules the poor world cannot invoke his name. In the decisive question of force, Las Casas never wavered; the subjugated people lead, in his words, "a just struggle, the lawful basis of which will be acknowledged by every reasonable and justice-loving man." The regime of the wealthy over the poor, which Las Casas was the first to describe, has not ended. The *Brief Account* is a look back into our own future.

Translated by Michael Roloff

4

Berlin Commonplaces

1. Revenant. A ghost is haunting Europe: the ghost of the revolution. The returnee is greeted like its great predecessor: with scorn and panic, skepticism and hysteria, and it also encounters—only in smaller doses—pacification and suppression. The doomsayers are at work; the manslaughterers are waiting for their turn.

What is being mentioned is only a shadow now. The revolution in Europe is not a material force. It gives a disembodied effect because it lacks a strong class basis. Many consider it a fad, the cause of the minority of a minority, that is the intellectuals. It is true: the ruling class in the metropolises has succeeded in melting down the political consciousness of the majority, in liquidating it. It is a sign of the suppression that rules our societies that political awareness has become the privilege of a minority and that only the minority of a minority makes use of this privilege.

But there's no shadow without a body, no ghost without a corpse. The shadow of the revolution is the shadow of another, greater one, of the hungering, plundered, and bomb-torn world. Their dead are coming to haunt us. The revolution in Europe until today is only the shadow of that revolution that Europe has tried vainly to beat down. Today Europe leaves this work—out of weakness, not out of insight—to the United States. Each victory and each defeat in this struggle edge us a little deeper into the shadow of the revolution. What is returning there, what disturbs the peace and refuses to be turned away is the future—inasmuch as the word still has a meaning, in Europe.

2. Lip reading. You can't be serious. That word already! *Revolution:* an expression that only the advertising world still uses. Revolution in the detergent market, revolution in the investment business. What goes beyond this is sick. Phantasts. Amok-runners. Troublemakers. Juvenile delinquents. Bleeding-hearts. Safety valve. Moth-eaten dusty slogans. Ironic shoulder shrugging on the surface, finger to the temple at the first scratch, and when the lacquer starts to flake off: fear and trembling, crying fit, where's the truncheon, it's getting serious. Slow motion: the camera seizes the passerby behind the barricade, who stops, turns around, shows surprise, slowly opens his mouth, there is no sound; zoom lens fetches the head, mouth is wide open now. The uninitiated are reminded of a soccer match and hear the word *score,* others who can read lips hear the cry for the gas chamber.

3. Foreign word [in Germany]. The revolution. A total change in the course or the connection of things. Thus one calls unusually large floods, earthquakes that alter large stretches of land, revolutions in nature, the Reformation a revolution in human understanding. Particularly the complete change in the constitution of a state, say when a monarchy becomes a republic, the succession is violently altered. The English, the French Revolution. In recent times one has tried to substitute a German word for this foreign word. The unhappiest choices one could probably make were *Umwälzung* and *Staatsumwälzung* because they don't express the concept of the matter and contain a harsh trope that is alien to our language.

Adelung 1807

4. Judgment by default. Everywhere, even in the U.S.A., the word *revolution* reminds people of their nation's best possibilities. In Germany it has remained a foreign word. The only victorious revolution we can call our own was imported by force of arms. The Germans did not make it, only administered it or suffered it to be administered on them. That has left its scars on this revolution, and there is nothing to indicate that the scars will disappear. Otherwise, the foreign word designates a long chain of historical omissions. At the latest, since 1789, travelers who have ventured to central Europe can report of a country whose political conditions testify to chronic underdevelopment.

> Is it so difficult to recognize that the German nation has not
> a life history but only a case history so far? (*Hebbel*)

5. Foreign product. I don't understand you. (My friend Z is thirty-nine; a lawyer at one time, he is now a professor, and as far as I can make out, shows agricultural workers how to manage a large farm. It would be called business administration over here; over there it most certainly is called something else. Z is a Cuban.)

All I have to do is say where I come from and I elicit immediate reflex movements as though I were running around with an unsheathed knife. What are you so afraid of? Of yourselves? Or do you really have so much to lose?

The revolution, you think, will deprive you of your shoehorns and your stewardesses, will close the discotheques and cut novels of Günter Grass. It rapes nuns, hangs pictures of tractors on the wall, and prohibits the NPD (*Nationalistische Partei Deutschlands*—West Germany's fascist party). In one word: it is the terror, pure and simple. Something like that might be okay for Cuba, but for Germany, God forbid. So you are on the side of humanity; everyone knows that. The revolution is the other per se, is infiltration, subversion, undermining, conspiracy, stab in the back. Something so furtive can only come from outside or from below, either from the East or the lower instincts.

And what if I tell you that it was made by human beings, the revolution, made in broad daylight, and that it is you who sit in the dark? Yes, someone replied to me in Kassel or Giessen, but we have a democracy. He also mentioned the past, which he wanted to overcome, so he said. Without a revolution? Well, just you try and show me how!

6. Ye olde Germany. In 1945, instead of doing the only thing that might have saved it, the revolution, Western Germany decided to convert. Moral transformation instead of political revolution, turnabout instead of coup d'état, stabilization of the social condition from above instead of revolution from below. Overcoming of the past instead of class warfare for the future. Reconstruction of the old reality, a new beginning as rhetoric.

The reasons are ascertainable. However, the historical moment was unique: the opportunity for an unbloody revolution, present at that time, will not return. The ruling class was discredited, the old state apparatus destroyed, the military defeated. However, Germany was exhausted. There was no workers' movement capable of concerted action. The masses were politically paralyzed by twelve years of dictatorship. The best that the country had to offer had fallen victim to the regime or had emigrated, and of those who returned, the politically more aware chose the eastern part of the country.

In the years after the war the Germans were blind to international class warfare. The international perspective was defined by events in their own country and by conflicts between the victorious powers. The colonial wars took place outside Germany's field of vision. China was an unknown quantity. The world had shrunk to a horizon of ruins: anyone who wanted to get farther than three miles from his home town needed a pass from the military authorities. The events in Africa, Asia, and Latin America were neither perceived nor could they be imagined. Banished into the overwhelming reality of their defeat, history seemed to stand still to the Germans.

7. **Blood money.** In the meantime the counterrevolution had already won its game. The currency reform, which the masses correctly understood as the decisive step, was the historical turning point. (That is the reason for the postwar period's fashion of not dating events before or after the defeat but before or after "the currency.") The economic consequences of this operation were clear; the political decisions implicit in it were not understood.

The cold war brought the return of West Germany into world politics, that is, on the side of the counterrevolution. The Stalinism of the Soviet Union, the Prague coup, the Berlin blockade, the politics of the SED (*Sozialistische Einheitspartei Deutschlands*) paralyzed all revolutionary alternatives. The total suspicion of ideology became a total ideology itself: monopoly power pretended to be social-market economy, mass consumption the embodiment of freedom, the reconstruction, which the working class paid for, a miracle that had to justify the sanctification of private property. Only one time was there real opposition: against the rearmament that in the long run was directed as much against the external as the internal enemy, that is, also against those masses whom it promised security. Yet the protest against the rearmament of the Federal Republic did not see this logic. Its motivation was profoundly unpolitical, consisting of emotional antipathy and moral scruples.

At the end of this development the intellectuals of the opposition asked themselves in all seriousness: Is there still a proletariat? Is there still a ruling class? Whereas they would have been more justified in asking: Is there still an intellectual opposition?

8. Contrast program. The ruling class is the only one that survived, unscathed, the German disaster for which it is responsible. Its heart is intact: financial and industrial capitalism, ministerial and legal bureaucracy, church and military infrastructure have secured the continuity of their personnel and resumed their old positions of power. (For purely geographical reasons, the old estate owners from the East sustained larger losses.) The ruling class was not weakened but strengthened by coopting a handful of managers who rose during the confusion of the postwar period and the addition of leading functionaries of the SPD (*Sozialdemokratische Partei Deutschlands*) and the union bureaucracy. Its class consciousness remains totally unfazed.

The price the ruling class had to pay for its survival was the Basic Law (*Grundgesetz*). Under duress of the Allies, German capitalism had to accept the rules of the game of formal democracy. Internally, it has never made its peace with this condition. Whoever listens, surprised, to the announcements of the industrial combines and the verbalizations of the high ministerial bureaucracy has missed the point that the ruling class in Germany always regarded the constitution as nothing more than a provisional annoyance. Its sudden conversion to democracy was never meant seriously. Only the dependent classes and the intelligentsia took it at face value, and their forebearance, unlimited naiveté, and blind trust has scarcely its equal in history.

The victory of the counterrevolution in West Germany did not occur by accident. A ruling class capable of ruining a nation without being taken to task for it and able to continue to govern while running into practically no opposition deserves to be taken seriously; it deserves the admiration of all cynics.

For its success it can thank: its decisiveness, its coherence, its farsightedness, its superior strategy, its worldwide outlook, its cooperation with international capitalism, its self-confidence, and its lack of scruples.

Its opponents can attribute their defeat to: their lack of daring, their fragmentation, their shortsightedness, their pathetic tactics, their provincial outlook, their isolation from the revolutionary movements around the world, their resignation and their idealism.

9. Closed due to inventory. After twenty years of opposition and of "the opposition," of social criticism and of "social criticism" it is time to take stock. A large percentage of West German intellectuals greeted with deceptive hopes the attempts by the Allies to create a functioning parliamentary democracy in this part of Germany. Those whom the Right called Leftists—and they were well-intentioned, peaceable, and patient—tried to take the constitution at its word and to reform the society of the Federal Republic through rational suggestions and by means of moral assent. They wanted to bring the ruling class to reason; they hoped that the Leviathan of late capitalism would be reasonable—if only sufficiently enlightened.

The Great Coalition* has put an end to this illusion. Since that time parliamentary democracy has been nothing but a sham in Germany. An organized opposition no longer exists. The constitutional sovereign, the people, is no longer in a position to remove the governing cartel. The Bundestag votes merely ratify the decisions of the cartel. Debates have become superfluous. The persecution of the extraparliamentary opposition has begun. Changes in the constitution, manipulation of the right to vote, and state-of-emergency laws serve the consolidation of this condition. The acid test of a government without the people and against the people has already been made: from the Fallex-Bunker[1] the commission of the ruling class has practiced lording it over the Basic Law. The civil war maneuvers of the Bundeswehr (armed forces) repre-

* Of SPD and CDU.

sent the high point of the arming against the internal enemy, at least so far.

These facts show that the political system of the Federal Republic is no longer repairable. One has either to consent to it or replace it by a new system. A third possibility is not in sight.

10. City tour. This alternative was not posited and developed in all its ramifications by the intellectuals of the opposition. On the contrary, for twenty years they sought to avoid it. The State with its show of force made the question of revolution the order of the day, and it was not the established writers, scientists, and publicists who accepted this challenge; it was the students. The first kernel of an opposition with a revolutionary orientation formed during the Berlin police pogroms this summer. The significance of this new opposition cannot be estimated right now. Its strategy is uncertain, its program vague, its numbers hardly overwhelming. Its chances for the future uncertain. But even now it has shown everyone who cares to look what this community is based on: on forcible repression; they have demonstrated that the state apparatus reaches for the truncheon and the pistol as soon as the sovereign begins to exercise his rights. And after twenty years of *Gruppe 47*, manifestos, anthologies, and election booths they have forced the oppositional intelligence to make its first audit.

11. Pauper's oath. The cash register was empty. The leftist intellectuals had been literarily assiduous and productive, yet politically profoundly uncreative. They consisted chiefly of "once-burnt" children, old social democrats, neoliberals, and late-Jacobins. The only theoretical basis uniting them was a vague negation, namely antifascism. These intellectuals remained bound to the historical trauma of 1945, fixated on specifically German complexes and events such as "collective guilt" and "the Wall," incapable of internationalism of any but the most superficial kind. Morality was more important to them than politics. The socialism to which they adhered remained nebulous if only for lack of detailed knowledge; its sociological education was minimal; its conflict with communism neurotic and obvious. Pacifism and philo-Semitism were dominant tendencies; they paid only belated attention to scientific, technological, and economic questions. In matters political they tended to react rather than act. Only in one area did they achieve any success whatsoever, and that not by accident either: in the defense of the freedom of the expression of opinion, that is, in representing their own interest and asserting their own privileges—certainly a legitimate, though scarcely a sufficient, political activity.

Decent, modest, and sentimental, always intent on preventing the worst or at least in delaying it, these star pupils of reformism for twenty years offered suggestions for improvement that were inherent in the system but no radical counterproposals. Perhaps they should have given less credence to the appellation their opponents lent them; for with the Left of other European countries the "leftist intellectuals" of Germany had sorrowfully little in common until recently; indeed, they could not even provide for the necessary exchange of international information and experiences. Nor did they produce a political theory worthy of the name. The defeat of the reformist intellectuals in Germany is complete. The Great Coalition of 1966 sealed it, the Berlin summer of 1967 * demonstrated it for everyone to see. It is all over with the fool's paradise; the time of the beautiful self-delusions has come to an end.

12. Not to be reproduced in any form. Is there such a thing as a revolutionary future for a technically highly developed industrial society? History cannot answer this question. The proletarian revolutions of the Old World, their victories and defeats, belong to the early phases of industrialization. They were carried out by an impoverished working class, led by a tightly organized class party. A centrally steered mass agitation, the formation of conspiratorial cadres, and the classic military tactic of the barricade and the street fight decided the outcome of the struggle. This model has not been employed a single time in a fully developed industrial society. Exceptions such as Czechoslovakia and East Germany don't count: what was victorious there was a revolution imported by force, stamped from a foreign model down to the last detail and dependent on an early stage of industrialization. A scheme that brought

---

* The beginning of the student revolt in West Germany.

rapid progress to countries such as Bulgaria and Rumania led to long-lasting economic stagnation, political repression, and cultural regression where the productive forces were more highly developed.

For the Western metropolises the old prerequisites are no longer valid; the old strategies of the revolution have become unusable. If these metropolises are to have a revolutionary future, the future will scarcely find models in the past: In Europe, the United States, and Japan the chief concern is no longer the liberation from social want but the liberation of social wealth that is already available. The ruling system has come to grips with the dearth in the metropolises, but not with the wealth. It explodes and disappears in waste, destruction, and repression.

13. Peacetime products. A revolution in Germany that would be nothing but a German revolution is not only improbable but unthinkable. A handful of guerrillas who operate in the highland of Bolivia are a phenomenon that matters to the whole world today. The strategists of the counterrevolution have made sure that the thesis of "socialism in one country" has been ruined once and for all. All political actions now stand and fall in the context of the international revolutionary movement, from the smallest demonstration to the great decisions that face the American people. That is why, and not for humanitarian reasons, the Vietnam war became the political event of the decade.

It is foreseeable that violence on the international scale will increase. Peace is a fiction in the metropolises under the prevailing social conditions. In reality we live in a permanent state of war, and the repercussions on our political situation will become more and more apparent every year. The forceful counterrevolutions in Asia, Africa, and Latin America will rebound to the wealthy lands. Whoever balances his account with huge catastrophes over there and a peaceful life over here, with genocide in foreign reaches and tolerance at home, with blind force to the outside and democratic conditions on the inside—that person is a fool.

14. Germany firsters. Each act of identification with the liberation movements of the Third World that conveniently forgets to check its own historical situation is premature and unfruitful. The rich countries have no farmers whose right to live as human beings is embodied in the fight for a handful of rice. Solidarity among intellectuals, too, remains pure rhetoric as long as it does not manifest itself in political actions whose usefulness can be proved.

The short-term interests of the working class in the United States and Europe are opposed to the interests of the guerrillas. The counterrevolution has made the working class participate, however miserably, in the earnings from its operations, and it leaves no doubts as to its methods: "Don't forget one thing: we are just two hundred million. There are three billion of them who are opposed to us. They want what we have. But they won't get it—not from us!" (Lyndon Johnson, 1967, to the American soldiers at Camp Stanley, South Korea; quoted from the *New York Review of Books,* February 23, 1967.) Every time an armament plant or military base is closed in the United States there are union protests and spontaneous strikes. While ten thousand students demonstrated in November 1967 against the presence on the campuses of recruiters from the Dow Chemical Company, the workers of this firm, which produced napalm for the Vietnam war, went on strike demanding better working conditions.

The conflict of interests that becomes evident here cannot be covered up with solidarity slogans. It shows the extent of the prevailing manipulation. Anyone who does not see that succumbs to a dangerous deception. The working class observes the utterances of intellectuals with a mistrust that is historically justified. Enlightenment is necessary but insufficient. The mind industry is in firm hands. The dependent classes will only begin to see through their enmeshment and recognize their long-term interests when conditions in the interior of the metropolises come to a head. Among those who are already able and who are therefore obligated to entertain such insights we find a romanticization of the Third World, which is useless and silly. Whoever ignores the experience of the guerrillas is a reactionary; whoever would like to imitate them uncritically is an illusionist. The sober mediation between the liberation movements in the Third World and the political action in the metropolis is a task whose difficulties have been scarcely recognized, not to mention solved, to date.

15. Bodyguards of reality. The stability of our social system is evidently threatened from the outside; regarded from the inside it seems limitless. As long as its technical productivity increases and as long as part of this growth spills over in the form of a growing standard of living the total concensus seems secure; the depoliticization of the masses continues; revolutionary opposition seems a quirk in an atmosphere of general affirmation. A highly paid corps of reality teachers meets it with crushing reminders of "reality," that is of the "movens quo," of which everyone is presumed to know the parameters. This concept of reality derives from the fiction that the historical process is foreseeable and controllable— in principle. What also corresponds to this is a quasi-scientific planning for the future (with premises inherent in the system) so as to guarantee an undisturbed course of history; that is, finally, the elimination of history altogether.

How little the strategies of the system believe in their own fictions can be garnered from their flow charts. The central function of their scenarios are surveillance, manipulation, and repression. The means the system employs to make itself unassailable demonstrate its susceptibility.

16. Physics lesson. *Crisis management.* A juggler is successful to the extent that he can maintain control over the force of gravity and the laws of mechanics. He is handling an extremely unstable, variable system of balls. His art consists of making the system appear stable. Training and skill enable him to do this. An ambitious juggler has the tendency to work with ever larger and more complicated systems. The number of balls and their weight increases; disks, rings, irregular shapes, unwieldy, huge, and tiny objects are added to the game. The public is intoxicated by the juggler's success; he is the greatest of them all, a manipulator without peer. Gravity seems eliminated, the stability of the system seems assured. However, one slip and the system collapses. The juggler is ruined.

Oscillatory circle. Twenty persons step on a suspension bridge that can hold two thousand persons; they manage to walk in such a way as to step in rhythm with the resonance frequency of the bridge, compared to whose mechanical strength they are practically impotent. Yet the oscillations that they impart to the bridge structure are augmented by regenerative feedback coupling; one can foresee the point when the bridge will collapse.

Reactor. A neutron produces further neutrons at each step along a chain reaction and in such a way that the average multiplier K is larger than one; a certain number of neutrons escape or are lost, which diminishes the K factor. To even out these losses a critical minimum is required to make up these losses; if K exceeds the value one, the number of reactions increases exponentially. Therefore control rods are affixed at certain places in the reactor to absorb the excess neutrons, keeping the K factor under control. Whoever knows these places and has access to them has control over the stability of the system. Whoever attacks the reactor with a sledgehammer produces superficial damage at most.

17. Green stamps. The social system of the metropolises has a limited capacity for integrating its internal and external opponents.

The conflicts with the poor external world are manifest and murderous. All attempts at integration by means of so-called development aid, the Point Four Program or the Alliance for Progress, have failed.

The system's internal latitude for operating without the use of force is diminishing too. Ironically enough, it is the ruling class's admirable ability to learn that makes for the constant shrinkage of its scope of operation. Planned capitalism can only survive if it succeeds in preventing profound economic and internal political crises, something that is solely possible by means of ever greater material and immaterial concessions to the dependent masses. These concessions, however, are irreversible. They can't be taken back without it coming to violent conflicts in the metropolises. In this manner, irrational "progress" liberates constantly increasing risks.

18. Snake at the breast. Such a risk, for example, lies in the increasing intellectualization of the industrial work process. This development, too, is irreversible and leads to an educational policy that for years on end liberates a growing percentage of the population under thirty from the production process. This growing population must be privileged on the one hand and kept under control on the other. The difficulties are self-evident. More and more, these privileged ones, the students and intellectuals, attack the system directly, an irony that planned capitalism had not intended and that therefore provokes its special fury. The logic of this process, however, is easy to see. The more the repression is refined and interiorized, the more self-censorship and self-piloting replace coercion and direct indoctrination, the more the suppressed accept their own suppression, yes, defend it; in the same degree does opposition to the system itself become a privilege, a cause that only those can afford who still have the opportunity to develop a consciousness that is not totally shackled to the compulsion to consume and the models of mass manipulation. The danger of being infected is foreseeable no matter which strategy is employed. One can try to crush this opposition, which consists primarily of the young and privileged. This method leads to internal political crises; besides, like decreasing the student population, it injures the technological process and with that, in the long run, economic growth. If, on the other hand, one lets these groups take the initiative, the possibility that at some point they will begin to create resonance oscillations cannot be ruled out.

19. Peripheral phenomena. Of course neither the students nor the intellectuals are "the revolutionary subject." As in earlier revolutions, the decision, in the final analysis, will be made by the dependent masses. However, history teaches just as clearly that it is invariably a minority that sets off the revolutionary process. Whoever lets himself be sent out on a search for this "subject" succumbs to mystification. This singular form makes no sense under present conditions. Rather, the ruling class sees itself confronted by a conglomeration of real and potential enemies that no longer allows of an unequivocal definition. These groups on the periphery are so disparate it seems grotesque: pupils, deserters, the unemployed, philosophers, hippies, students, Negroes, automation pensioners, old-time Communists, "guest workers," dissatisfied women, miners, Eastertime marchers—a list that can be increased or diminished at will depending on local circumstances. However, it is clear that the class basis of this opposition to the system is weak and not unified. The system does not see itself confronted by a growing, homogeneous, firmly entrenched organization commanding a clear strategy. Rather, it finds itself in the position of the juggler who has to juggle an increasing number of disparate balls. The weakness of such an opposition is only too apparent;

on the other hand it is difficult to control just because it is so decentralized. Self-sufficiency, sudden fluctuations, great spontaneity, incalculable threats and pullbacks, changes in concentration and dispersion make its suppression difficult. The possibility of chain reactions cannot be excluded.

Under conditions of increasing external instability one can imagine a situation when these peripheral groups recognize that it is the system itself that is fighting with its back to the wall at the periphery of the world. If a situation like that should arise, the masses and their passivity, which the system has cultivated, can become fateful for it. Then the question will be reversed: the ruling class will look vainly for a counterrevolutionary subject that it might mobilize for its purposes.

20. A friend in need. Theory sans practice means to adopt a wait-and-see attitude. Any halfway analytically schooled mind is in a position to produce an infinite number of reasons that suggest waiting, that say that it is either too early or too late. If only for that, every theory not covered, corrected, and propelled by actions is worthless. One must also mistrust every analysis that purports to provide precise information about the possibilities presently obtaining. A theory capable of making such predictions does not exist, and one is justified in asking whether it is even imaginable.

Under our circumstances the most insignificant political action can lead to new recognitions. In recent times even seemingly ambiguous, blind, yes nonsensical, acts by the smallest groups have provoked occurrences that had the effect of a bugle call.

No abstract insight into the repressive character of the system can replace the physical experience of repression. Police, legal and secret-service systems are the most important friends and assistants of the opposition to the system. The system's mortal fear can only be understood in terms of one's own personal fear. Destruction of bourgeois respectability, economic pressure, surveillance, financial penalties, arrests, prison, immediate physical threat: through these means the coercive state apparatus has already formed a hard core of oppositionists. Thousands will graduate from this academy of the revolution in the coming years. With that the system will make itself enemies for the rest of its life. The experiences being gathered in police stations, courts, and prisons today are the only genuine citizenship lessons that the republic has to offer.

21. Living lie. Liberals of every persuasion pretend to defend the constitution, yet the sacredness they would like to ascribe to it is that of a sacred cow. What the liberals protect is the right of the constitution to die, untrammeled, of hunger.

What is to be said against the liberals is this: the constitution is the living lie of the system. There exists a gaping disparity between the guarantees of the constitution and the interests of the ruling class, which can no longer be covered up. The Basic Law (*Grundgesetz*) guarantees the inviolability of the individual, the right to form coalitions, the right to free expression of opinions, the right to strike, and the right to resist. These provisions threaten the very existence of the system. The constitution is itself a danger to the state.

That is why the committee that governs in Bonn has undertaken fifteen changes in the Basic Law within eighteen years, why leading members of the committee had already publicly expressed their scorn for the constitution back in the fifties. That is why this committee has made laws that are unconstitutional. That is why this committee has already made a dry run of how one governs without the Basic Law. That is why this committee has decided to disenfranchise the Basic Law by means of the State of Emergency Law (*Notstandsgesetz*).

The constitution is a pledge that the ruling class neither wants nor is in a position to keep. Only the revolution can redeem it.

22. All rights reserved. Every argument, whether the opposition to the system should employ indirect, legal or illegal, violent or nonviolent methods, is superfluous. The opposition is lost as soon as it commits itself in advance to one or the other and acknowledges the limits that its opponents stake out. Its tactic must consist of putting these very rules into question, of fitting its means to the situation, of always finding fresh means, of testing, dropping, picking up again. It must keep the initiative and utilize the element of surprise. It must operate at the limits of legality and constantly transgress the limits in both directions. Regarding the use of force: it does not emanate from the people but is employed by the state apparatus. It has always been there. One can avoid it, one can outfox it, but one cannot eliminate it for moral reasons. It is a moral problem for the revolution in only one respect: all revolutions to date have let themselves be infected by the inhumanity of their opponents. The problem is serious; but it can only be solved by those who make the revolution. The revolutionaries are not going to let themselves be advised by their opponents.

23. Sylvan solitude. Radicalism is a dirty word in Germany. We have, so the brooks warble in the liberals' forest retreat, understanding for your problems; but you are isolating yourselves, you are going too far, you are forfeiting your sympathies. However, first of all, think of the Fascists. You must always think of the Fascists. You're helping them, you're driving the people into their arms. That's why we advise you: stop your nonsense, why not join us, no one sees you here, here you find understanding, here you don't produce a backlash, here you don't do any harm, our forest still has plenty of room.

It is too bad that Fascism won't listen to this reasoning either; or does anyone seriously believe that Hitler and his patrons would have resigned if the Communist party had voluntarily dissolved itself in 1929? Was Tucholsky the reason for Goebbels? Would history have stopped cold in its tracks had he kept his mouth shut?

That is what the argument comes down to: to the longing for complete stasis, the general moratorium. A little consideration for the liberals and Ho Chi Minh will embrace General Westmoreland instead of forfeiting their potential sympathy.

24. Party insignia. The weakest point of the opposition to the system is its inability to develop new organizational forms. It is quite apparent that the old form of the cadre party is no longer useful. The Communist parties in the Western metropolises degenerated Stalinistically; they have no internal democracy and no useful external program. Their unity has been dearly bought at the price of opportunism. They offer no revolutionary perspective.

Since the opposition to the system lacks a strong class basis in the metropolises, the founding of a party is unthinkable. At any event, the parliamentary way to socialism is, as the Greek example demonstrated, a chimera. But the old models no longer suffice—

also for internal reasons. Real democracy, decentralization of the decisions, cooperation instead of subordination—these elementary demands that the opposition makes of any future society it must first try to realize in the forms of its own organization.

25. Checkback. There is no revolutionary science for the present and the future of the metropolises. We have the classics from the last century, Lenin and Trotsky, news from the Far East and Latin America. From California we imported Marcuse. Our own resources provide us with interpretations of Beckett's *Endgame,* dissertations on the psychology of National Socialism, commentaries on Hegel and other arrangements for piano.

We need investigations that develop revolutionary alternatives for the solution of all important political and social questions; a science that knows our requirements and takes our wishes seriously, whose imagination liberates itself from the ostensible models, which has the courage for a new concrete utopia.

Therefore, the earlier we clarify three obvious misunderstandings, so much the better.

We are not entertaining that favorite question: whether we are being genuinely "constructive." In this country that question is always raised as though one must answer it within the terms of the system; asking it, one is supposed to be able to ascertain the "negative" or "positive" aspects of a proposition and not its concrete capacity for threatening the system. Used in this manner, the question about the constructive nature of this or that point is transparently fraudulent. Still, it also contains an element of truth. Whoever refuses to have his conceptions made more precise by comparison with another society, be it for reasons of methodological scruples, be it with the argument that only once it is victorious can the revolution provide information about its own future, not only forfeits all ability to convince with anything he says: he also admits his own unfruitfulness.

Nor are we practicing the fashionable art of prognostication, which worships facts and which invariably ends up postulating a prolongation of the current state of affairs; and it is neither a question of joining the prevailing cult of experts that maintains that, say, lacking a detailed knowledge of milk production in

Schleswig-Holstein, one has no right to discuss economics, or that one should not discuss politics without having spent a month studying the Vietnam hearings transcripts and without having informed oneself with on-the-spot helicopter investigations: that kind of argument is a positivistic con game. In matters revolutionary every man is an expert who refuses to let himself be intimidated by the "material pressure" of a repressive social system that has long since become invalid.

However, the options available to any man in the future must first be exposed and explored. That is not happening. Ignorance and dilettantism dominate the field.

What possibilities of self-government exist in a technically highly developed industrial society? To what extent and how can one decentralize large and complicated production and distribution systems? How can one technically and institutionally secure the participation of everyone in the political and economic decisions that concern them? How can the social work be divided with a minimum of regimentation? How can the technological process be kept under such control as to create the opportunity for reestablishing psychologically and biologically bearable living conditions? Which possibilities for the regulation of social conflict can be developed? Which parts of the old state apparatus can be dissolved at once and which have to be revamped? How can schools and institutions of higher learning be absorbed in society, so that the work process becomes a learning process? We don't know.

26. Horror film. The specter of the revolution imparts unnecessary dread into millions of our fellow citizens. The revolution—that is the bloody hand, censorship, the GPU, the camp, barbed wire, the ration card, confiscation. It is not the fascism whose every aspect we have experienced that produces this dread, but the revolution that failed to occur. As long as the opposition to the system is solely interested in demonstrating its own protest but not the social possibilities; as long as it does not understand how to arouse the deepest wishes and desires of the masses; as long as it abandons the masses to that dread that the mind industry suggests to it fresh each day, and that is the dread of its own wishes and desires, the revolution in Germany will remain an apparition.

27. Refresher course for advanced students. "Imperialism and reactionaries are paper tigers: that is their nature. That is the basis of our strategic considerations. On the other hand, they are also living tigers, steel tigers, real tigers: they eat men. That is the basis of our tactical considerations."

Short-term hopes are futile. Long-term resignation is suicidal.

Postscript: These notes are called "commonplaces" because they don't belong to any one individual; "Berlin" commonplaces because they have been demonstrated in the streets of this city. I note them down in the hope that they will become "German" commonplaces. Inasmuch as they are critical, they are meant as much for myself as for others.

Translated by Michael Roloff

Part Three

SOCIOLOGY AND ECOLOGY

1

Tourists of
the Revolution

The European Left manifests an arbitrary and ideological relationship to the socialistically governed countries with its discussions about revisionism and antirevisionism, "accomplishments" and "deformations"; and anyone who pays close attention to these discussions often finds it difficult to localize the voices he hears—as though the speakers were ventriloquists from whom issued something like a socialist *Weltgeist*. When such a dislocation occurs, the fabric of the conversation is deprived of something that requires foremost consideration: the role of the observer that devolves on the Western Left with respect to those countries where socialism has found—if not its realization—at least serious attempts in that direction.

No matter what attitude or position one takes toward these countries—and they run the gamut from blind identification to vitriolic dislike—the verdicts are invariably reached *from the outside.* No one who returns from a sojourn in socialism is a genuine part of the process he tries to describe. Neither voluntary commitment nor the degree of solidarity with which one behaves, no propaganda action, no walk through the cane fields and schools, factories and mines, not to mention a few moments at the lectern or a quick handshake with the leader of the revolution, can deceive about the fact.

The less the traveler understands this and the less he questions his own position, the greater and more justified will be the animosity that the voyager into socialism encounters from the very onset—from both sides. Such as in these lines:

THE TRAVELERS

They come in the clothes of the affluent society,
a thorn in whose side they are, whose "unreliable elements,"
fitted out with academic titles,
writing books for the departments of sociology
of the best universities
(which underwrite the cost).
They get their visas in a jiffy,
are informed about antiwar campaigns,
about protests against the Vietnam war, in short:
they are treading the righteous path of history.
While they lounge in the shiny seats
of the international airports,
each flight they take an illegal act,
they feel pleasantly subversive,
their conscience is clean.
They are the comfortable travelers of the wave of the future,
with Rolleiflex cameras, perfectly suited
for the tropical light,
for underdevelopment;
with information charts for objective interviews,
if, however (of course), something less than impartial,
for they love the struggle,
the guerrillas,
the zafras,
the hardships of life,
the vulgar Spanish of the natives.

After two or three weeks
(that's the maximum)
they write books about guerrillas
or the Cuban national character,
about the hardships of life or
the vulgar Spanish of the natives.

Provided with systems, with methods,
they are obviously frustrated
by the missing sexual freedom in Cuba,
by the unfortunate puritanism of the revolution,
and they define that state of affairs
with honest melancholy
as the abyss between theory and practice.
In private (not in their book or at the round table)
they admit that they cut more cane
than the best machetero (that guy took a siesta all day).
These fourteen-day heroes declare
that the people in the inns want to dance,
that the intellectuals (completely depoliticized)
are still able to write poetry;
the night before their flight back, lying next to their women,
they believe
they have developed supernatural muscles.
They go at it like blacks, as though they were depraved.
The girls, pregnant every five years,
are delirious with these unaccustomed husbands,
now insatiable.
At home they look at slides
that show the family hero
surrounded by natives, fraternally embraced (. . .)

Heberto Padilla [1]

The travelers whom Padilla describes bear the distinctive features of the sixties; and perhaps the only ones who can judge how
accurate and appropriate his observations and arguments are are
those whom they are aimed at. But the mistrust that manifests
itself in his text is not of today's vintage, nor of yesterday's. It
exists since the existence of two established social systems and it
is encountered by anyone who moves more or less freely between
the two. This mistrust has hardened in the course of the last fifty
years. It contains layers upon layers of past experiences, the rec-
ollection of misjudgments that have long since become a tradition
with the Left in the capitalist societies.

However, the phenomenon cannot be gotten rid of by rhetoric
alone. (Padilla's text, too, contains its hidden ambivalence.) What

makes a more precise investigation necessary are the objective effects that these journeys into socialism have had over the years. These effects, of course, have nothing to do with the significance of the individual travelers who were not up to the role they were asked to play, nor with the import of their (mostly superficial) observations and their (frequently threadbare) arguments. What lends these reports significance and why they continue to play a certain, though diminishing, role has to do with the isolation of the socialist countries from the outside world. This exclusion is one element in international class warfare and, depending on how that conflict has gone since 1917, it has assumed the forms of blockade, ostracism, military cordon sanitaire, "iron curtain," the Wall, and so on. This condition finds its administrative equivalent in travel restrictions, different forms of censorship, anti-emigration edicts, and complicated permission procedures of all kinds. The extent to which these measures were made necessary by socialist transformations, how far they have become bureaucratically institutionalized and are politically superfluous are questions that cannot be investigated here; nor can they be resolved in principle or once and for all time.

In any event, the consequences are serious. The flow of communication between the socialistically governed countries and the outside world is disrupted. Socialism becomes an internal and secretive affair, only accessible to those who have the opportunity to peek behind the mystifying façade. Ignorance and manipulation become the rule. These consequences don't necessarily devolve primarily to the disadvantage of the class enemy. On the contrary: the governments and monopolies of the capitalist world have news and spy services that are in a position to make up the information deficit. On the other hand, the Left is thrown back on anachronistic forms of communication if it is dissatisfied with the information and deformation provided by the bourgeois media. Among these surrogates the trip, the visit, the eyewitness report play an important role. The sources of error of this kind of information nexus are self-evident, and we shall try to name them. Considered as a whole, it is paradoxical that the social-socialist movements in the West have been generally dependent on individual views when it came to finding out something about collective life and production procedures; that is, for information about huge industrialization processes they have had to rely on a preindustrial messenger service. No wonder the wanderers frequently cut a ridiculous figure. The puny flow of information is scarcely their fault. It has objective causes.

Now that the old difficulties have not disappeared but have become surpassable, and every one of us can travel to the USSR almost at will, to Bulgaria, the GDR, and Czechoslovakia, the criticism of the travelers also turns against those who stay at home. A lack of curiosity is spreading among the West European Left that, at first glance, is astonishing and that requires an explanation. Year after year, many of the comrades go to Sardinia, to Greece, or to Amsterdam; however, they assiduously shun contact with the Hungarian or Ukrainian reality. These avoidance strategies, too, have their prehistory. Even during the thirties and forties many Communists preferred, if possible, to avoid the USSR, which they praised in their writings as the true home of the working class—even when this country was open to them at all times. For this, however, they had more concrete reasons than present travelers. Brecht, for example, stayed only a few weeks in the USSR during his trip from Finland to California, avoiding contact with Soviet reality as much as possible—evidently so as not to endanger himself. Today many comrades fear contact for other reasons. And sheer disinterest on the part of the politically active is probably not one of them. What those who remain behind are afraid of, rather, are their own ill bodings. They don't even let it get as far as contact with the reality of the socialist countries so as not to endanger their own fragile convictions. That is not to say that the others leave their fears behind when they journey into socialism. On the contrary: the same concern that keeps some at home others drag around with them. It's part of their moral hand baggage. The inquisitive ones, too, have developed their defense mechanisms in the last fifty years—to soften the shock when a purely imagined reality encounters a historical one. The first to characterize this operation was Lev Trotsky:

> Today the book market of all civilized countries overflows with books on the Soviet Union. . . . The literature dictated by blind hatred assumes an increasingly smaller proportion; a considerable portion of the new works on the Soviet Union

on the other hand, are acquiring an increasingly benign if not enchanted air. . . . The publications of the "Friends of the Soviet Union" fall into three main categories. Dilettantistic journalism of a descriptive genre, more or less 'leftist' reports, constitute the great majority of articles and books. Then we find publications of humanitarian, pacifistic, and lyrical communism that, if anything, are even more pretentious. In third place stands the economic schematization in the spirit of the old German lectern socialism. . . .

What unites these three categories despite their differences is their obeisance to the fait accompli and their preference for soporific generalizations. They are incapable of rebelling against their own capitalism and are therefore that much more eager to support themselves with a revolution that is already subsiding. Before the October Revolution not one of these people or their spiritual ancestors seriously asked themselves in what manner or form socialism would realize itself. Therefore, it becomes that much easier for them to acknowledge what they find in the USSR as socialism. This not only provides them with a progressive appearance, but also with a certain moral fiber, which, however, does not commit them to anything. This kind of contemplative, optimistic, anything-but-destructive literature, which presumes that all troubles are over, has a very calming effect on the readers' nerves and therefore is readily accepted. In this way an international school, which might be called *Bolshevism for the enlightened bourgeoisie*, or in a strict sense *socialism for radical tourists*, is imperceptively coming into existence.[2]

Trotsky's analysis, however, leaves untouched one centrally important aspect of the matter: *the institutional side* without which the "Tourism of the Revolution" remains incomprehensible. Whoever overlooks this side sooner or later arrives at a moralizing attitude that fixes on the character of a single individual. All one finds out this way is that X is naive, Y corrupt, and Z a hypocrite. But this explains nothing and nothing is won by it.

The institutional basis of "radical" or "revolutionary" tourism is the *delegacija* system. *Delegacija* actually means nothing but delegation, but the word has acquired a special meaning in Russian and designates official travelers of all kinds, even if they appear by themselves or in small groups; and it is by no means necessary for these people to have been delegated by anyone.

The following elements—inasmuch as they affect travelers from outside the country—are what make up the system:

1. The *delegate* is not undertaking the trip on his own account. He is invited. Normally he does not pay his own expenses. He is the guest and is therefore under the aegis of the unwritten laws of hospitality. From a material viewpoint this arrangement can lead to corruption; from a moral viewpoint to a defusing of criticism.

2. The *delegate* has to deal with hosts who occupy a monopolistic position. Paid-for trips also exist in capitalist countries; governments, organizations, and firms particularly like to invite journalists, a procedure considered a normal aspect of public relations. But usually the traveler is not dependent on such invitations; he can also travel without them. In contrast, the invitation as a *delegate* was (in every) and is (in some) countries the only possibility of acquiring a visa, the local currency, a room, and transportation.

3. Compared to the general population, the *delegate* is in every respect a privileged person. When there is a shortage he enjoys precedence over the natives; hotel rooms, seats in public transportation, cars and chauffeurs are reserved for him; during longer stays he is permitted to buy at special shops; admission to special events normally off limits to others and considerable sums of money are often made available to him.

4. The *delegate* is always cared for by an organization. He isn't supposed to—no, he isn't allowed to—worry about anything. Usually he receives a personal guide who functions as translator, nanny, and watchdog. Almost all contact with the host country is mediated through this companion, which makes distinct the *delegate's* segregation from the social reality surrounding him. The companion is responsible for the traveler's *program*. There is no traveling without a *program*. The guest may express his wishes in this respect; however, he remains dependent on the organization that invited him. In this respect he is treated as though he were still under age. The combination of being spoiled and impotent is reminiscent of infantile situations. Such visitors' lack of self-sufficiency can reach utter helplessness; it seems as though this state of affairs meets with the approval of the responsible organizations. The socialist countries have institutions that specialize in this kind of work; they are usually called "Society for the Friendship with the People" or something on that order. But all other organizations—from state apparatus and party apparatus to the

women's organizations—have sections that take care of official guests.

The *delegacija* system is a Russian invention. It has its beginnings in the early twenties, and one can't assume that it was the intention from the start to pull the wool over the foreigners' eyes and to put them in a position that would lead to an inevitable loss of contact with reality. Anyone who assumes this kind of conspiracy demonizes a complicated relationship by inventing a theory that doesn't even completely apply today, when it has become difficult to distinguish between cynicism and experience. For even now a delegate who, say, goes to Hungary, Cuba, or the Georgian Republic, will encounter completely genuine expressions of hospitality, and the trouble people take on his behalf not only serves to shield him from reality but also to protect him from situations that he might be unable to handle by himself. This was even more the case during the Russian civil war; that is, during the periods when the system was being created and when it was nearly impossible for a foreigner to travel to Russia without running the danger of dying from hunger, freezing to death, or being shot.

But that is just one side of the coin. Also, one should not forget that no cheaper or more effective means for influencing the outside world has ever been devised than the *delegacija* system. That is certainly one reason why it has spread from Russia over half the world. A few early examples give proof of its effectiveness. The first report is from Victor Serge and refers to the year 1920.

> The II. Congress of the Communist International continued its work in Moscow. Foreign colleagues and delegates lived in a hotel in the center of the city, the Djelovoi Dvor, which is situated at the end of a long boulevard whose one side consists of the white battlement-crowned wall of the Kitai-Gorod. Medieval portals beneath one nearby old tower lead to the Warvarka, where the legendary house of the Romanovs stands. From there we went to the Kremlin, a city within the city, all of whose entrances have guards that control the passes. The twin power of the revolution, the Soviet government and the International, were meeting there in the palaces of the autocracy, amidst the Byzantine churches. The only city that the foreign delegates did not get to know—and their lack of interest in this respect confused me—was the living Moscow with its hunger rations, its arrests, its filthy prison stories, its black-market façades. Luxuriously fed amidst the

general misery (although, in fact, one served them too many rotten eggs), led through museums to exemplary kindergartens, the delegates of world socialism gave the impression of being on vacation or traveling as tourists through our wasted, besieged republic. I discovered a new form of unawareness, Marxist unawareness. A German party leader, athletic and full of optimism, said to me quite simply that "the internal contradictions of the Russian revolution contain nothing surprising" for a Marxist, and in that he was undoubtedly right; but he used that general truth as an umbrella to avoid the immediate appearance of reality—which has its importance despite everything. The majority of the Bolshevized-Left Marxists assumed this complacent attitude. For them the words *dictatorship of the proletariat* magically explained everything without their ever thinking of asking where the dictatorial proletariat was and what it was thinking, feeling, and doing. . .

All in all, the foreign delegates were actually a disappointing crowd that delighted in valuable privileges in a famished country; they were quick to be enthusiastic but mentally lazy. One saw among them few workers and many politicians. "How happy they are," Jacques Mesnil said to me, "that they can finally watch parades from the official rostrum."[3]

The following observations of Franz Jung fall into the same period:

> Hunger also left its mark at the headquarters of the International, the Hotel Lux. Almost the entire intellectual and political elite of Europe and the world that stood close to socialism was presented to the Kremlin via the Hotel Lux—invited guests of honor of the government, sympathizers who had been advised to make the trip to Moscow, and leading members of various Communist parties who had been ordered to Moscow.
>
> In May 1920, the food supply system of Hotel Lux had broken down. The distinguished hotel guests sat at long tables in the spacious dining room but could get nothing except tea with which everyone could provide himself from the samovars, which stood about everywhere. Several times a day, at irregular intervals, large bowls of caviar were placed on the tables together with plates of lox, but no bread and no kasha. Anyone who took the time to wait with his tea was bound to get caviar and lox at some point during the day.
>
> The prominent guests were very indignant at that time, most of them because they had upset stomachs due to the caviar

and lox. They mentioned among themselves that if they were
at the head of the government of the victorious revolution
the food supply would be better organized, especially in the
quarters of the government guests such as the Hotel Lux—
they would see to that. They talked about this from early in
the morning till late at night, at tea before the steaming sam-
ovar, while waiting for the next bowls full of caviar and plates
with lox.[4]

Seven years later the contradictions within Soviet society had
become even more acute and the blindness of certain visitors assumed grotesque proportions:

All opponents of 1927 went to the end of their terrible road,
each in his own way no matter whether they let themselves
be constantly humiliated out of loyalty to the party or put up
constant resistance out of loyalty for socialism. . . .
    What a crass contrast to these men were the foreigners,
famous writers, Communist delegates, liberal guests of high
rank who celebrated the tenth anniversary of the revolution
in Moscow at that time! And they gave us lectures on how
to be clever! Paul Marion (the future undersecretary of state
in Pétain's government), member of the central committee of
the Communist party of France, was scattering boulevard bon
mots about Moscow, knew how to appreciate the young
Russian women, and tried to explain to me that we were
utopian; he himself saw the mistakes of the Communist
movement very clearly, but continued to support it because
'despite everything, it was the only force. . . .' He was just
an average Frenchman—without intelligence—who was primarily interested in always coming out smelling like a rose.
All in all: buyable. . . .
    I met Barbusse, with whom I was corresponding, in the
Hotel Metropole, guarded by an interpreter-secretary (from
the GPU) and supported by a very pretty secretary doll. . . .
I was coming from the overcrowded rooms of the suburbs,
from which comrades disappeared every night. I saw their
women, whose eyes were much too red and clouded with fear
for me to feel very indulgent toward the great official foreign
guests who were coming on tour; besides, I knew who had
been chased from the hotel to accommodate the great writer.
. . . Barbusse had a large emaciated and supple body topped
by a small, waxen, hollow-cheeked face with suffering lips.
Right away I had a very different impression of him, primarily concerned not to be pinned down to anything, not to see

anything that might have pinned him down against his will, concerned to conceal thoughts that he wasn't allowed to express, evading every direct question, always elusive, with uncertain glances, describing curves in the air with his slim hands while uttering words such as *depths, breadth, augmentation,* and all this so as to make himself in fact the accomplice of the stronger side. But since one didn't know yet whether the struggle had really been decided, he had just dedicated one of his books to Trotzky, but didn't dare visit him so as not to compromise himself. When I mentioned the repression, he acted as though he had a headache, as though he didn't understand, as though he were rising to wondrous heights of thought: "Tragic fate of the revolution, breadth, depths, yes yes . . . oh my friend!" With a kind of cramp in my jaw I noticed that I was facing the human incarnation of hypocrisy (Victor Serge).[5]

Examples such as these would probably enable one to develop a comparative psychology of such "Friends of the Soviet Union" and other countries, as well as of their trusting listeners at home; however, so as to become politically relevant, such an analysis would have to go beyond individual idiosyncrasies and search out the historically determined elements of the wishful thinking and their blindness to reality and their corruption. The point is not to discover that "man is evil," but why professed socialists let themselves be politically blackmailed, morally bribed, and theoretically blinded, and not just a few individuals, but in droves. Such a reckoning of course cannot confine itself to an investigation of the "Tourism of the Revolutionaries"; this phenomenon, after all, is only one of the symptoms.

Let us return to the objective, institutional side of the *delegacija* business. The last example contains a suggestion on how the system developed between 1920 and 1927; that is, from its crude beginnings to a far-flung, highly differentiated apparatus. Henri Barbusse, after all, was not a comrade; no central committee ever sent him to Moscow to the Comintern. Although he scarcely represented more than himself, he was received as a state guest. Yes, it is questionable in what sense, if any, he even belonged to the Left; his social position, his habits, his actions, and his thinking characterize him rather as a typical bourgeois intellectual. And this was what constituted his political usefulness to the Soviet leadership at that time. The greater the precision with which the socialist bureaucracies learned to calculate such tactical victories, the more far-reaching their attempts to utilize the "Tourism of the Revolutionaries" as part of their political purposes. Under such circumstances it was inevitable that the *delegacija* system became differentiated. Varying categories of visitors, running the gamut from reactionary journalists to deserving party members and ultraleftist sectarians, were assigned to different organizations, fitted out with carefully graded privileges and then sluiced through the country. A renegade who is an expert in these matters describes how the system functions in practice:

A free-lance writer ranked somewhere near the bottom of the hierarchy. However, I was not a simple free-lance; I had an "organisation"—the MORP—which, being affiliated to the Comintern, was situated somewhere in the middle range of the pyramid. Moreover, I was a Party member, which improved my grading; but only a member of the German, not the Russian Party, which lowered it. I also carried on me a letter from *Agitprop Ekki* (Department of Agitation and Propaganda of the Executive Committee of the Communist International) which again considerably improved my grading.

Such "to whom it may concern" letters serve as a kind of passport in the Soviet Union. It is on their strength that the citizen obtains his permits, his accommodation, ration card, and so on. Accordingly, these letters are very carefully worded and graded, to convey the exact degree of priority to which the bearer is entitled. Mine was a "strong" letter, signed by the head of *Agitprop Ekki*, Comrade Gopner, in person. It said that I was a delegate of the Revolutionary Writers' League of Germany, and that I was travelling under the sponsorship of the Comintern.

On the other hand, I was also a bourgeois foreign correspondent, working for several important newspapers, and duly accredited as such with the Press department of *Narkomindyel,* the Ministry of Foreign Affairs. This placed me in one of the top grades on another side of the pyramid, as it were. It entitled me to accommodation in *Intourist* Hotels where such existed; to travel in the "soft class" on trains; and to buy my food at *Insnab,* the co-operative stores reserved for the diplomatic corps, the foreign Press and foreign technical advisers. I disliked availing myself of these bourgeois privileges, but as I was travelling alone through remote and famine-stricken regions of the country, it was often the only way of obtaining food and shelter.

I was careful never to show my bourgeois, *Narkomindyel,* documentation at the Party offices and factories that I visited, nor to travelling companions, for the immediate result would have been to arouse distrust and suspicion. On the other hand, I never showed my Comintern letter to hotel managers, railway officials and co-operative store managers—it would have deprived me of the preferential treatment for bourgeois tourists who have to be humoured for reasons of propaganda. Such double existence was not regarded as dishonourable. On the contrary, it reflected the basic dualism of *"Narkomindyel* line" and *"Comintern line"*—the two aspects of the Soviet Union as a respectable international power, and as a clandestine centre of the world revolution. To bear this duality constantly in mind was one of the first lessons taught to every Party member.

Thus I traveled symbolically in two different guises, and literally with one set of documents in my right-hand pocket, another in my left-hand pocket. I never mixed them up, thanks to the simple memorising device that the Comintern was "on the left."

Even so, it would have been impossible for me to travel alone without falling back on the help of the only organisation that functioned efficiently everywhere throughout the country: the GPU. In every railway station in the Soviet Union there was a GPU Commissariat which maintained a minimum of order in the chaos. The function of the "Station GPU" was not political surveillance, but to act as railway officials, travel agents and information centres for official travellers. When I got out of the train in a new town, I went straight to the Station GPU, presented my papers, and was provided, as a matter of routine, with those basic necessities which no individual traveller can obtain without the "organisation" behind him: a room or bed, ration-card, means of transportation. My sponsors were the Comintern and the Foreign Ministry, neither of which had branch offices in small places; so the Station GPU took me under its wing until it was able to hand me over to the care of the slow-moving local Party Committee or Government Guest House. In short, the Station GPU had none of the sinister associations of that notorious body, of which it formed a kind of administrative public-service branch. It was, as I have said, the only efficient institution throughout the country, the steel framework which held the pyramid together . . .[6]

Between 1925 and 1939 a great number of European intellectuals went, like Koestler, on a search for the coming time. The enormous dissemination that the literature produced by these "Friends of the Soviet Union" enjoyed was due to a massive need for concrete utopias—which the Soviet Union seemed to embody at that time. These books were by no means solely designed for the proletariat inasmuch as it was organized within the Communist parties, but also, and even primarily, for the petit bourgeois intellectuals and the new "middle class" of employees who felt that capitalism endangered their existence. What secured a broad public for the "Tourism of the Revolution," therefore, was its bourgeois traits. The more euphoric, the more welcome this literature was: its illusions, which seem defects to us, were perhaps the basis of its success.

Of course, this literature never dominated the field. Since we are dealing with the Left or "leftist" tourism, we will disregard the flood of anti-Soviet hate literature that the West produced after the October Revolution. It goes almost without saying that the wars of intervention and the economic and political pressures found their ideological complement in the press, in books, and in films; that capitalism did not forego a propagandistic counteroffensive. Yet the Left, too, produced documents of disillusion and vehement criticism of Soviet conditions alongside the literature of illusion. Such testimony begins to appear occasionally as early as the twenties. Particularly the anarchists published early reports of their experiences that shed a critical light on developments in the USSR. Examples of this are the books by Rudolf Rocker (*My Disillusionment in Russia,* New York, 1923), Alexander Berkman (*The Bolshevik Myth. Diary 1920–24,* New York, 1925), and Emma Goldman (*Living My Life,* New York, 1934). Of course, these reports were written at a time when the *delegacija* system was still unknown, and only a small minority of people took any notice of them.

The French-Romanian writer Panait Istrati was presumably the first apostate among the "radical tourists." As honorary president of the Society of Friends of the USSR, he had been invited to attend the tenth anniversary of the October Revolution in Moscow and had been received like a State guest. He aired his disappointment in a report *Après seize mois en URSS,* which was published in 1929 in Paris. This report manifests the radical turnabout from one extreme to the other that is characteristic of the anti-Communist utterances of many former pilgrims. Not a single argument muddies the flow of Istrati's confessions; the newly found disgust is only the reverse of the former blind belief. It is just as helplessly emotional and politically ignorant: "History," Istrati states very calmly, "confronts the workers with the question not whether they want socialism in fifteen years but whether they want their freedom at once." [7]

Istrati's piece, however, was only a bumbling predecessor of an entire wave of critical reports and analyses that began to appear in the thirties against the idolization of Stalinist USSR. The most sensational of these nay-sayings was by André Gide.

This famous man joined the Communist party at the age of sixty-three and then participated actively in the fight that helped the United Front to a short-lived victory in 1936. That same year he traveled to Moscow as guest of the Soviet Writers' Union and from there through large parts of the Union. The two books, which he published after his return, *Retour de l'URSS* and *Retouches à mon retour de l'URSS* (both Paris, 1936 and 1937 respectively), had a bomblike effect. Within one year more than a hundred thousand copies were sold and there were translations into fifteen languages.

What happened to André Gide in Russia? Nothing but the same treatment that his predecessors had enjoyed and taken little notice of; except that Gide was not Barbusse—on the contrary; for the first time the *delegacija* system revenged itself on its inventors.

And indeed what disturbed me most when I got there, was not so much to find imperfections, as to meet once again with the advantages I had wanted to escape from, the privileges I had hoped were abolished. Certainly I thought it natural that a guest should be received as well as possible and everywhere shown the best. But what astonished me was that there was such a gap between this best and the common lot; such excessive privilege beside so mediocre or so bad an ordinary. . . .

And of course I see that without any actual attempt at corruption it may very well be advantageous for the Soviet government to make the way smooth for artists and writers and for all who will sing its praises; but I also see only too well how advantageous it may be for the writer to approve a government and a constitution that favor him to such an extent. This at once puts me on my guard. I am afraid of letting myself be seduced. The excessive advantages I am offered over there frighten me. I did not go to the USSR to meet with privileges over again. Those that awaited me were flagrant.

And why should I not say so?

I had learnt from the Moscow newspapers that in a few months more than four hundred thousand copies of my books had been sold. I leave you to calculate the percentage of author's rights. And the articles so richly paid for! If I had written dithyrambs on the USSR and Stalin, what a fortune! . . .

These considerations would not have restrained my praise; neither will they prevent my criticisms. But I confess that the extraordinarily privileged position (more so than in any other country in Europe) granted to anyone who holds a pen—provided he writes in the proper spirit—contributed not a little to open my eyes. Of all the workers and artisans in the USSR writers are much the most favored. Two of my traveling companions (each of them had the translation of one of his books in the press) searched the shops for antiques, curiosities, bric-a-brac—something on which to spend the thousands or so rubles they had cashed and knew they would not be able to take away with them. As for me, I could hardly make any impression on an enormous balance, for everything was offered me gratis. Yes, everything; from the journey itself to my packets of cigarettes. And every time I took out my billfold to settle a hotel or restaurant bill, to pay an account, to buy stamps or a newspaper, the delightful smile and authoritative gesture of our guide stopped me. "You're joking! You are our guest, and your five companions too."

No, I had nothing to complain of during the whole course of my tour in the USSR, and of all the spiteful explanations that have been invented to invalidate my criticisms, that which tried to put them down to the score of personal dissatisfaction is certainly the most absurd. I had never before traveled in such sumptuous style. In special railway carriages or the best cars, always the best rooms in the best hotels, the most abundant and the choicest food. And what a welcome! What attentions! What solicitude! Everywhere acclaimed, flattered, made much of, feasted. Nothing seemed too good, too exquisite to offer me. I should have been ungracious indeed to repulse such advances; I could not do so; and I keep a marvelous remembrance of it all, the liveliest gratitude. But these very favors constantly brought to mind privileges, differences where I had hoped to find equality.

When, after escaping with great difficulty from official receptions and official supervision, I managed to get into contact with laborers whose wages were only four or five rubles a day, what could I think of the banquet in my honor that I could not avoid attending? An almost daily banquet at which the abundance of the hors d'œuvre alone was such that one had already eaten three times too much before beginning the actual meal; a feast of six courses which used to last two hours and left you completely stupefied. The expense! Never having seen a bill, I cannot exactly estimate it, but one of my companions who was well up in the prices of things calculates that each banquet, with wines and liqueurs, must have come to more than three hundred rubles a head. Now there were six of us—seven with our guide; and often as many hosts as guests, sometimes many more.[8]

Gide's criticism of Soviet society is based in many respects on thoroughly bourgeois premises, most distinctly where he laments the country's "uniformity" and its inhabitants lack of the "personal touch." For example, when he notices that Soviet citizens "own little private property" and when this outrages him he strikes an involuntary comic note. Brecht made some comments on this subject at the time, comments that should give "radical tourism" something to think about—above and beyond the case of Gide:

The French writer André Gide has enriched the great book of his confessions with a further chapter. A tireless Odysseus, he has provided us with the report of a new venture, however without being able to divulge on board which ship this report was composed and where this ship is traveling to.

Everyone who watched what he was writing at the time when he was preparing his last mistake had to look forward with considerable apprehension to his departure for the new continent. He greeted it as an individualist, primarily as an individualist.

He set out like someone who is looking for a new country, tired of the old one, doubtlessly eager to hear his own yelp of joy, but what he was really looking for was *his* new country, not an unknown but a known country, not one that others but one that he himself had built, and in his head at that. He did not find this country. It apparently does not exist on this planet.

He set out far too unprepared. But he did not travel untouched. He did not only bring the dust on his shoes. Now he is disappointed, not about the fact that the country does not exist but about the fact that this is not his country. One must understand this: after his trip he was in a position to say this land is like so and so, its people do this and that, I don't quite understand. He expected a verdict of himself; he was one of the crowd that looked expectantly at him. He probably lacked the intention from the very beginning to communicate what this land is like, but rather intended to convey what he is like, and that didn't take much time, this booklet was written quickly. He sat down and wrote . . . "Everyone's happiness evidently consists only in depersonalization. The happiness of everyone is only achieved at the price of the individual. To be happy you must be uniform."

Here he broaches the question about the well-being of the people, and he is right: there probably never was a regime that so calmly admitted as the criterion of its effect the question whether the people are happy, and that means the many. Gide recognizes their happiness, he describes it in many places in his book, but immediately doubts whether what looks like happiness to him is happiness; that is, what he himself always calls happiness. He saw happy persons, in great numbers, but they were "depersonalized." They were happy, but they were uniform. They lacked nothing to be happy, but Gide lacked something. Thus he reaches no new insight about happiness except perhaps that it is a scarce commodity. The reality he saw did not warp his measuring rod, which he brought and took back with him. He did not come back happy, but as a personality. Also, what he called personality he will go on calling personality; he saw one country that lacked it: one sixth of the earth.

He is skeptical toward other classes. Toward the concept of personality, toward his own, thoroughly bourgeois, concept of personality he is not skeptical. Here people are living under completely new, unheard-of conditions; for the first time the masses are in control of the means of production, making it impossible for individuals to use their talents to exploit others. Perhaps those personalities decay that were formed under other conditions and new kinds of personalities begin to form, that are meant for other kinds of social work, with other differentiations? Such personalities he would not call personalities.[9]

Brecht's critique of Gide is marked by rationality and equanimity, something one cannot claim for the reaction of the Communist parties. From now until the end of his life they were to call Gide a hyena, a perverse purveyor of filth, and a mixer of poisons. Rereading his books today one must admit, however reluctantly, that they have outlasted much of what his Marxist opponents put on paper at that time. Probably only the crassest fanatic would disagree with some of his observations about bureaucracy and repression, official mendacity, and the privilege business. Gide was certainly wrong in considering himself a Communist; certainly he was unschooled in theory and politically naive and his taking sides was sentimental. Still, his idealism did not keep him from publishing the following table in which the approved representatives of the Diamat simply couldn't develop any interest at all:

	MINIMUM & MAXIMUM INCOME	USUAL INCOME
Workers	from 70–400 rubles	125–200 rubles
Small employees	80–250 rubles	130–180 rubles
Domestics	50–60 rubles (of course including room and board)	
Middle-rank officials and technicians, specialists, and those in "very responsible positions"	300–800 rubles	
High officials, certain professors, artists, and writers	1500–10,000 rubles and more; some, it is indicated, receive between 20,000 to 30,000 rubles per month.[10]	

There is a very simple reason why Gide's yellowed critique is not only acceptable but still readable today: it is his complete solidarity. This solidarity with the Russian workers and farmers is colored by Protestant moralism and is not devoid of idealistic mist; yes, at times it is so simple as to be awkward. Still, it provides the decisive criterion. It is this solidarity that distinguishes Gide's report from the tirades of the other disillusioned ones, that separates him once and for all from the anti-Communist filth of the cold war, as well as from the arrogant know-it-all attitude and the malicious gleefulness that survives in some writers of the Left to this day.

Of course, one cannot compare today's attitude quite that simply with those of yesterday. Much has changed since Gide's days also with respect to traveling in countries such as the Soviet Union. The infrastructure has improved, tourism has become a firmly established social institution—above and beyond caring for state guests of the revolution. The Intourist Bureau, the football club, the Ministry of Foreign Trade, the Writers' Union—every organization today has its specialists who take care of the *delegacija* unobtrusively and routinely. The GPU no longer exists and to mention its successor is considered bad form as much on the part of the hosts as the guests.

The USSR also is no longer the favorite travel objective of "radical" or "revolutionary tourists." The interest of this peculiar and ambiguous group has fallen on younger revolutions, on the non-European transitional societies.

The goals have changed, but the objective as well as subjective mechanism has remained the same. What Gide wrote before his trip to the Soviet Union is still valid:

> The stupidity and insidiousness of the attacks on the USSR is largely responsible for our conducting its defense with a certain willfulness. These yapping dogs will begin to praise the way things are going in Russia at the very moment when we will stop doing so, because their praise will only be for the compromises and slander, for the deviations from the original objective, which abet the gleeful exclamation: "There, you see!" [11]

The objections which are meant to prevent any criticism of the socialist transitional societies have scarcely changed since Gide enumerated them in 1937:

> (1) that the malpractices I have pointed out are exceptions to the rule from which one shouldn't draw any conclusions (because one cannot deny them);
> (2) that in order to admire the present state of affairs one needs only to compare it to the previous one, the condition before the conquest (mean to say: before the revolution)
> (3) that everything I complain about has profound ontological reasons that I have been unable to fathom: passing temporary evils in view of an imminent and that much greater state of well-being. [12]

The sterile debate between the admirers and defenders is being continued at any price, even at that of solidarity with the peoples who are being discussed, inasmuch as there is any room left for them between arrogance and loss of a sense of reality. Trotzky's dictum is still valid: "What really hides behind the 'official friends' ' animosity to criticism is not so much concern for the fragility of socialism as the fragility of their own sympathy for socialism." Here, then, a recent example of this state of affairs:

China after the Cultural Revolution is what Maria Antonietta Macciocchi calls her report; a more fitting title would be *Marie Antoinette in Wonderland*. For this book by an Italian Communist party delegate tells us less about China (where the author traveled together with her husband, the foreign political editor of *Unità*) than it does about the petit-bourgeois mentality characteristic of so many party intellectuals. Her blindness toward the situation at the workplace, her incomprehension of production relationships and of human and social costs entailed by them, and her typical admiration of the colorful and sensuous aspect of goods becomes evident from the description the author gives of a silk-weaving plant in Hangchow that produces "fifteen color" Mao pictures in large series: "The thousand machines are spinning briskly always in the same rhythm, and from the looms pour the great beards of Marx and Engels, the pointed goatee of Lenin, the face of Mao with his forage cap. Then the gobelins showing historical events: Mao at the proclamation of the 20th of May; Mao in a bathrobe before the famous crossing of the Yangtze. . . . The poems of Mao, too, are printed in black and white. . . . The factory has 1700 workers who work three shifts, day and night, to satisfy the demand."

We too have visited this factory. But we didn't only see the "glowing colors" of the large and small Mao pictures. The workers are standing in dark places where one ruins one's eyes and are exposed to incredible noise. The day shift lasts 8½ hours, the night shift 6½ hours. Seven days of vacation per year. Fifty-six days maternity leave including delivery time. Staggered wages, premiums as work incentives, preferential treatment for the drafting teams as compared with the producers. The Communist delegate has heard and seen nothing of this. She doesn't lose a word over it. When we met her recently and asked her about this discrepancy she said vehemently: "Perhaps you don't know Italian factories?" "Of course," we replied, we know them as well as American and Soviet factories; but it never occurred to us to claim that Italy, the USA or the USSR are socialist countries.

For Macciocchi, on the other hand, China is an ideal socialist country which "manifests an entirely new model of industrialization." This is due to the fact that she spent less time in the factories than in the company of functionaries who took her to the best restaurants in Peking.[14]

It is no accident but the political consequence of such an attitude that the great majority of "radical tourists" assiduously ignore the true situation of the working class in the socialistically governed countries. This striking disinterest is only barely concealed by means of declamatory slogans. The usual visits to factories and kolkhozes tend to meet the indifference of these visitors at least halfway. They cannot and are not set up to break through the social segregation of the guests, whose contact is limited to designated individuals from the functionary class and to foreigners who live in the same hotels. This umbrella is so effective that most of the political tourists don't have the slightest idea of the working conditions even after weeks or months in the host country. Ask them about wages and working hours, protection against unlawful dismissal, housing assignments, the number of shifts worked and the premium system, living standards and rationalization, and usually they have no answer. (In Havana I kept meeting Communists in the hotels for foreigners who had no idea that the energy and water supply in the working quarters had broken down during the afternoon, that bread was rationed, and that the population had to stand two hours in line for a slice of pizza; meanwhile the tourists in their hotel rooms were arguing about Lukács.)

In any event, there are indications that the Western travelers' awareness of problems is increasing. More and more reporters try to dispense with the ideological veil their status foists on them. Of course, one is more easily blinded when it is a question of one's own privileges. Even where the political intent of these privileges goes undetected one senses them more and more as a moral scandal, and they become problematical at least in this respect, as in the following reflections by Susan Sontag, who visited Hanoi in spring 1968:

> . . . Hence, the store to which we were taken the third day to get tire sandals and have us each fitted for a pair of Vietnamese trousers. Hieu and Phan told us, with an almost proprietary pride, that this was a special store, reserved for for-

eigners (diplomatic personnel, guests) and important government people. I thought they should recognize that the existence of such facilities is "un-Communist." But maybe I'm showing here how "American" I am.

I'm troubled, too, by the meals at the Thong Nhat. While every lunch and dinner consists of several delicious meat and fish courses (we're eating only Vietnamese food) and whenever we eat everything in one of the large serving bowls a waitress instantly appears to put another one on our table, ninety-nine percent of the Vietnamese will have rice and bean curd for dinner tonight and are lucky to eat meat or fish once a month. Of course I haven't said anything. They'd probably be mystified, even insulted, if I suggested that we shouldn't be eating so much more than the average citizen's rations. It's well known that lavish and (what would be to us) self-sacrificing hospitality to guests is a staple of Oriental culture. Do I really expect them to violate their own sense of decorum? Still, it bothers me. . . . It also exasperates me that we're driven even very short distances; the Peace Committee has rented two cars, in fact—Volgas—that wait with their drivers in front of the hotel whenever we're due to go anywhere. The office of the NLF delegation in Hanoi, which we visited the other day, was all of two blocks from the hotel. And some of our other destinations proved to be no more than fifteen or twenty blocks away. Why don't they let us walk, as Bob, Andy, and I have agreed among ourselves we'd feel more comfortable doing? Do they have a rule: only the best for the guests? But that kind of politeness, it seems to me, could well be abolished in a Communist society. Or must we go by car because they think we're weak, effete foreigners (Westerners? Americans?) who also need to be reminded to get out of the sun? It disquiets me to think the Vietnamese might regard walking as beneath our dignity (as official guests, celebrities, or something). Whatever their reason, there's no budging them on this. We roll through the crowded streets in our big ugly black cars—the chauffeurs blasting away on their horns to make people on foot and on bicycles watch out, give way. . . . Best, of course, would be if they would lend us, or let us rent, bicycles. But though we've dropped hints to Oanh more than once, it's clear they don't or won't take the request seriously. When we broach it, are they at least amused? Or do they just think we're being silly or impolite or dumb?[15]

The only traveler I know who has thought the problem of "radical tourism" through to the end is the Swede Jan Myrdal. With a conscientiousness that makes a veritably puritanical impression compared to the usual sloppiness in these matters, he gave an account (in his book *Report from a Chinese Village,* written in 1962 and published the following year) of the circumstances of his trip and his own situation. His reflections, therefore, and their exemplary character justify a longer quote.

We financed our journey to China and our travels in China with our own resources. We probably could have become "invitees"; the Chinese suggested this to us on several occasions, when we spoke of reducing our expenses, and that we did not do so was less because we thought that we would be corrupted—I have never believed myself to be easily corruptible and I don't think that I change my opinions because of small economic gains—but I intensely dislike the international junkets, the pleasure trips at public expense. The big powers, the Soviet Union, the United States, China, France, Great Britain, are all subjecting the writers of small countries like Sweden (and of each other) to well-intentioned economic pressure through different forms of free travel "with all expenses paid." Even if I don't think I would be corrupted, I'm against the whole tendency. It has a perverting influence on the intellectual morals of the writer, it runs counter to the free expression of ideas. I can't stop this tendency, but I can at least say no for myself. I distrust free-loaders whether they are capitalists, communists, liberals, conservatives, anarchists or just plain sellers of words. I have never liked being grateful to anybody. And I can't understand how the public—that after all pays for it—can put up with this spectacle of politicians, writers and sundry "public figures" banqueting their way around the world on a spree of phrases.

But as my funds were by no means unlimited and as there were, and are, few facilities in China today for the tourist with a slim pocketbook, this led to certain conflicts. . . . I'm not criticizing the Chinese; in every country in which I have lived I have had to take up a discussion with the bureaucracy in order to be left in peace to do my work. The Chinese officials were reasonable and it took rather less time to convince them than it has taken in many other countries; also there was no question of corruption. They followed their regulations and I wanted to have these regulations changed.

One of the prerequisite conditions for traveling in China today is that you accept interpreters and guides. We were given ours by the Chinese People's Association for Cultural Relations with Foreign Countries. I will come back to the question of interpreters, but I just want to point out that you either accept this condition or you don't travel outside Peking, Canton, Shanghai—and more often than not, not even there. I don't like this. But it is a tendency that is spreading from country to country. Even in Sweden we are starting to take in "invitees," give them guides and see to it that they keep looking at what we want to show them. I'm disturbed by this tendency. It gives strength to my fears that we, all over the world, are moving towards a more "supervised" form of existence. But in this case I could not just say no, find a third way out or shift the emphasis. Either I have my travel supervised—or I stay at home, quite probably supervised in one way or another even there. However much I dislike it, I have to accept this condition. . . .

Our chief interpreter was Pei Kwang-li. She had come with us from Peking. She was the most flexible, the best linguist and the most hard-working of the interpreters I had come across in China. I had tried several interpreters before getting hold of her, and we had been working together for about two weeks when we arrived at the village. She was supposed to go back to Peking from Yenan and it was only after some quite hard discussion that I managed to take her with me to Liu Ling. She was of great help to me in the village. She was friendly and cheerful and interested in the work. I gathered that she was afterwards criticized for her work with me. When we came back to Peking, she went away on vacation and after that she was not so friendly, natural and relaxed as she had been during the month in Liu Ling. She later on—when the book was finished—interpreted for us during our trip to Yunnan and during that trip she was cold, formal, dogmatic and even (which in China says much) quarrelled violently with us on the grounds that we showed "anti-Chinese" opinions. As our "anti-Chineseness" was our opinions about toil and sweat and peasant hunger that she had understood so well in Liu Ling, I cannot explain this change in her behaviour otherwise than that she had through "criticism and self-criticism" come to evaluate us and our work in a different way and change her opinions about our way of working. Because of this I got rather less information in Yunnan than I had hoped for.

The authorities in Yenan were very eager that we should not sleep in the village. They promised to arrange for us to be ferried there and back every day. We wanted, of course, to live in the village, we even demanded to be allowed to do so. The "Old Secretary" of the village strongly supported us. To him it was a point of honour. After some discussion the Yenan authorities were (with some reluctance) convinced of our point of view. (The reluctance can be interpreted in many ways, one of them is that the Yenan authorities wanted us to be as comfortable as possible. They probably wanted to be kind. It is not their fault that their kindness would have made this book impossible.) We then lived in a stone cave (normally the party secretary's office) and I worked in another (the brigade's conference-room). Since we lived in a cave in a village of caves and ate the village food and the whole time associated with the villagers, it would be easy to say that we lived as one of the people. But that would be a romantic and thus mendacious description of reality. We were the first foreigners to have lived in the village, and the village honour required that our cave should be whitewashed and that we should eat well. We lived considerably better than the villagers. . . . As a guest in a village you eat well, you also eat with a certain reverence, because you know that you are eating the fruits of the toil and sweat of the people around you. But you never say so to your hosts. There is pride in toil. There is nothing "objective" about food in a poor peasant village. It does not come out of a tin, neither is it something you carry with you from the city. But I was not one of the villagers. And I was not living like a Chinese peasant. . . .

The decision to have an upper limit to the interviews, i.e., not to continue far up in the bureaucratic structure above the village, was contained in the idea of the book itself. But first I had thought of including at least some representative from Yenan, who could give the slightly larger picture of the village in its setting. I even tried to make that interview and spent one morning in Yenan interviewing the local party secretary, a young man. Unfortunately he was too dogmatic, too official to be of any value. (And this is a typical problem all over Asia: the middle echelon of bureaucracy is mostly young and dogmatic and narrow-mindedly inexperienced. The old experienced peasants are illiterate, the bright young administrators are already high up and the old intellectual generation of revolutionaries or "national figures" are slowly fading away.) I don't blame the young bureaucrat from Yenan. He ran true to type, but when he flatly stated: "We have here in our part never had any difficulty, never committed a mistake, never made a fault and we have no problems today," I broke off the interview with a few nice, pleasant phrases, and decided that he was not to be included in the book and that I had better go back to the village and talk with the peasants.[16]

Despite the careful thoughts Myrdal has addressed to the problems that the "observation" of a transitional society creates, and as convincing as his report seems, he cannot provide us with a general solution to these difficulties. Such a solution not only presumes a different attitude on the traveler's part but also a change in the objective conditions. The *delegacija* system will not disappear until the isolation of the socialistically governed countries is overcome and until the foreigner's as well as the indigenous worker's freedom of movement has been guaranteed. When everyone is free to choose his own companion—or decide to dispense with him; when the infrastructure is sufficiently developed to insure lodging, transportation, and food for everyone who is under way, when the total dependence on guides and controlling institutions has vanished—then the *delegacija* business will not necessarily cease of its own accord, but dependency, bribery, segregation from the working population, reality loss, and uncritical ingratiation, as well as the privileges that are its material substratum, will become straitjackets that everyone who does not feel comfortable can discard.

Such a development is foreseeable, that is, as an unplanned and perhaps unwished-for but necessary complement of a policy of global coexistence—whose questionable sides, incidentally, are no secret. But to ascertain its positive aspects does not mean to capitulate to the two-dimensional theories of convergence so much in favor with bourgeois observers. However, it is conceivable that the Left in the West will not use the opportunities that are becoming manifest here. Little speaks for the fact that those who adhere to socialism in the West will take up the confrontation with the attempt to realize it. Now that the objective difficulties are decreasing and it is becoming less and less a question, in many countries, of endangering anyone by talking with them, now that traveling is ceasing to be an individual privilege, it should be possible to launch a massive attack on this overdue task that no one has performed as yet: the analysis of socialist societies or those that go by that name. Individual messengers cannot undertake such an investigation. We have tried to detect the reason for their failure. But whoever curses the "radical tourism" of the last fifty years in order to conceal his own disinterest will find it difficult to reply to the question that is put to him when he is having his beer, or at street-corner meetings or at demonstrations, the question: "Why don't you go live in the East?"

Translated by Michael Roloff

2

A Critique of
Political Ecology

Ecology as Science

As a scientific discipline, ecology is almost exactly a hundred years old. The concept emerged for the first time in 1868 when the German biologist Ernst Haeckel, in his *Natural History of Creation,* proposed giving this name to a subdiscipline of zoology—one that would investigate the totality of relationships between an animal species and its inorganic and organic environment. Compared with the present state of ecology, such a proposal suggests a comparatively modest program. Yet none of the restrictions contained in it proved to be tenable: neither the preference given to animal species over plant species, nor to macro- as opposed to micro-organisms. With the discovery of whole ecosystems, the perspective Haeckel had had in mind became untenable. Instead, there emerged the concept of mutual dependence and of a balance between all the inhabitants of an ecosystem, and in the course of this development the range and complexity of the new discipline have grown rapidly. Ecology became as controversial as it is today only when it was decided to include a very particular species of animal in its researches—man. While this step brought ecology unheard-of publicity, it also precipitated it into a crisis about its validity and methodology, the end of which is not yet in sight.

Human ecology is, first of all, a hybrid discipline. In it cate-

186

gories and methods drawn from the natural and social sciences have to be used together without this in any way theoretically resolving the resulting complications. Human ecology tends to suck in more and more new disciplines and to subsume them under its own research aims. This tendency is justified not on scientific grounds, but because of the urgency of ecology's aims. Under the pressure of public debate ecology's statements in recent years became more and more markedly prognostic. This "futurological deformation" was totally alien to ecology so long as it considered itself to be merely a particular area of biology. It must be clearly understood that this science has now come to lay claim to a total validity—a claim it cannot make good. The more far-reaching its conclusions, the less reliable it is. Since no one can vouch for the accuracy of the enormous volume of material from every conceivable science on which its hypotheses are constructed, it must—precisely to the degree that it wishes to make global statements—confine itself to working syntheses. One of the best known ecological handbooks—*Population, Resources, Environment* by Paul and Anne Ehrlich—deploys evidence from the following branches of sciences either implicitly or explicitly: statistics, systems theory, cybernetics, games theory and prediction theory; thermodynamics, biochemistry, biology, oceanography, mineralogy, meteorology, genetics; physiology, medicine, epidemology, toxicology; agricultural science, urban studies, demography; technologies of all kinds; theories of society, sociology, and economics (the latter admittedly in a most elementary form). The list is not complete. It is hard to describe the methodological confusion that results from the attempt at a synthesis of this sort. If one starts from this theoretical position there can, obviously, be no question of producing a group of people competent to deal with it. Henceforth, when push comes to shove, we are all ecologists; and this, incidentally, is what makes the statements in this article possible.

The Central Hypothesis

What till recently was a marginal science has within a few years become the center of bitter controversies. This cannot be explained merely by the snowballing effect of the mass media. It is connected with the central statement made by human ecology—a statement that refers to the future and is therefore at one and the same time prognostic and hypothetical. On the one hand, everyone is affected by the statement, since it relates to the existence of the species; on the other, no one can form a clear and final judgment on it because, in the last resort, it can only be verified or proved wrong in the future. This hypothesis can be formulated as follows: the industrial societies of this earth are producing ecological contradictions, which must in the foreseeable future lead to their collapse.

In contradistinction to other earlier theories of catastrophe this prognosis does not rest on linear, monocausal arguments. On the contrary, it introduces several synergetic factors. A very simplified list of the different strains of causality would look something like this:

1. Industrialization leads to an uncontrolled growth in world population. Simultaneously, the material needs of that population increase. Even given an enormous expansion in industrial production, the chances of satisfying human needs deteriorate per capita.

2. The industrial process has up to now been nourished from sources of energy which are not in the main self-renewing; among these are fossil fuels as well as supplies of fissile material such as uranium. In a determinable space of time these supplies will be exhausted; their replacement through what are basically new sources of energy (such as atomic fusion) is theoretically conceivable, but not yet practically realizable.

3. The industrial process is also dependent on the employment of mineral raw materials—above all of metals—which are not self-renewing either; their exploitation is advancing so rapidly that the exhaustion of deposits can be foreseen.

4. The water requirements of the industrial process have reached a point where they can no longer be satisfied by the natural circulation of water. As a result, the reserves of water in the ground are being attacked; this must lead to disturbances in the present cycle of evaporation and precipitation and to climatic changes. The only possible solution is the desalination of sea-water; but this is so energy-intensive that it would accelerate the process described in number 2 above.

5. A further limiting factor is the production of foodstuffs. Neither the area of land suitable for cultivation nor the yield per acre

can be arbitrarily increased. Attempts to increase the productivity of farming lead, beyond a certain point, to new ecological imbalances, e.g. erosion, pollution through poisonous substances, reductions in genetic variability. The production of food from the sea comes up against ecological limits of another kind.

6. A further factor—but only one factor among a number of others—is the notorious "pollution" of the earth. This category is misleading insofar as it presupposes a "clean" world. This has naturally never existed and is moreover ecologically neither conceivable nor desirable. What is actually meant are disequilibriums and dysfunctionings of all kinds in the metabolism between nature and human society occurring as the unintentional side effects of the industrial process. The polycausal linking of these effects is of unimaginable complexity. Poisoning caused by harmful substances—physiological damage from pesticides, radioactive isotopes, detergents, pharmaceutical preparations, food additives, artificial manures, trace quantities of lead and mercury, fluoride, carcinogens, gene mutants, and a vast quantity of other substances are only one facet of the problem. The problem of irreversible waste is only another facet of the same question. The changes in the atmosphere and in the resources of land and water traceable to metabolic causes such as production of smog, changes in climate, irreversible changes in rivers and lakes, oceanographic changes must also be taken into account.

7. Scientific research into yet another factor does not appear to have got beyond the preliminary stages. There are no established critical quantifications of what is called "psychic pollution." Under this heading come: increasing exposure to excessive noise and other irritants, the psychical effects of overpopulation, as well as other stress factors which are difficult to isolate.

8. A final critical limit is presented by "thermal pollution." The laws of thermodynamics show that, even in principle, this limit cannot be crossed. Heat is emitted by all processes involving the conversion of energy. The consequences for the global supply of heat have not been made sufficiently clear.

A basic difficulty in the construction—or refutation—of ecological hypotheses is that the processes invoked do not take place serially but in close interdependence. That is also true of all attempts to find solutions to ecological crises. It often, if not always, emerges that measures to control one critical factor lead to another getting out of control. One is dealing with a series of closed circuits, or rather of interference circuits, which are in many ways linked. Any discussion that attempted to deal with the alleged "causes" piecemeal and to disprove them singly would miss the core of the ecological debate and would fall below the level the debate has reached in the meantime.[1]

Yet even if there exists a certain, but by no means complete, consensus that the present process of industrialization must lead *ceteris paribus* to a breakdown, three important questions connected with the prognosis are still open to debate. The first concerns the time scale involved. Estimations of the point in time at which a galloping deterioration of the ecological situation may be expected differ by a factor of several centuries. They range from the end of the 1980s to the twenty-second century. In view of the innumerable variables involved in the calculations, such divergencies are not to be wondered at. (For example, the critics of the MIT report *The Limits of Growth* have objected to its conclusions on the grounds that the mathematical model on which it is based is much too simple and the number of variables too limited.) A second controversial point is closely related to the first: namely that the relative weighting to be given to the individual factors blamed for the catastrophe is not made clear. This is a point at issue, for example, in the debate between Barry Commoner and Paul Ehrlich. While the latter considers population growth to be the "critical factor," the former believes that the decisive factor is modern industrial technology. An exact analysis of the factors involved comes up against immense methodological difficulties. The scientific debate between the two schools therefore remains undecided.

Thirdly, it is obviously not clear what qualifies as an environmental catastrophe. In this connection one can distinguish a number of different perspectives dictated by expectation or fear. There are ecologists who concern themselves only with mounting dangers and the corresponding physiological, climatic, social, and political "disturbances"; others, like the Swedish ecologist Gösta Ehrensvärd, contemplate the end of social structures based on industrialization; some prognoses go further—those of what in the

United States are called "doomsters" talk of the dying out of the human species or the disappearance from the planet of a whole series of species: primates, mammals, and vertebrates. The tone in which the respective ecological hypotheses are presented ranges correspondingly from the mildest reformist warnings to deepest resignation. What is decisive for the differences between them is naturally the question of how far the process of ecological destruction and uncontrolled exploitation is to be regarded as irreversible. In the literature, the answer to this question is made to depend on the one hand on an analysis of the factors involved and on the other on temporal parameters. The uncertainty which is admitted to prevail on these two points means that there is no prospect of a firm answer. Authors like Ehrensvärd, who start from the premise that the end of industrial societies is at hand, and are already busy with preparations for a post-industrial society—one which, it should be added, contains a number of idyllic traits—are still in the minority. Most ecologists imply that they consider that the damage done so far is reversible, if only by tacking on to their analyses proposals to avert the catastrophe of which they are the prophets. These proposals will need to be critically examined.

The Ecological "Movement"

Ecology's hypotheses about the future of industrialization have been disseminated, at least in industrialized capitalist countries, through the mass media. The debate on the subject has itself to some extent acquired a mass character, particularly in the Anglo-Saxon and Scandinavian countries. It has led to the rise of a wide, although loosely organized, movement whose political potential is hard to estimate. At the same time the problem under discussion is peculiarly ill-defined. Even the statements of the ecologists themselves alternate between the construction of theories and broad statements of *Weltanschauung*, between precise research and "totalizing" theories linked to a philosophy of history. The thinking of the ecological groups therefore gives the impression of being at once obscure and confused. The very fact that it is disseminated by the mass media means that the debate generally loses a great deal of its stringency and content. Subordinate questions such as that of recycling refuse or "pollution" are treated in isolation; hypotheses are presented as unequivocal truths; spectacular cases of poisoning are sensationally exploited; isolated results of research are given absolute validity and so on. Processing through the sewage system of industrialized publicity has therefore, to some extent, led to further pollution of a cluster of problems that, from the start, cannot be presented in a "pure" way. This lack of clarity is propagated in the groups that are at present actively occupied with the subject of ecology, or rather with its *disjecta membra*, with what is left of it. The most powerful of these groups is that of the technocrats who, at all levels of the state apparatus and also of industry, are busy finding the speediest solutions to particular problems—"quick technological fixes"—and implementing them. This they do whenever there is a considerable potential for economic or political conflict—and only then. These people consider themselves entirely pragmatic—that is to say, they are servants of the ruling class now in power—and cannot be assumed to have a proper awareness of the problem. They can be included in the ecological movement only insofar as they belong—as will be demonstrated—to its manipulators and insofar as they benefit from it. The political motives and interests in these cases are either obvious—as with the Club of Rome, a consortium of top managers and bureaucrats—or can easily and unequivocally be established.

What is less unequivocal is the political character of a second form of ecological awareness and the practice that corresponds to it. Here it is a matter of smaller groups of "concerned and responsible citizens," as they say in the United States. The expression points, as does its German parallel, "citizens' initiative," to the class background of those involved in it. They are overwhelmingly members of the middle class and of the new petty bourgeoisie. Their activities have generally modest goals. They are concerned with preserving open spaces or trees. Classes of schoolchildren are encouraged to clean up litter on beaches or recreation grounds. A boycott of nonbiodegradable packaging is organized, etc. The harmless impression made by projects of this kind can easily blind us to the reserves of militancy they conceal. There only needs to be a tiny alteration in the definition of goals and these groups spontaneously begin to increase in size and power. They are then able to prevent the carrying through of large-scale projects, such as the siting of an airport or an oil refinery, to force high-tension cables to be laid underground or a highway to be diverted. But even achievements of this magnitude only represent the limits of their effectiveness for a time. If the hypotheses of the ecologists should come even partially true, the ecological action groups will become a force of the first order in domestic politics and one that can no longer be ignored. On the one hand, they express powerful and legitimate needs of those who engage in these activities; on the other hand, they set their sights on immediate targets, which are not understood politically, and they incline to indulge in social illusion. This makes them ideal fodder for demagogues and interested third parties. But the limited nature of their initiatives should not conceal the fact that there lies within them the seed of a possible mass movement.

Finally, there is that part of the ecological movement that considers itself to be its hard core but that, in fact, plays a rather marginal role. These are the "eco-freaks." These groups, which have mostly split off from the American protest movement, are engaged in a kind of systematic flight from the cities and from civilization. They live in rural communes, grow their own food, and seek a "natural way of life," which may be regarded as the simulation of pre- or postindustrial conditions. They look for salvation in detailed, precisely stipulated dietary habits—eating "earth food"—and agricultural methods. Their class background corresponds to that of the hippies of the 1960s—of reduced middle-class origin, enriched by elements from peripheral groups. Ideologically, they incline toward obscurantism and sectarianism.

On the whole one can say that in the ecological movement—or perhaps one should say movements—the scientific aspects, which derive predominantly from biology, have merged in an extremely confused alliance with a whole series of political motivations and interests, which are partly manifest, partly concealed. At a deeper level one can identify a great number of sociopsychological needs, which are usually aroused without those concerned being able to see through them. These include: hopes of conversions and redemption, delight in the collapse of things, feelings of guilt and resignation, escapism, and hostility to civilization.

In these circumstances it is not surprising that the European Left holds aloof from the ecological movement. It is true that it has incorporated certain topics from the environmental debate in the repertory of its anticapitalist agitation; but it maintains a skeptical attitude to the basic hypothesis underlying ecology and avoids entering into alliances with groups that are entirely oriented toward ecological questions. The Left has instead seen its task to be to face the problem in terms of an ideological critique. It therefore functions chiefly as an instrument of clarification, as a tribunal that attempts to dispel the innumerable mystifications that dominate ecological thinking and have encouraged it. The most important elements in this process of clarification, which is absolutely necessary, are listed and discussed below.

The Class Character of the Current Ecological Debate

The social neutrality to which the ecological debate lays claim, having recourse as it does so to strategies derived from the evidence of the natural sciences, is a fiction. A simple piece of historical reflection shows just how far this class neutrality goes. Industrialization made whole towns and areas of the countryside uninhabitable as long as 150 years ago. The environmental conditions at places of work, that is to say in the English factories and pits, were—as innumerable documents demonstrate—dangerous to life. There was an infernal noise; the air people breathed was polluted with explosive and poisonous gases as well as with carcinogenous matter and particles that were highly contaminated with bacteria. The smell was unimaginable. In the labor process contagious poisons of all kinds were used. The diet was bad. Food was adulterated. Safety measure were nonexistent or were ignored. The overcrowding in the working-class quarters was notorious. The situation regarding drinking water and drainage was terrifying. There was in general no organized method for disposing of refuse.

> . . . When cholera prevailed in that district [Tranent, in Scotland] some of the patients suffered very much indeed from want of water, and so great was the privation, that on that calamitous occasion people went into the ploughed fields and gathered rain water which collected in depressions in the ground, and actually in the prints made by horses' feet. Tranent was formerly well-supplied with water of excellent quality by a spring above the village, which flows through a sand-

bed. The water flows into Tranent at its head . . . and is received into about ten wells, distributed throughout the village. The people supply themselves at these wells when they contain water. When the supply is small, the water pours in a very small stream only. . . . I have seen women fighting for water. The wells are sometimes frequented throughout the whole night. It was generally believed by the population that this stoppage of the water was owing to its stream being diverted into a coal-pit which was sunk in the sand-bed above Tranent.[2]

These conditions, which are substantiated by innumerable other sources from the nineteenth century, would undoubtedly have presented a "neutral observer" with food for ecological reflection. But there were no such observers. It occurred to no one to draw pessimistic conclusions from these facts about the future of industrialization. The ecological movement has only come into being since the districts the bourgeoisie inhabit and their living conditions have been exposed to those environmental burdens that industrialization brings with it. What fills their prophets with terror is not so much ecological decline, which has been present since time immemorial, as its universalization. To isolate oneself from this process becomes increasingly difficult. It deploys a dialectic that in the last resort turns against its own beneficiaries. Pleasure trips and expensive packaging, for example, are by no means phenomena that have emerged only in the last decades; they are part of the traditional consumption of the ruling classes. They have become problematic, however, in the shape of tourism and the litter of consumerism; that is, only since the laboring masses have shared them. Quantitative increase tips over into a new quality— that of destruction. What was previously privilege now appears as nightmare and capitalist industry proceeds to take tardy, if still comparatively mild, revenge on those who up to now had only derived benefit from it. The real capitalist class, which is decreasing in numbers, can admittedly still avoid these consequences. It can buy its own private beaches and employ lackeys of all kinds. But for both the old and the new and the petty bourgeoisie such expenditure is unthinkable. The cost of a private "environment" that makes it possible to escape to some extent from the consequences of industrialization is already astronomical and will rise more sharply in the future.

It is after all easy to understand that the working class cares little about general environmental problems and is only prepared to take part in campaigns where it is a question of directly improving their working and living conditions. Insofar as it can be considered a source of ideology, ecology is a matter that concerns the middle class. If avowed representatives of monopoly capitalism have recently become its spokesmen—as in the Club of Rome— that is because of reasons that have little to do with the living conditions of the ruling class. These reasons require analysis.

The Interests of the Eco-industrial Complex

That the capitalist mode of production has catastrophic consequences is a commonplace of Marxism, which also not infrequently crops up in the arguments of the ecological movement. Certainly the fight for a "clean" environment always contains anticapitalist elements. Nevertheless, fascism in Germany and Italy have demonstrated how easily such elements can be turned round and become tools in the service of the interests of capital.[3] It is therefore not surprising that ecological protest, at least in Western Europe, almost always ends up with an appeal to the state. Under present political conditions this means that it appeals to reformism and to technocratic rationality. This appeal is then answered by government programs that promise an "improvement in the quality of life," without of course indicating whose life is going to be made more beautiful, in what way, and at whose expense. The state only "goes into action when the earning powers of the entrepreneur are threatened. Today the environmental crisis presents a massive threat to these interests. On the one hand it threatens the material basis of production—air, earth, and water—while on the other hand it threatens man, the productive factor, whose usefulness is being reduced by frequent physical and mental illnesses."[4] To these have to be added the danger of uncontrollable riots over ecological questions as the conditions in the environment progressively deteriorate.

On the question of state intervention and "environmental protection from above," the Left's ideological critique displays a remarkable lack of historical reflection. Here too it is certainly not a question of new phenomena. The negative effects of environmental damage on the earning power of industry, the struggle over the off-loading of liability, over laws relating to the environment and over the range of state control can be traced back without much difficulty to the early period of English industrialization; a remarkable lack of variation in the attitude of the interests involved emerges from such a study. The previously quoted report on the water supply and the drainage problems in a Scottish mining village is taken from an official report of the year 1842—a report that incidentally was also quoted by Engels in his book *The Condition of the English Working Class.* The chairman of the commission of inquiry was a certain Sir Edwin Chadwick, a typical predecessor of the modern ecological technocrats. Chadwick was a follower of the utilitarian political philosopher and lawyer Jeremy Bentham, of whom Marx said: "If I had the courage of my friend H. Heine, I would call Mr. Jeremiah a genius at bourgeois stupidity."[5] James Ridgeway, one of the few American ecologists capable of intervening in the present environmental discussion with political arguments, has dealt thoroughly with Chadwick's role.[6] Then as now the rhetoric of the ecological reformers served to cloak quite concrete connections between a variety of interests. The technological means with which this "reform from above" operates have also altered less than one might think.[7]

But a historical perspective fails in its object if it is used to reduce modern problems to the level of past ones. Ridgeway does not always avoid this danger: he tends to restrict himself to traditional ecological questions such as water pollution and the supply of energy. Without meaning to do so he thereby reduces the extent of the threatened catastrophe. It is true that there were environmental crises before this and that the mechanisms of reformist managements set up to deal with the crises can look back on a long history. What has to be kept in mind, however, is that the ecological risks have not only increased quantitatively, but have taken on a new quality.

In line with the changes that have taken place in the economic basis, this also holds true for environmental pollution and state intervention. In its present form monopoly capitalism is inclined, as is well known, to solve its demand problems by extravagant expenditure at the cost of the public exchequer. The most obvious examples of this are unproductive investments in armaments and in space exploration. Industrial protection of the environment emerges as a new growth area, the costs of which can either be off-loaded on to prices or are directly made a social charge through the budget in the form of subsidies, tax concessions, and direct measures by the public authorities, while the profits accrue to the monopolies. "According to the calculations of the American Council of Environmental Quality at least a million dollars is pocketed in the course of the elimination of three million dollars worth of damage to the environment."[8]

Thus, the recognition of the problems attendant on industrial growth serves to promote a new growth industry. The rapidly expanding eco-industrial complex makes profits in two ways: on the straightforward market, where consumer goods for private consumption are produced with increasing pollution, and in another where that same pollution has to be contained by control techniques financed by the public. This process at the same time increases the concentration of capital in the hands of a few international concerns, since the smaller industrial plants are not in the position to provide their own finance for the development of systems designed to protect the environment.

For these reasons the monopolies attempt to acquire influence over the ecological movement. The MIT study commissioned by the Club of Rome is by no means the only initiative of this kind. The monopolies are also represented in all state and private commissions on the protection of the environment. Their influence on legislation is decisive, and there are numerous indications that even apparently spontaneous ecological campaigns have been promoted by large firms and government departments. There emerges a policy of "alliances from above," whose demagogic motives are obvious.[9]

By no means all ecological movements based on private initiative put themselves at the service of the interests of capital with such servility. That is demonstrated by the fact that their emergence has often led to confrontations with the police. The danger of being used is, however, always present. It must also be remembered that the interests of capital contain their own contradictions. Ecological controversies often mirror the clash of interests of different groups of entrepreneurs without their initiators always being clear as to the stakes involved in the campaigns. A long process of clarification will be necessary before the ecological movement has reached that minimum degree of political consciousness that it would require finally to understand who its enemy is and whose interests it has to defend.[10]

Demography and Imperialism

Warnings about the consequences of uncontrolled population growth—the so-called population explosion—also contain ideological motives and behind the demands to contain it are concealed political interests that do not reveal themselves openly. The neo-Malthusian arguments that authors such as Ehrlich and Taylor have been at pains to popularize found expression at a particular moment in time and in a quite particular political context. They originate almost exclusively from the North American sources and can be dated to the late 1950s and early 1960s—a time, that is to say, when the liberation movements in the Third World began to become a central problem for the leading imperialist power. (On the other hand the rate of increase in population had begun to rise much earlier, in the 1930s and 1940s.)

That this is no mere coincidence was first recognized and expressed by the Cubans.

At that time (1962) the Population Council in New York, supported by the Population Reference Bureau, Inc. in Washington, launched an extensive publicity campaign for neo-Malthusianism with massive financial help from the Ford and Rockefeller foundations, which contributed millions of dollars. The campaign pursued a double goal, which may even be attained: the ruling classes of Latin America were to be persuaded by means of skillful propaganda based on the findings of the FAO and work done by numerous, even progressive scientists, that a demographic increase of 2.5 per cent in Latin America would lead to a catastrophe of incalculable dimensions. The following excerpts from the report of the Rockefeller Foundation for 1965 are typical of this literature *made in the USA*; "the pessimistic prediction that humanity is soon likely to be stifled by its own growth increasingly confronts all attempts to bring about an improvement in living standards. . . . It is clear that mankind will double in numbers in the lifetime of two generations unless the present growth tendency is brought under control. The results will be catastrophic for innumerable millions of individuals." The Population Reference Bureau expresses itself even more un-equivocally: "The future of the world will be decided in the Latin American continent, in Asia and Africa, because in these developing territories the highest demographic rates of growth have been registered. Either the birth rates must be lowered or the death rate must rise again if the growth is to be brought under control. . . . The biologists, sociologists, and econo-mists of the Bureau have forecast the moment when Mal-thus' theory will return like a ghost and haunt the nations of the earth" (P.R.B. press statement of October 1966).

The Cuban report also quotes Lyndon B. Johnson's remark to the effect that "five dollars put into birth control is more useful in Latin America than a hundred dollars invested in economic growth." [11] It adds, "A comment on this cynical statement seems to us to be superfluous."

Indeed, not much intelligence is needed to discover behind the benevolent pose of the Americans both strong political motivation and the irrational fears that are responsible for the massive at-tempt by official and private groups in the United States to export birth control to the countries of the Third World. The imperialist nations see the time coming when they will be only a small mi-nority when compared to the rest of the world, and their govern-ments fear that population pressures will become a source of po-litical and, in the last analysis, military power. Admittedly, fears of another kind can be detected underneath the rational calcula-tions: symptoms of a certain panic, the precursors of which are easily recognizable in history. One has only to think of the hyster-ical slogans of the heyday of imperialism—"The Yellow Peril"—and of the period of German fascism—"the Red Hordes." The "politics" of population have never been free of irrational and racist traits; they always contain demagogic elements and are al-ways prone to arouse atavistic feelings. This is admittedly true not only for the imperialist side. Even the Cuban source does not stop at the extremely enlightening comment that has been quoted but continues as follows:

> Fidel Castro has spoken on the question many times. We re-call his words now: "In certain countries they are saying that only birth control provides a solution to the problem. Only

capitalists, the exploiters, can speak like that; for no one who is conscious of what man can achieve with the help of technology and science will wish to set a limit to the number of human beings who can live on the earth. . . . That is the deep conviction of all revolutionaries. What characterized Malthus in his time and the neo-Malthusians in our time is their pessimism, their lack of trust in the future destiny of man. That alone is the reason why revolutionaries can never be Malthusians. *We shall never be too numerous,* however many of us there are, if only we all together place our efforts and our intelligence at the service of mankind, a mankind which will be freed from the exploitation of man by man." [12]

In such phrases not only does the well-known tendency of the Cuban revolution to voluntarism find expression together with a rhetoric of affirmation; but there is also the tendency to answer the irrational fears of the imperialist oppressor with equally irrational hopes. A materialist analysis of concrete needs, possibilities, and limits cannot be replaced by figures of speech. The Chinese leadership recognized that long ago and has therefore repeatedly modified its earlier population policy, which was very similar to the Cuban one in its premises. As far as the neo-Malthusians in the United States are concerned, a violent conflict has been raging for several years over their theses and their motivation.

The Problem of Global Projection

A central ideological theme of the ecological debate as it is at present conducted—it is perhaps at its very heart—is the metaphor of "spaceship earth." This concept belongs above all to the repertory of the American ecological movement. Scientific debates tend to sound more sober, but their content comes to the same thing: they consider the planet a closed and global eco-system.

The degree of "false consciousness" contained in these concepts is obvious. It links up with platitudes, which are considered "idealistic" but to which even that word is misapplied: "The good of the community takes precedence over the good of the individual," "We are all in the same boat," and so on. The ideological purpose of such hasty global projections is clear. The aim is to deny once and for all that little difference between first class and steerage, between the bridge and the engine room. One of the oldest ways of giving legitimacy to class domination and exploitation is resurrected in the new garb of ecology. Forrester and Meadows, the authors of the MIT report, for instance, by planning their lines of development from the start on a world scale, and always referring to the spaceship earth—and who would not be taken in by such global brotherliness?—avoid the need to analyze the distribution of costs and profits, to define their structural limitations and with them the wide variation between the chances of bringing human misery to an end. For while some can afford to plan for growth and still draw profits from the elimination and prevention of the damage they do, others certainly cannot. Thus, under accelerated state capitalism, the industrial countries of the northern territories of the world can maintain capital accumulation by diverting it to antipollution measures, to the recycling of basic raw materials, to processes involving intensive instead of extensive growth. This is denied to the developing countries, which are compelled to exploit to the utmost their sources of raw materials and, because of their structural dependence, are urged to continue intensive exploitation of their own resources. (It is worth quoting in this connection the remark of a Brazilian Minister of Economics to the effect that his country could not have enough pollution of the environment if that was the cost of giving its population sufficient work and bread.) [13]

The contradictions that the ecological ideologies attempt to suppress in their global rhetoric emerge all the more sharply the more one takes their prognoses and demands at face value. What would be the concrete effect, for instance, of a limitation of the consumption of energy over the whole of spaceship earth such as is demanded in almost all ecological programs?

Stabilization of the use of energy—certainly, but at what level? If the average per-capita consumption of a United States citizen is to serve as a measure, then a future world society stabilized at this level would make an annual demand on the available reserves of energy of roughly 350×10^{12} kilowatt hours. The world production of energy would then be almost seven times as great as at present and the thermal, atmospheric, and radioactive pollution would increase to such a degree that the consequences would be unforeseeable; at the same time the available reserves of fossil fuel would disappear. If one chooses the present world average instead of the energy standard of the United States today as a measure of a future "stable" control of energy, then the exploitation of the available source of energy and the thermal, chemical, and radioactive effects in the environment would settle at a level only slightly higher than at present and one that would perhaps be sustainable well into the future. The real question would then be, however, how the available energy should be distributed globally. In arithmetical terms the solution would look something like this: the developing countries would have to have three times as much energy at their disposal as they do today; the socialist countries could by and large maintain their present level of consumption; but the highly industrialized countries of Europe and the United States would have to reduce their consumption enormously and enter upon a period of *contraction*.[14]

It must be clear that redistributions of such magnitude could be put through only by force: this is bound to hold good not only in international but also in national terms. Admittedly, the captains of industry, gathered together in the Club of Rome, appear to have another view of conditions on board the ship in which we are supposed to be sitting. They are clearly not plagued by doubts as to their own competence and qualities of leadership. On the contrary, they assert: "Very few people are thinking about the future from a global point of view."[15] This minority leaves no doubt that they are determined to adjust their view of the world to suit their own interests. The scarcer the resources, the more one has to take this view in distributing them; but the more one adopts this view of the world, the fewer people can be considered for this high office.

An ecologist who finds himself confronted by objections of this kind will generally attempt to counter them by changing the terms of the argument. He will explain that his immediate task is to deal with a condition that exists in fact; this is a task that takes precedence over future distribution problems that it is not his task to solve. On a factual level, however, it is impossible not to treat the problem on a global scale; indeed it is inevitable. The pollution of the oceans or of the atmosphere, the spread of radioactive isotopes, the consequences of man-made changes in climate—all these are *actually,* and not merely in an ideological sense, worldwide and global phenomena and can be understood only as such.

While that is true, it does not help much. So long as ecology considered itself to be a branch of biology it was always conscious of the dialectical connection between the whole and the part; far from wishing "merely" to investigate life on earth, it saw itself as a science of interdependence and attempted to investigate the relations between individual species, the ecological subsystem in which they live, and the larger systems. With the expansion of its research aims, its claims to hegemony, and the consequent methodological syncretism, human ecology has forfeited that ability to differentiate that characterized its founders. Its tendency to hasty global projection is in the last analysis a surrender in the face of the size and complexity of the problem it has thrown open. The reason for this failure is not difficult to determine. An ecologist researching the conditions of life in a lake has solid methodological ground to stand on; ecological arguments begin to become shaky only when the ecologist involves his own species in them. Escape into global projection is then the simplest way out. For, in the case of man, the mediation between the whole and the part, between subsystem and global system, cannot be explained by the tools of biology. This mediation is social, and its explication requires an elaborated social theory and at the very least some basic assumptions about the historical process. Neither the one nor the other is available to present-day ecologists. That is why their hypotheses, in spite of their factual core, so easily fall victim to ideology.

Environmental Apocalypse
as an Ideological Pawn

The concept of a critique of ideology is not clearly defined—nor is the object it studies. It is not only that "false consciousness" proliferates in extraordinary and exotic luxuriance given the present conditions under which opinions are manufactured, but it also possesses the suppleness of a jellyfish and is capable of protean feats of adaptability. So far we have examined the most widely diffused components of environmental ideology chiefly with regard to the interests that they at once conceal and promote. This would have to be distinguished from an evaluation in terms of an ideological critique that sees the ecological debate as a symptom that yields conclusions about the state of the society that produces it. So that nothing may be omitted, interpretations of this kind will now be briefly surveyed, although it is doubtful whether that will bring to light any new perspectives.

From this point of view, the preoccupation with ecological crisis appears as a phenomenon belonging entirely to the superstructure—namely an expression of the decadence of bourgeois society. The bourgeoisie can conceive of its own imminent collapse only as the end of the world. Insofar as it sees any salvation at all, it sees it only in the past. Anything of that past that still exists must be preserved, must be conserved. In earlier phases of bourgeois society this longing for earlier cultural conditions was concentrated on "values" that either did obtain previously or were believed to have done so. With the progressive liquidation of this "inheritance," e.g. religion, the search for the roots of things, which is now thought to reside in what is left of "nature," becomes radicalized. In its period of decadence the bourgeoisie therefore proclaims itself to be the protector of something it itself destroyed. It flees from the world that, so long as it was a revolutionary class, it created in its own image, and wishes to conserve something that no longer exists. Like the sorcerer's apprentice, it would like to get rid of the industrialization to which it owes its own power. But since the journey into the past is not possible, it is projected into the future: a return to barbarism, which is depicted as a preindustrial idyll. The imminent catastrophe is conjured up with a mixture of trembling and pleasure and awaited with both terror and longing. Just as, in German society between the world wars, Klages and Spengler sounded the apocalyptic note, so in the Anglo-Saxon lands today the ecological Cassandras find a role as preachers calling a class that no longer believes in its own future to repentance. Only the scale of the prophecies has changed. While Klages and Spengler contemplated the decline of Europe, today the whole planet must pay for our *hubris*. Whereas in those days a barbarian civilization was to win terrible victories over a precious culture, today civilization is both victim and executioner. What will remain, according to the prophecies, is not an inner but a physical desert. And so on. However illuminating such excesses may occasionally sound, they cannot advance beyond a point of view that is little more than that of the history of ideas. Besides, they do not carry much conviction in view of the fact that the dominant monopolies of the capitalist world show no signs of becoming aware of their presumed decadence. Just as German industry in the 1920s did not allow itself to be diverted from its expansion, so IBM and General Motors show little inclination to take the MIT report seriously. Theories of decline are a poor substitute for materialist analyses. If one explores their historical roots it usually emerges, as in the case of Lukács, that they are nourished by that very idealism they claim to criticize.

The Critique of Ideology
as an Ideology

The attempt to summarize the Left's arguments has shown that its main intervention in the environmental controversy has been through the critique of ideology. This kind of approach is not completely pointless, and there is no position other than Marxism from which such a critical examination of the material would be possible. But an ideological critique is only useful when it remains conscious of its own limitations: it is in no position to handle the object of its researches by itself. As such it remains merely the interpretation of an interpretation of real conditions and is therefore unable to reach the heart of the problem. Its characteristic gesture of "unmasking" can turn into a smug ritual, if attention remains fixed on the mask instead of on what is revealed beneath it. The fact that we name the interests that lie behind current demographic theories will not conjure the needs of a rapidly growing population out of existence. An examination of the advertising campaigns of the enterprises involved does not increase the energy reserves of the earth by a single ton. And the amount of foreign matter in the air is not in any way reduced if we draw attention to the earlier history of pollution in the working-class quarters of Victorian England. A critique of ideology that is tempted to go beyond its effective limits itself becomes an ideology.

The Left in West Germany has so far been scarcely conscious of this danger, or at least has not thought about it adequately, although it is by no means new in historical terms. Even Marxist thinking is not immune to ideological deformations, and Marxist theory too can become a false consciousness if, instead of being used for the methodical investigation of reality through theory and practice, it is misused as a defense against that very reality. Marxism as a defensive mechanism, as a talisman against the demands of reality, as collection of exorcisms—these are tendencies that we all have reason to take note of and to combat. The issue of ecology offers but one example. Those who wish to deprive Marxism of its critical, subversive power and turn it into an affirmative doctrine generally dig in behind a series of stereotyped statements that, in their abstraction, are as irrefutable as they are devoid of results. One example is the claim that is proclaimed in the pages of every other picture magazine, irrespective of whether it is discussing syphilis, an earthquake, or a plague of locusts—"Capitalism is to blame!"

It is naturally splendid that anticapitalist sentiments are so widespread that even glossy magazines cannot avoid them altogether. But it is quite another question how far an analysis that a priori attributes every conceivable problem to capitalism deserves to be called Marxist, and what the political effect of this is. Its commonplace nature renders it harmless. Capitalism, so frequently denounced, becomes a kind of social ether, omnipresent and intangible, a quasi-natural cause of ruin and destruction, the conjuring up of which can have a positively neutralizing effect. Since the concrete problem at hand—psychosis, lack of nursery schools, dying rivers, air crashes—can, without precise analysis of the exact causes, be referred to the total situation, the impression is given that any specific intervention here and now is pointless. In the same way, reference to the need for revolution has become an empty formula, the ideological husk of passivity.

The same holds true for the thesis that ecological catastrophe is unavoidable within the capitalist system. The prerequisite for all solutions to the environmental crisis is then the introduction of socialism. No particular skill is involved in deducing this answer from the premises of Marxist theory. The question, however, is whether it adds up to more than an abstract statement that has nothing to do with political praxis and that allows whoever utters it to neglect the examination of his concrete situation.

The ideological packaging of such statements is dispelled at once, however, if one asks what exactly they mean. The mere question of what is meant by "capitalism" brings to light the crassest contradictions. The comfortable structure of the commonplace falls apart. What is left is a heap of unresolved problems. If one understands by capitalism a system characterized by private ownership of the means of production, then it follows that the ecological problem, like all the other evils of which "capitalism" is guilty, will be solved by nationalization of the means of production. It follows that in the Soviet Union there can be no environmental problems. Anyone who asserts the contrary must be prepared to be insulted if he produces a bundle of quotations from *Pravda* and *Izvestia* about the polluted air of the Don Basin or the filthy Volga as evidence. Such a comparison of systems is forbidden—at least by Marxists like Gerhard Kade:

> For all those who are embarrassed by the question of the relationship between bourgeois capitalist methods of production and the destruction of the environment, a well-proven argument can be produced from that box of tricks where diversionary social and political tactics are kept. Scientists talk of comparing the two systems: standard commonplace minds immediately think of the filthy Volga, the polluted air of the Don Basin, or of that around Leuna. A whole tradition lies behind this. There is no social or political issue, from party conferences to reports on the state of the nation, where the diversionary effectiveness of such comparisons between systems has not already proved its worth. Whatever emerges from the increasing number of inquiries into environmental pollution in the socialist countries is dressed up scientifically and becomes a useful weapon in a situation where demands for replacement of the system begin to threaten those who have an interest in upholding present conditions. "Go to East Germany if you don't like it here" or "Throw Dutschke over the Wall" are the socially aggressive forms adopted by that diversionary maneuver.[16]

Critique of ideology as ideology: the position that lays the blame on "capitalism" is defended here at the cost of its credibility. Moreover, the fact that in the socialist countries destruction of the environment has also reached perilous proportions is not even disputed, merely ignored. Anyone who is not prepared to go along with this type of scientific thinking is guilty of drawing analogies between the systems and is denounced as an anticommunist, a sort of ecological Springer. The danger that such a denatured form of Marxism will establish a hold on the masses is admittedly slight. The relationship of the German working class to its own reality is not so remote as to exclude the possibility of a comparative examination. In the face of such narrowness, one must

> bear in mind that capitalism as a historical form and as a system of production cannot be identified with the existence of a class of owners. It is an all-embracing social mode of production arising from a particular type of accumulation and reproduction that has produced a network of relationships between human beings more complicated than any in the history of man. This system of production cannot simply be done away with by dispossessing private capitalists, even when this expropriation makes it possible in practice to render that part of surplus value available for other purposes that is not used for accumulation. The socialist revolution cannot be understood merely as a transfer of ownership leading to a more just distribution of wealth, while other relationships remain alienated and reified. On the contrary, it must lead to totally revolutionized relationships between men and between men and things—that is to say, it must revolutionize the whole social production of their lives. It will either aim to transcend the proletariat's situation, of alienation, of the division between work and its profit, the end of commodity fetishism or it will not be the socialist revolution.[17]

Only such a view of capitalism, i.e., as a mode of production and not as a mere property relationship, allows the ecological problem to be dealt with in Marxist terms. In this connection the categories of use value and exchange value are of decisive importance. The disturbance of the material interchange between man and nature is then revealed as the strict consequence of capitalist commodity production.[18] This is a conclusion that makes the ideological ban on thought unnecessary and explains why ecological problems survive in the socialist countries too. After all, the contradiction between use value and exchange value is not superseded any more than wage labor and commodity production. "Socialist society has remained a transitional society in a very precise meaning of the word—a social form in which the capitalist mode of production, compounded with new elements, continues to exist and exercises a decisive pressure on the political sphere, on relations between human beings and on the relationship between rulers and ruled."[19] No less decisive is the pressure that the persistence of the capitalist mode of production exercises on the relationship between man and nature—a pressure that, on very similar lines to industrial production in the West, also leads to the destruction of the environment in the countries where the capitalist class has been expropriated.

The consequences of this position are extremely grave. It is true that it is possible in this manner to derive the catastrophic ecological situation from the capitalist mode of production; but the more fundamental the categories, the more universal the result. The argument is irrefutable in an abstract sense, but it remains politically impotent. The statement "capitalism is to blame" is correct in principle, but threatens to dwindle into an abstract negation of the existing order of things. Marxism is not a theory that exists in order to produce eternal verities; it is no good Marxists being right "in principle," when that means the end of the world.

Perhaps one has to remember that Marx represented *historical* materialism. From that it follows that the time factor cannot be eliminated from his theories. The delay in the coming of revolution in the overdeveloped capitalist lands is therefore not a matter of theoretical indifference. But that it was delayed does not in any way falsify the theory; for Marx certainly regarded the proletarian revolution as a necessary but not an automatic and inevitable consequence of capitalist development. He always maintained that there are alternatives in history, and the alternatives facing the highly industrialized societies were long ago expressed in the formula: socialism or barbarism. In the face of the emerging ecological catastrophe this statement takes on a new meaning. The fight against the capitalist mode of production has become a race with time, which mankind is in danger of losing. The tenacity with which that mode of production still asserts itself fifty years after the expropriation of the capitalist class in the Soviet Union indicates the kind of time dimensions we are discussing. It is an open question how far the destruction it has wrought here on earth and continues to wreak is still reversible.

In this situation one must be relentless in critically examining certain elements in the Marxist tradition. First of all, one must examine to what extent one is dealing with original elements of Marxist thought or with later deformations of theory. Compared with the range of such questions the "preservation of the classics" seems a trifling matter. Catastrophes cannot be combated by quotations.

To begin with, one must examine critically the concept of material progress that plays a decisive part in the Marxist tradition. It appears in any case to be obsolete in that it is linked to the technical optimism of the nineteenth century. The revolutions of the twentieth century have throughout led to victory in industrially underdeveloped countries and thereby disproved the idea that the socialist revolution was tied to a certain degree of "ripeness" and to "the development of the productive forces," or was actually the outcome of a kind of natural necessity. On the contrary, it has been demonstrated that "the development of the productive forces" is not a linear process to which political hopes can be attached.

> Until a few years ago most Marxists accepted the traditional view that the development of the productive forces was by its nature positive. They were persuaded that capitalism, in the course of its development, would provide a material base that would be taken over by a socialist society—one on which socialism could be constructed. The view was widely diffused that socialism would be more easily developed the higher the development of the productive forces. Productive forces such as technology, science, human capabilities and knowledge, and a surplus of reified labor would considerably facilitate the transition to socialism.
>
> These ideas were somewhat mechanistically based on the Marxist thesis of the sharpening of the contradictions between the productive forces on the one hand and the relationships of production on the other. But one can no longer assume that the productive forces are largely independent of the relationship of production and spontaneously clash with them. On the contrary, the developments of the last two decades lead one to the conclusion that the productive forces were formed by the capitalist productive relationships and so deeply stamped by them that any attempt to alter the productive relationships must fail if the nature of the productive forces— and not merely the way they are used—is not changed.[20]

Beyond a certain point, therefore, these productive forces reveal another aspect that till now was always concealed and reveal themselves to be destructive forces, not only in the particular sense of arms manufacture and in-built obsolescence, but in a far wider sense. The industrial process, insofar as it depends on these deformed productive forces, threatens its very existence and the existence of human society. This development is damaging not only to the present but the future as well, and with it, at least as far as our "Western" societies are concerned, to the utopian side of communism. If nature has been damaged to a certain, admittedly not easily determinable, degree and that damage is irreversible, then the idea of a free society begins to lose its meaning. It seems completely absurd to speak in a short-term perspective, as Marcuse has done, of a "society of superabundance" or of the abolition of want. The "wealth" of the overdeveloped consumer societies of the West, insofar as it is not a mere mirage for the bulk of the population, is the result of a wave of plunder and pillage unparalleled in history; its victims are, on the one hand, the peoples of the Third World and, on the other, the men and women of the future. It is therefore a kind of wealth that produces unimaginable want.

The social and political thinking of the ecologists is marred by blindness and naïveté. If such a statement needs to be proven, the review of their thinking that follows will do so. Yet they have one advantage over the utopian thinking of the Left in the West, namely the realization that any possible future belongs to the realm of necessity not that of freedom and that every political theory and practice—including that of socialists—is confronted not with the problem of abundance, but with that of survival.

What Ecology Proposes

Most scientists who handle environmental problems are not visible to the general public. They are highly specialized experts, exclusively concerned with their carefully defined research fields. Their influence is usually that of advisers. When doing basic research they tend to be paid from public funds; those who have a closer relationship with industry are predominantly experts whose results have immediate application. Most nonspecialists, however, aim to achieve direct influence on the public. It is they who write alarmist articles that are published in magazines such as *Scientific American* or *Science*. They appear on television, organize congresses, and write the bestsellers that form the picture of ecological destruction that most of us have. Their ideas as to what should be done are reflected in the reforms promised by parties and governments. They are in this sense representative of something. What they say in public cannot decide how valid their utterances are as scientific statements; yet it is worthwhile analyzing their proposals, for they indicate where the lines of scientific extrapolation and dominant "bourgeois" ideology intersect.

The Americans Paul and Anne Ehrlich are among the founders of human ecology and are still among its most influential spokesmen. In their handbook on ecology they summarize their proposals under the heading "A Positive Program," excerpts from which are extremely revealing.

> 2. Political pressure must be applied immediately to induce the United States government to assume its responsibility to halt the growth of the American population. Once growth is halted, the government should undertake to regulate the birthrate so that the population is reduced to an optimum size and maintained there. It is essential that a grass-roots political movement be generated to convince our legislators and the executive branch of the government that they must act rapidly. The programme should be based on what politicians understand best—votes. Presidents, Congressmen, Senators, and other elected officials who do not deal effectively with the crisis must be defeated at the polls and more intelligent and responsible candidates elected.

> 3. A massive campaign must be launched to restore a quality environment in North America and to *de-develop the United States*. De-development means bringing our economic system (especially patterns of consumption) into line with the realities of ecology and the world resource situation. . . . Marxists claim that capitalism is intrinsically expansionist and wasteful, and that it automatically produces a monied ruling class. Can our economists prove them wrong? . . .

> 5. It is unfortunate that at the time of the greatest crisis the United States and the world has ever faced, many Americans, especially the young, have given up hope that the government can be modernized and changed in direction through the functioning of the elective process. Their despair may have some foundation, but a partial attempt to institute a "new politics" very nearly succeeded in 1968. In addition many members of Congress and other government leaders, both Democrats and Republicans, are very much aware of the

problems outlined in this book and are determined to do something about them. Others are joining their ranks as the dangers before us daily become more apparent. These people need public support in order to be effective. The world cannot, in its present critical state, be saved by merely tearing down old institutions, even if rational plans existed for constructing better ones from the ruins. We simply do not have the time. Either we will succeed by bending old institutions or we will succumb to disaster. Considering the potential rewards and consequences we see no choice but to make an effort to modernize the system. It may be necessary to organize a new political party with an ecological outlook and national and international orientation to provide an alternative to the present parties with their local and parochial interests. The environmental issue may well provide the basis for this.

6. Perhaps the major necessary ingredient that has been missing from a solution to the problems of both the United States and the rest of the world is a goal, a vision of the kind of Spaceship Earth that ought to be and the kind of crew that should man her. . . .[21]

This is not the only case of a serious scientist presenting the public with a program of this kind. On the contrary. Page upon page could be used to document similar ideas. They can be seen as a consensus of what modern ecology has to offer in the way of suggestions for social action. A collection of similar statements would only repeat itself; and we will therefore confine ourselves to one further piece of evidence. The following quotation is from a book by the Swede Gösta Ehrensvärd, a leading biochemist, in which he attempts a comprehensive diagnosis of the ecological situation. His therapeutic ideas are summarized as follows.

"We are not *compelled* to pursue population growth, the consumption of energy, and unlimited exploitation of resources to the point where famine and worldwide suffering will be the results. We are not *compelled* to watch developments and do nothing and to pursue our activities shortsightedly without developing a long-term view." The catastrophe can be avoided, he says, "if we take certain measures *now* on a global scale. These measures could stabilize the situation for the next few centuries and allow us to bring about, with as little friction as possible, the transition from today's hectically growing industrialized economy to the agricultural economy of the future. The following components of a crash program are intended to gain time for the necessary global restructuring of society on this earth.

"1. Immediate introduction of worldwide rationing of all fossil fuels, above all of fluid resources of energy. Limitation of energy production to the 1970 level. Drastic restrictions on all traffic, insofar as it is propelled by fluid fuels and is not needed for farming, forestry, and the long-distance transport of raw materials.

"2. Immediate total rationing of electricity.

"3. Immediate cessation of the production of purely luxury goods and other products not essential for survival, including every kind of armament.

"4. Immediate food rationing in all industrial countries. Limitation of all food imports from the developing countries to a minimum. The main effort in terms of development policies throughout the world to be directed toward agriculture and forestry.

"5. Immediate imposition of the duty to collect and recycle all discarded metal objects, and in particular to collect all scrap.

"6. Top priority to be given to research on the development of energy from atomic fusion as well as to biological research in the fields of genetics, applied ecology, and wood chemistry.

"7. Creation of an international center to supervise and carry through action around the six points listed above. This center to have the duty to keep the inhabitants of this earth constantly informed through the mass media of the level of energy and mineral reserves, the progress of research, and the demographic situation."[22]

A Critique of the
Ecological Crash Program

In their appeals to a world whose imminent decline they prophesy, the spokesmen of human ecology have developed a missionary style. They often employ the most dramatic strokes to paint a future so black that after reading their works one wonders how people can persist in giving birth to children, or in drawing up pension schemes. Yet at the conclusion of their sermons, in which the inevitability of the End—of industrialization, of civilization, of man, of life on this planet—is convincingly described if not proved, another way forward is presented. The ecologists end up by appealing to the rationality of their readers; if everyone would grasp what is at stake, then—apparently—everything would not be lost. These sudden turnabouts smack of conversion rhetoric. The horror of the predicted catastrophe contrasts sharply with the mildness of the admonition with which we are allowed to escape. This contrast is so obvious and so central that both sides of the argument undermine each other. At least one of them fails to convince: either the final exhortation, which addresses us in mild terms, or the analysis, which is intended to alarm us. It is impossible not to feel that those warnings and threats, which present us with the consequences of our actions, are intended precisely to soften us up for the conversion that the anxious preacher wishes to obtain from us in the end; conversely, the confident final resolution should prevent us from taking too literally the dark picture he has painted and from sinking into resignation. Every parish priest is aware of this noble form of verbal excess; and everyone listening can easily see through it. The result is (at best) a pleasurable *frisson*. Herein may lie the total inefficacy of widely distributed publications maintaining that the hour will soon come not only for man himself, but for his whole species. They are as ineffective as a Sunday sermon.

In its closest details, both the form and content of the Ehrlichs' argument are marked by the consciousness (or rather the unconsciousness) of the WASP, the white, Protestant, middle-class North American. This is especially obvious in the authors' social and political ideas: they are just as *unwilling* to consider any radical interference with the political system of the United States as they are *willing* to contemplate the other immense changes they spell out. The U.S. system is introduced into their calculations as a constant factor: it is introduced not as it is, but as it appears to the white member of the middle class, that is to say in a form that has been transformed out of recognition by ideology. Class contradictions and class interests are completely denied: the parliamentary mechanism of the vote is unquestionably considered to be an effective method, by means of which all conceivable conflicts can be resolved. It is merely a question of finding the right candidate and conducting the right campaigns, of writing letters and launching a few modest citizens' activities. At the most extreme, a new parliament will have to be set up. Imperialism does not exist. World peace will be reached through disarmament. The political process is posed in highly personalized terms: politics is the business of the politicians who are expected to carry the "responsibility." Similarly, economics is the business of the economists, whose task is to "draw up" a suitable economic system—this, at least, one has the right to ask of them. "Marxism" appears only once, as a scarecrow to drive recalcitrant readers into the authors' arms. All that this crude picture of political idiocy lacks are lofty ideas: the authors are not averse to making good the lack. What is needed is a "vision," since only relatively "idealistic programs" still offer the possibility of salvation. Since the need is so great, there will be no lack of offers, and the academic advertising agency promptly comes up with the cliché "Spaceship Earth," in which the armaments industry and public relations join hands. The depoliticization of the ecological question is now complete. Its social components and consequences have been entirely eliminated.

Concrete demands can now cheerfully be made. There is no danger that they may be implemented with disagreeable consequences. A brake on population increase, de-development of the economy, draconian rationing can now be presented as measures that, since they are offered in a spirit of enlightened, moral common sense, and are carried out in a peaceful, liberal manner, harm no interests or privileges and demand no changes in the social and economic system. Ehrensvärd presents the same demands in more trenchant, apparently radical terms—those of the coolly calculating scientist. Like the Ehrlichs, his arguments are so unpolitical as to be grotesque. Yet his sense of reality is strong enough for him to demand privileges for himself and his work—that is to say, the highest priority for the undisturbed continuation of his research. One particular social interest, if a very restricted one, thereby finds expression: his own.

"Many of the suggestions," say the Ehrlichs, "will seem 'unrealistic,' and indeed this is how we view them."[23] The fact that not even the authors take their own "crash program" seriously at least makes it clear that we are not dealing with madmen. The reason they seek refuge in absurdity is that their competence as scientists is limited precisely to the theoretical radius of the old ecology, that is to say, to a subordinate discipline of biology. They have extended their researches to human society, but they have not increased their knowledge in any way. It has escaped them that human existence remains incomprehensible if one totally disregards its social determinants; that this lack is damaging to all scientific utterances on our present and future; and that the range of these utterances is reduced whenever these scientists abandon the methodology of their particular discipline. It is restricted to the narrow horizons of their own class. The latter, which they erroneously regard as the silent majority, is in fact a privileged and very vocal minority.

Conclusions:
Hypotheses Concerning a Hypothesis

There is a great temptation to leave matters there and to interpret the forecast of a great ecological crisis as a maneuver intended to divert people from acute political controversy. There are even said to be parts of the Left that consider it a luxury to trouble themselves with problems of the future. To do that would be a declaration of bankruptcy; socialist thinking has from the beginning been oriented not toward the past, but toward the future. Herein lay one of its real chances of success. For, while the bourgeoisie is intent on the short-term interests of the accumulation of capital, there is no reason for the Left to exclude long-term aims and perspectives. As far as the competence of the ecologists is concerned, it would be a mistake to conclude that, because of their boundless ignorance on social matters, their statements are absolutely unfounded. Their methodological ineptitude certainly decreases the validity of their overall prognoses; but individual lines of argument, which they found predominantly on the causality of the natural sciences, are still usable. To demonstrate that they have not been thought through in the area of social causes and effects is not to refute them.

> The ideologies of the ruling class do not reproduce mere falsifications. Even in their instrumental form they still contain experiences that are real insofar as they are never optimistic. They promise the twilight of the gods, global catastrophe, and a last judgment; but these announcements are not seen

to be connected with the identification and short-term satis-
factions that form part of their content.[24]

All this applies admirably to the central "ecological hypothesis"
according to which if the present process of industrialization continues naturally it will in the foreseeable future have catastrophic
results. The central core of this hypothesis can neither be proved
nor refuted by political discussion. What it says is of such importance, however, that what one is faced with is a calculation like
Pascal's wager. So long as the hypothesis is not unequivocally refuted, it will be heuristically necessary to base any thinking about
the future on what it has to say. Only if one behaves "as if" the
ecological hypothesis were valid, can one test its social validity—a
task that has scarcely been attempted up to now and of which
ecology itself is clearly incapable. The following reflections are
merely some first steps along this path. They are, in other words,
hypotheses based on other hypotheses.

A general social definition of the ecological problem would have
to start from the mode of production. Everywhere where the capitalistic mode of production obtains totally or predominantly—
that is to say, where the products of human labor take the form
of commodities—increasing social want is created alongside increasing social wealth. This want assumes different forms in the
course of historical development. In the phase of primitive accumulation it expresses itself in direct impoverishment caused by extensive exploitation, extension of working hours, lowering of real
wages. In the cyclical crises, the wealth that has been produced by
labor is simply destroyed—grain is thrown into the sea and so on.
With the growth of the productive powers the destructive energies
of the system also increase. Further want is generated by world
wars and armaments production. In a later phase of capitalistic
development this destructive potential acquires a new quality. It
threatens all the natural bases of human life. This has the result
that want appears to be a socially produced natural force. This
return of general shortages forms the core of the "ecological crisis." It is not, however, a relapse into conditions and circumstances from the historical past, because the want does not in any
sense abolish the prevailing wealth. Both are present at one and
the same time; the contradiction between them becomes ever
sharper and takes on increasingly insane forms.

So long as the capitalist mode of production obtains—that is to say not merely the capitalist property relationships—the trend can at best be reversed in detail but not in its totality. The crisis will naturally set in motion many processes of adaptation and learning. Technological attempts to level out its symptoms in the sense of achieving a homeostasis have already gone beyond the experimental stage. The more critical the situation becomes, the more desperate will be the attempts undertaken in this direction. They will include: abolition of the car, construction of means of mass transport, erection of plants for the filtration and desalinization of seawater, the opening up of new sources of energy, synthetic production of raw materials, the development of more intensive agricultural techniques, and so on. But each of these steps will cause new critical problems; these are stopgap techniques, which do not touch the roots of the problem. The political consequences are clear enough. The costs of living accommodations and space for recreation, of clean air and water, of energy and raw materials will increase explosively as will the cost of recycling scarce resources. The "invisible" social costs of capitalist commodity production are rising immeasurably and are being passed on in prices and taxes to the dependent masses to such a degree that any equalization through controlling wages is no longer possible. There is no question, needless to say, of a "just" distribution of shortages within the framework of Western class society: the rationing of want is carried out through prices, if necessary through gray or black markets, by means of corruption and the sale of privileges. The subjective value of privileged class positions increases enormously. The physiological and psychic consequences of the environmental crisis, the lowered expectation of life, the direct threat from local catastrophes can lead to a situation where class can determine the life or death of an individual by deciding such factors as the availability of means of escape, second houses, or advanced medical treatment.

The speed with which these possibilities will enter the consciousness of the masses cannot be predicted. It will depend on the point in time at which the creeping nature of the ecological crisis becomes apparent in spectacular individual cases. Even dramatic phenomena such as have principally appeared in Japan—the radioactive poisoning of fishermen, illnesses caused by mercury and cadmium—have not yet led to a more powerful mobilization of the masses because the consequences of the contamination have become apparent only months or years later. But once, at any point in the chain of events, many people are killed, the indifference with which the prognoses of the ecologists are met today will turn into panic reaction and even into ecological rebellions.

There will of course be organizational initiatives and political consequences at an even earlier stage. The ecological movement in the United States, with its tendency to flee from the towns and industry, is an indication of what will come, as are the citizens' campaigns that are spreading apace. The limitations that beset most of these groups are not fortuitous; their activity is usually aimed at removing a particular problem. There is no other alternative, for they can only crystallize round particular interests. A typical campaign will, for example, attempt to prevent the siting of an oil refinery in a particular district. That does not lead, if the agitation is successful, to the project being canceled or to a revision of the policy on energy; the refinery is merely built where the resistance of those affected is less strongly expressed. In no case does the campaign lead to a reduction of energy consumption. An appeal on these grounds would make no sense. It would fall back on the abstract, empty formulas that make up the "crash programs" of the ecologists.

The knot of the ecological crisis cannot be cut with a paper-knife. The crisis is inseparable from the conditions of existence systematically determined by the mode of production. That is why moral appeals to the people of the "rich" lands to lower their standard of living are totally absurd. They are not only useless but cynical. To ask the individual wage earner to differentiate between his "real" and his "artificial" needs is to mistake his real situation. Both are so closely connected that they constitute a relationship that is subjectively and objectively indivisible. Hunger for commodities, in all its blindness, is a product of the production of commodities, which could only be suppressed by force. We must reckon with the likelihood that bourgeois policy will systematically exploit the resulting mystifications—increasingly so, as the ecological crisis takes on more threatening forms. To achieve this, it only needs demagogically to take up the proposals of the ecologists and give them political circulation. The appeal to the common good, which demands sacrifice and obedience, will be taken up by these movements together with a reactionary populism, determined to defend capitalism with anticapitalist phrases.

In reality, capitalism's policy on the environment, raw materials, energy, and population will put an end to the last liberal illusions. That policy cannot even be conceived without increasing repression and regimentation. Fascism has already demonstrated its capabilities as a savior in extreme crisis situations and as the administrator of poverty. In an atmosphere of panic and uncontrollable emotions—that is to say, in the event of an ecological catastrophe that is directly perceptible on a mass scale—the ruling class will not hesitate to have recourse to such solutions. The ability of the masses to see the connection between the mode of production and the crisis in such a situation and to react offensively cannot be assumed. It depends on the degree of politicization and organization achieved by then. But it would be facile to count on such a development. It is more probable that what has been called "internal imperialism" will increase. What Negt and Kluge have observed in another connection is also relevant to the contradiction between social wealth and social poverty, which is apparent in the ecological crisis: "Colonialization of the consciousness or civil war are the extreme forms in which these contradictions find public expression. What precedes this collision, or is a consequence of it, is the division of individuals or of social groups into qualities that are organized against each other."[25]

In this situation, external imperialism will also regress to historically earlier forms—but with an enormously increased destructive potential. If the "peaceful" methods of modern exploitation fail, and the formula for coexistence under pressure of scarcity snaps, then presumably there will be new predations, competitive wars, wars over raw materials. The strategic importance of the Third World, above all of those lands that export oil and nonferrous metals, will increase and with it their consciousness that the metropolitan lands depend on them. The "siege" of the metropolises by the village—a concept that appeared premature in the 1950s—will acquire quite new topicality. It has already been unmistakably heralded by the policy of a number of oil-producing countries. Imperialism will do everything to incite the population of the industrialized countries against such apparent external enemies whose policy will be presented as a direct threat to their standard of living, and to their very survival, in order to win their assent to military operations.

Talk in global terms about "Spaceship Earth" tells us almost nothing about real perspectives and the chances of survival. There are certainly ecological factors whose effect is global; among these are macroclimatic changes, pollution by radioactive elements, and poisons in the atmosphere and oceans. As the example of China shows, it is not these overall factors that are decisive, but the social variables. The destruction of mankind cannot be considered a purely natural process. But it will not be averted by the preachings of scientists, who only reveal their own helplessness and blindness the moment they overstep the narrow limits of their own special areas of competence. "The *human* essence of nature first exists only for *social* man; for only here does nature exist as the *foundation* of his own *human* existence. Only here has what is to him his *natural* existence become his *human* existence, and nature become man for him. Thus *society* is the unity of being of man with nature—the true resurrection of nature—the naturalism of man and the humanism of nature both brought to fulfilment." [26]

If ecology's hypotheses are valid, then capitalist societies have probably thrown away the chance of realizing Marx's project for the reconciliation of man and nature. The productive forces that bourgeois society has unleashed have been caught up with and overtaken by the destructive powers released at the same time. The highly industrialized countries of the West will not be alone in paying the price for the revolution that never happened. The fight against want is an inheritance they leave to all mankind, even in those areas where mankind survives the catastrophe. Socialism, which was once a promise of liberation, has become a question of survival. If the ecological equilibrium is broken, then the realm of Freedom will be further off than ever.

Translated by Stuart Hood

3

On the Inevitability
of the Middle Classes:
A Sociological Caprice

T hat you who are reading this are reading it is almost proof in itself: proof that you belong. Please forgive, dear reader, this direct address. (Proof is perhaps an exaggeration.) I grant you that "in the following remarks" I will be claiming more than I can prove—for example, that there is such a thing as the middle class. Without batting an eye. After all, *middle class* is a phrase like any other, even if it sounds old-fashioned (like *dear reader*), and the fact that it is mostly said in a tone of annoyance, of disgust even, is not my fault. That has always been the case—at least since Ludwig Börne, himself a member of the middle classes, introduced the term into the German political vocabulary around 1830.

Without any scruples, without having ploughed through the "literature", i.e., a few tens of thousands of pages on the concept of class in M., E., and X., I would further claim that the class referred to here can only be defined in terms of what it is not, in other words as the class that is neither nor.*

Permit me—not out of curiosity, but simply in the hope of making myself understood—to ask some questions of you.

* M.–Marx, E.–Engels

—Do you live, or could you live, from the income of capital invested in production?

—No? You see, I suspected as much.

—But does that mean that you live exclusively from selling your work by the hour to a capitalist who makes a profit from it?

—Yes? Are you sure?

—No scholarships, then? No bank interest? Honoraria? Subsidies? Expense accounts? Profit margins? Royalties? Rents? Commissions?

No educational trust fund; no extra cash from home? No tenured job? Home of your own? Reimbursement for financial outlays? No private means of production, not even a home library? In a word, no income derived from surplus value created by others?

Once again I beg your pardon for these pedantic and insistent questions.

Perhaps it is not the thing that bothers you, but the term. It sounds pathetic: middle class. If it embarrasses you, you aren't alone. This is the reason why the people I am referring to and amongst whose number I count myself have thought up any number of other names for what I am talking about. Just check below the ones that appeal to you:

Old, new upper, lower, middle, "cultivated" middle classes;

Artisans, tradesmen (small), petty bourgeoisie;

White-collar workers (secretaries, administrative assistants, etc.);

Civil servants, state employees, bureaucrats;

Managers, "specialists," technocrats, technological intelligentsia;

Self-employed, independent professionals;

Academics, intellectuals (creative, scientific, etc.).

You see, I don't want to tread on anyone's toes. I'm just inviting you to see this, if at all possible, as referring to you, and asking you, for simplicity's sake, to permit me to use the inclusive first-person plural. Thank you.

We belong to a class, then, that neither controls nor possesses what really matters—the famous means of production—and that doesn't create what also matters—the famous surplus value (or only indirectly or tangentially, a point that may be avidly debated in college seminars but is by no means as vexed as people try to make out). This is exactly how inexact the whole thing is. The middle class is not one of the principal parties in the (famous) antagonism; it is neither the ruling nor the exploited class, but the class in between, the class left over, the floating remainder.

A most burdensome remainder, especially for those who like to have a neat, clear-cut view of things. For the floating class is always the disturbing class. Its existence is constantly upsetting theory and practice. For a number of other reasons that will perhaps concern us later, there has been no lack of attempts in the course of the last hundred years to get rid of this scandal, to liquidate the middle classes. To a certain extent, it was said, one could leave this job to the (iron) laws of history. It was and still is said here and there that one part of our class, the smaller one, would all by itself lump itself with the goats, rise to the upper classes, and in consequence vanish along with that doomed group; the other part, by far the larger of course, would find itself on the side of the sheep and there would reap the fruits of socialism: these deserving ones would by virtue of the (famous) laws of capitalism become proletarianized, though not necessarily quite of their own free will. The increasingly small group of undeserving ones would then just have to be made to disappear. Our ancestors, insofar as they belonged to the class described here, doubtless heard this message and believed passionately in this prophecy, with fear and trembling.

It did not come to pass. Whatever may have happened to the middle class, its apocalypse has not taken place. Neither progressive concentration of capital nor chronic inflation, neither scientific and technological progress nor wars and crises have finished it off. Not even the introduction of a kind of socialism has been able to remove the unstable class in the Soviet Union, Eastern Europe, or the Third World. On the contrary, it has produced middle-class citizens of a new type, the middle-class offspring of the victorious revolution, big bosses, cadres, functionaries: strange mutations, unheard-of manifestations of a "new class" suspiciously like the old.

But even in capitalist societies the good old, bad old middle class has not remained unchanged. The Victorian image of the small tradesman, the shop owner, the would-be cultured, the dignitary no longer plays a major role as it did in the past. (Though one look at the German parliament reveals that this type has by no means died out.) But effortlessly, it seems, the middle class has made good all these losses; indeed it has quantitatively expanded, as persistently and unnoticeably as crabgrass. With every structural change in society its roots have, so to speak, sent out new runners. The scientific take-over of production, the growth of the tertiary and quaternary sectors of the economy, the expansion of private and public administration, the growth of the consciousness industry, of pedagogical and medical institutions—the middle class has been a part of it all. And after every political revolution it has installed itself immediately in the new state and party apparatus and has not only defended its social status and possessions, but expanded them.

There seems to be at present no theory that could explain the survival, the staying-power, the historical success of this class. We need to explain, for a start, the mere fact that the middle class has been plainly and persistently underestimated, and this for at least 150 years. No one has contributed more to this denigration than the middle class itself. This doubtless has to do with its own peculiar class consciousness. Ambivalent from the outset, it can be described today, if at all, only as a lack of consciousness pure and simple. For just as the class can be defined analytically only *ex negativo,* so it understands itself *ex negativo.* The middle-class citizen claims to be anything but "middle class." He seeks to establish his identity not by siding with his class, but by distinguishing himself from it, by denying it. He disclaims precisely what binds him to his peers. Only the difference is allowed to stand: a "middle-class" person is always someone else. This strange self-hatred is like a magic cloak. With its help the class as a whole has almost made itself invisible. For it there can be no question of solidarity or collective action: it will never develop a consciousness of itself as a class. The result of this repressive strategy is, subjectively, that the middle class is not taken seriously in social terms; objectively, this prevents the development of clearly defined, encompassing, political class structures. The social image of the middle class is rather like a chameleon. And the more the class increases, the less recognizable it becomes.

Perhaps there never was such a divided, splintered class. The extreme objective and subjective fragmentation of the middle class is no mystery. It is the result of its economic position and of its prehistory. Its relation to the means of production is always extremely derivative and indirect. One result of this is that the class is crippled by an inability actually to take over politically. This class can and will not become the ruling class, and even this very impotence has been strangely internalized. The middle-class citizen both rejects and worships power; but this just means that he delegates it and perceives it only in its delegated form—by administering it, justifying it, and questioning it. But the smaller the actual ruling class becomes, the more it needs the middle class to expand and transmit its dominance. Were this not the case, the working class would long since have ceased to be kept in check. Thus the political influence of the middle classes must be defined *ex negativo,* as a kind of unarticulated veto power. This explains their interest in the formal aspects of politics, procedures, regulations, legalistic rules, and modes of intercourse.

The middle class's inability to unify and act concertedly has, however, another side to it. Its manifold nature, its thousandfold categorization according to status, profession, and possessions is also the cause of its persistence, its energy and aggressiveness. This is an advantage in social evolution, a factor of self-preservation. In biological systems the principle obtains that a species is the less destructible the greater its variability, its genetic pool. An analogous rule of thumb also holds for society. A social monolith can survive changes in historical conditions less readily than an assorted and manifold group. Ability to adjust to prevailing conditions—ideologically despised and energetically denigrated precisely by the middle classes as lack of character and opportunism—increases without a doubt the survival chances of a social class. No one possesses these qualities to a greater degree than the middle class. No social niche is too small, too peripheral, too exposed for it. To grasp every opportunity and never to be definitively pinned down: that is the only thing that this class has learned from its ever-changing history.

It has long since taken leave of its former social character, the comfortable, stick-in-the-mud, placidly philistine ways of its first golden age. (Though it is a question in how far this preference for self-satisfied stasis is actually historically founded, even the old petty bourgeoisie of the nineteenth century was a nervous, high-strung class easily provoked and outraged, prone to turn sporadically radical, to get suddenly worked up, critical out of resentment and courageous out of anxiety. It was the petty bourgeoisie that created the cliché of the philistine, and it was from the petty bourgeoisie that the bohemian class, whose specialty was horrifying other petits bourgeois, largely recruited itself.)

Today this class is teeming with believers in progress, and no one is more anxious to take advantage of the newest trend. It is always up to date. No one can change his ideologies, his clothes, his modes of behavior more rapidly than the middle-class citizen. He is the new Proteus, ever eager to learn something new—even to the point of losing his identity. Always fleeing the old-fashioned, he is constantly hastening to catch up with himself.

Political defeats may shatter the class consciousness of the worker; but it is impossible to deprive him of the complacent conviction of his own necessity. The upper class, too, thinks of itself as indispensable. The middle class, on the other hand, constantly has to struggle with a sense of its own superfluity. Cynicism is the privilege of the ruling class. But the self-suppressing class is concerned with justification; it is constantly seeking its own meaning. It is as ingenious as it is amoral, though ever in need of morality. In rationalization and self-doubt it has attained a state of solitary mastery. But its self-criticism and self-rejection are of limited extent. A class cannot get rid of itself. Thus the doubts, the exhaustion of the middle-class function, in the last analysis, as a stimulus and a pleasure. To shake its complacency is child's play. But to turn it from itself is an impossibility. The middle class is constantly questioning itself: it is the experimental class par excellence. But this self-critical process serves only to sustain and expand its own sphere. There is a method to its self-undermining: purposefully, it is put to the service of a strategy that in fact clings to the illusion of security.

How can we explain the central position the middle class maintains in all highly industrialized societies of today? Our class has neither capital nor direct access to the means of production; it is as far removed as ever from political and economic power. Does it not know wherein its strength lies? Or is it just afraid of letting the cat out of the bag? The answer is too pat, too simple, too obvious: it is the middle class that has the cultural hegemony today in all highly industrialized societies. It has become the model class, the only one to mass-produce the forms of everyday living and make them binding upon others. It is the one that takes care of innovation. It decides what is thought beautiful and desirable; it decides what is thought. (The dominant thoughts are no longer those of the dominant class, but those of the middle class.) It invents ideologies, sciences, technologies. It decides what "goes" in what we call our private lives. It is the only class that produces art and fashion, philosophy and architecture, criticism and design.

Mass consumption as a whole has been decisively shaped by concepts developed by the middle class. Brand-name products and advertising are projections of its consciousness. All the social characteristics of the middle class can be found in generalized form in consumer society: energy and isolation, progress as a kind of panic reaction, formalism and ceaseless innovation, superfluity and the need to define oneself. We need only look at the two consumer products that are prototypical of our civilization: the television set and the private automobile. Only the middle classes could have dreamed up these remarkable objects.

Equally impressive are middle-class achievements in the sphere of nonmaterial production. The apparatus of the superstructure is occupied on all sides by members of our class, and almost all "fashions," "trends," and "movements" that occur in highly industrialized societies have been inspired, supported, and inculcated by the middle classes: from tourism to do-it-yourself, from avant-garde art to urban studies, from the student movement to ecology, from cybernetics to feminism, from competitive sports to the "sexual revolution," and so on and so forth. Every alternative movement in our culture has been promptly disarmed and absorbed by the middle classes—we need only think, for example, of rock music, originally (like its predecessor, jazz, fifty years before) an autonomous expression of proletarian youth. Even ideologies such as anarchism or Marxism that were originally quite subversive today have been largely coopted by the middle classes.

Just how the "experimental class" has arrived at its cultural hegemony could only be explained by a thorough, materialistic analysis. A high degree of industrialization is certainly a necessary, though perhaps not sufficient, condition. The middle-class cultural model presupposes a certain social wealth. Not until production has become highly organized can the social sphere of distribution, circulation, and administration extend in such a way as to give rise to a broad middle class. By the same token, it is only with increasing concentration and centralization of capital that the ruling class shrinks sufficiently for it to lose its cultural dominance.

The frenetic productivity and innovative potential of the middle class can be explained, however, simply by the fact that it has no other choice. It is "intelligent," "talented," "innovative" because its survival depends on it. Those in power don't need all this: they get others to do their inventing for them; they "buy" intelligence and "develop" talent. By contrast, any attempt at autonomous productivity is systematically eradicated from the proletariat. "It's not your job to think!" was the cry hurled at production workers by F. W. Taylor, an early member of the middle class and the father of rationalization; and naturally it has stayed this way, not just in the West. Thus the fabulous talent of the middle classes, like most of their other qualities, is to be explained *ex negativo*.

A quite different question, however, is what makes the cultural hegemony of the middle class so irresistible. How could it become a universal model, emulated by millions? What distinguishes this model? What are the qualities that have enabled it to eliminate, on both the national and international levels, virtually all alternative models?

It is a commonplace to say that the European proletariat bears the mark of middle-class culture in its way of life and aspirations. But even the former upper-class way of life has been completely liquidated by middle-class culture: its former luxuries have been reduced to the format of the glossies; its "exclusive" standard is merely that of a middle-class person who can afford a more expensive brand. On the other hand, it is just a question of time before the electric toothbrush takes over the slums. And even now there is no Oriental bazaar, no Malayan or Caribbean market that has not long since been infiltrated by the relics of middle-class culture. The economic basis of this general invasion is well known; the middle classes did not create it. But what any purely economic perspective fails to take into account is the cultural dimension of this development. (Pier Paolo Pasolini has given a model explanation of this for Italy.)

So the question remains: What is so unique, so seductive about the automatic cigarette lighter, the taste of Pepsodent, concrete poetry, the home workshop, "Sesame Street," concentrated lemon juice, behaviorism, *Emanuela,* deodorants, sensitivity training, Polaroid cameras, shop-window displays, parapsychology, *Peanuts,* metallic paint, nylon shirts, science fiction, skyjacking, and digital watches that no one, no nation and no class from Kamchatka to Tierra del Fuego, is immune to it? Is there no antidote to the ingenious ideas of our class? Will no one, not even the Congolese, be saved the trouble of equipping themselves with underpants designed by a French couturier? Must even the Vietnamese take valium? Is there no escape from behavior modification, the Concorde, Masters and Johnson, bedroom communities, and curricular reform? And the living-room set in stain-resistant imitation leather ("it breathes") with loose polyurethane cushions, attached buttons, quality foam-rubber suspension and cotton padding, decorative buckles, modular sections, easy-glide chrome-plated casters, this fabulously beautiful, reasonably priced piece that persistently dogs me and is constantly lying in wait for me, always there first, like the tortoise in the fable—at birthday parties, on television, in the two-room apartment of a Turkish worker in a Berlin suburb, in *Der Spiegel,* at the dentist's, on my safari vacation, in party pamphlets, in department-store specials, on the beautiful blue Danube, in the White House, and at the town dump—is there no help, will it roll on inevitably, this incarnation of all the rosy dreams of our class, until it has reached the bazaars of Damascus and the airport in Shanghai? Perhaps it has arrived there long since.

Translated by Judith Ryan

4

Two Notes on
the End of the World

I

The apocalypse is part of our ideological baggage. It is an aphrodisiac. It is a nightmare. It is a commodity like any other. You can call it a metaphor for the collapse of capitalism, which as we all know has been imminent for more than a century. We come up against it in the most varied shapes and guises: as warning finger and scientific forecast, as collective fiction and sectarian rallying cry, as product of the leisure industry, as superstition, as vulgar mythology, as a riddle, a kick, a joke, a projection. It is ever present, but never "actual": a second reality, an image that we construct for ourselves, an incessant product of our fantasy, the catastrophe in the mind.

All this it is and more, as one of the oldest ideas of the human species. Thick volumes could have been written on its origins, and of course such volumes actually have been written. We know likewise all manner of things about its checkered history, about its periodic ebb and flow, and the way these fluctuations connect with the material process of history. The idea of the apocalypse has accompanied utopian thought since its first beginnings, pursuing it like a shadow, like a reverse side that cannot be left behind: without catastrophe no millennium, without apocalypse no paradise. The idea of the end of the world is simply a negative utopia.

233

But even the end of the world is no longer what it used to be. The film playing in our heads, and still more uninhibitedly in our unconscious, is distinct in many respects from the dreams of old. In its traditional coinings, the apocalypse was a venerable, indeed a sacred, idea. But the catastrophe we are so concerned with (or rather haunted by) is an entirely secularized phenomenon. We read its signs on the walls of buildings, where they appear overnight, clumsily sprayed; we read them on the printouts spewed forth by the computer. Our seven-headed monster answers to many names: police state, paranoia, bureaucracy, terror, economic crisis, arms race, destruction of the environment. Its four riders look like the heroes of Westerns and sell cigarettes, while the trumpets that proclaim the end of the world serve as theme music for a commercial break. Once people saw in the apocalypse the unknowable avenging hand of God. Today it appears as the methodically calculated product of our own actions, and the spirits whom we hold responsible for its approach we call reds, oil sheikhs, terrorists, multinationals; the gnomes of Zürich and the Frankensteins of the biology labs; UFOs and neutron bombs; demons from the Kremlin or the Pentagon: an underworld of unimaginable conspiracies and machinations, whose strings are pulled by the all-powerful cretins of the secret police.

The apocalypse was also once a singular event, to be expected unannounced as a bolt from the blue: an unthinkable moment that only seers and prophets could anticipate—and, of course, no one wanted to listen to their warnings and predictions. Our end of the world, on the other hand, is sung from the rooftops even by the sparrows; the element of surprise is missing; it seems only to be a question of time. The doom we picture for ourselves is insidious and torturingly slow in its approach, the apocalypse in slow motion. It is reminiscent of that hoary avant-garde classic of the silent cinema, in which we see a gigantic factory chimney crack up and collapse noiselessly on the screen, for a full twenty minutes, while the spectators, in a kind of indolent comfort, lean back in their threadbare velvet seats and nibble their popcorn and peanuts. After the performance, the futurologist mounts the stage. He looks like a poor imitation of Dr. Strangelove, the mad scientist, only he is repulsively fat. Quite calmly he informs us that the atmospheric ozone belt will have disappeared in twenty years' time, so that we shall surely be toasted by cosmic radiation if we are lucky enough to survive until then; unknown substances in our milk are driving us to psychosis; and with the rate at which world population is growing, there will soon be standing room only on our planet. All this with Havana cigar in hand, in a well-composed speech of impeccable logic. The audience suppresses a yawn, even though, according to the Professor, the disaster looms imminently ahead. But it's not going to come this afternoon. This afternoon, everything will go on just as before, perhaps a little bit worse than last week, but not so that anyone would notice. If one or another of us should be a little depressed this afternoon, which cannot of course be ruled out, then the thought might strike him, irrespective of whether he works in the Pentagon or the underground, irons shirts or welds sheet metal, that it would really be simpler if we were rid of the problem once and for all; if the catastrophe really did *come*. However, this is out of the question. Finality, which was formerly one of the major attributes of the apocalypse, and one of the reasons for its power of attraction, is no longer vouchsafed us.

We have also lost another traditional aspect of the end of the world. Previously, it was generally agreed that the event would affect everyone simultaneously and without exception: the never-satisfied demand for equality and justice found in this conception its last refuge. But as we see it today, doom is no longer a leveler; quite the opposite. It differs from country to country, from class to class, from place to place. While it is already overtaking some, others can watch it on television. Bunkers are built, ghettos walled in, fortresses erected, bodyguards hired, on a large scale as well as a small. Corresponding to the country house with burglar alarms and electric fences, we have whole countries, on the international scale, that fence themselves in while others go to ruin. The nightmare of the end of the world does not end this temporal disparity; it simply radicalizes it. Its African and Indian versions are overlooked with a shrug of the shoulders by those not directly affected—including the African and Indian governments. At this point, finally, the joke comes to an end.

II

Dear Balthasar,

When I wrote my comment on the apocalypse—a work that I confess was not particularly thorough or serious—I was still unaware that you were also concerned with the future. You complained to me on the telephone that you were "not really getting anywhere." That sounded almost like an appeal for help. I know you well enough to understand your dilemma. Today it is only the technocrats who are advancing toward the year two thousand full of optimism, with the unerring instinct of lemmings, and you are not one of their number. On the contrary, you are a faithful soul, always ready to assemble under the banner of utopia. You want as much as ever to hold fast to the principle of hope, for you wish us well: i.e., not only you and me, but humanity as a whole.

Please don't be angry if this sounds ironic. That isn't my fault. You would have liked to see me come rushing to your aid. My letter will be disappointing for you, and perhaps you even feel that I am attacking you from behind. That isn't my intention. All I would like to suggest is that we consider things with the cuffs off.

The strength of left-wing theory of whatever stamp, from Babeuf through to Ernst Bloch, i.e., for more than a century and a half, lay in the fact that it based itself on a positive utopia that had no peer in the existing world. Socialists, Communists, and anarchists all shared the conviction that their struggle would introduce the realm of freedom in a foreseeable period of time. They "knew just where they wanted to go and just what, with the help of history, strategy and effort, they ought or needed to do to get there. Now, they no longer do." I read these lapidary words recently in an article by the English historian Eric Hobsbawm. But this old Communist does not forget to add that "In this respect, they do not stand alone. Capitalists are just as much at a loss as socialists to understand their future, and just as puzzled by the failure of their theorists and prophets."

Hobsbawm is quite correct. The ideological deficit exists on both sides. Yet the loss of certainty about the future does not balance out. It is harder to bear for the Left than for those who never had any other intention but to hang on at any price to some snippet of their own power and privileges. This is why the Left, including you, dear Balthasar, go in for grumbling and complaining.

No one is ready any more, you say, or in a position either, to put forward a positive idea that goes beyond the horizon of the existing state of affairs. Instead of this, false consciousness is rampant; the stage is dominated by apostasy and confusion. I remember our last conversation about the "new irrationalism," your lamenting over the resignation that you sense on all sides, and your tirades against the flippant doomsters, shameless pessimists, and apostles of defeatism. I shall be careful not to contradict you here. But I wonder whether one thing has not escaped you in all this: the fact that in these expressions and moods there is precisely what you were looking for—an idea that goes beyond the limits of our present existence. For, in the last analysis, the world has certainly not come to an end (or else we could not talk about it); and so far no conclusive proof has reached me that an event of this kind is going to take place at any clearly ascertainable point in time. The conclusion I draw from this is that we are dealing here with a utopia, even if a negative one; and I further maintain that, for the historical reasons I mentioned, left-wing theory is not particularly well-equipped to deal with this kind of utopia.

Your reactions are only further evidence for my assumption. The first stanza of your song, in which you bewail the prevailing intellectual situation, is promptly followed by the second, in which you enumerate the scapegoats. For such an old hand at theory as yourself, it is not difficult to lay hands on the guilty parties: the ideological opponent, the agents of anticommunism, the manipulation of the mass media. Your arguments are in no way new to me. They remind me of an essay that came to my attention a few years back. The author, an American Marxist by the name of H. C. Greisman, came to the conclusion that "the images of decline of which the media are so fond are designed to hypnotize and stupefy the masses in such a way that they come to see any hope of revolution as meaningless."

What is striking in this proposition is above all its essential defensiveness. For a hundred years or so, as long as it was sure of its ground, classical Marxist theory argued the very opposite. It did not see the images of catastrophe and visions of doom of the time simply as lies concocted by some secret seducers and spread among the people, but sought rather to explain them in social terms, as symbolic depictions of a thoroughly real process. In the 1920s, to take just one example, the Left saw the attraction that Spengler's historical metaphysics had for the bourgeois intelligentsia in precisely this way: *The Decline of the West* was in reality nothing more than the imminent collapse of capitalism.

Today, on the other hand, someone like yourself no longer feels his views confirmed by the apocalyptic fantasy, but instead feels threatened, reacting with last-ditch slogans and defensive gestures. To be quite frank, dear Balthasar, it seems to me that the result of these obeisances is rather wretched. I don't mean by this that it is simply false. You do not, of course, fail to resort to the well-tried path of ideological criticism. And it is child's play to show that the rise and fall of utopian and apocalyptic moods in history correspond to the political, social, and economic conditions of the time. It is also uncontestable that they are exploited politically, just like any other fantasy that exists on a mass scale. You need not imagine you have to teach me the ABCs. I know as well as you that the fantasy of doom always suggests the desire for miraculous salvation; and it is clear to me, too, that the Bonapartist savior is always waiting in the wings, in the form of military dictatorship and right-wing putsch. When it is a question of survival, there have always been people all too ready to place their trust in a strong man. Nor do I find it surprising that those who have called for one more or less expressly, in the last few years, should include both a liberal and a Stalinist: the American sociologist Hellbroner and the German philosopher Harich. It is also beyond doubt that the apocalyptic metaphor promises relief from analytical thought, as it tends to throw everything together in the same pot. From the Middle East conflict to a postal strike, from punk style to a nuclear-reactor disaster, anything and everything is conceived as a hidden sign of an imaginary totality: catastrophe "in general." The tendency to hasty generalization damages that residual power of clear thought that we still have left. In this sense, the feeling of doom does in fact lead only to mystification. It goes without saying that the new irrationalism that so troubles you can in no way solve the real problems. On the contrary, it makes them appear insoluble.

This is all very easy to say, but it does not help matters all that much. You try and fight the fantasies of destruction with quotations from the classics. But these rhetorical victories, dear Balthasar, remind me of the heroic feats of Baron von Münchhausen. Like him, you want to reach your goal alone and unafraid; and to avoid departing from the correct straight line, you too are ready in case of need to leap onto a cannonball.

But the future is not a sports ground for hussars, nor is ideological criticism a cannonball. You should leave it to the futurologists to imitate the boastings of an old tin soldier. The future that you have in mind is in no way an object of science. It is something that exists only in the medium of social fantasy, and the organ by which it is chiefly experienced is the unconscious. Hence the power of these images that we all produce, day and night: not only with the head, but with the whole body. Our collective dreams of fear and desire weigh at least as heavy, probably heavier, than our theories and analyses.

The really threadbare character of customary ideological criticism is that it ignores all this and wants to know nothing of it. Has it not struck you that it has long ceased to explain things that do not fit our schemas, and started to taboo them instead? Without our having properly noticed, it has taken on the role of watchdog. Alongside the state censorship of the law-and-order people there are now ranged the mental-hospital orderlies of the Left in the social and human sciences, who would like to pacify us with their tranquilizers. Their maxims are: 1. Never concede anything. 2. Reduce the unfamiliar to the familiar. 3. Always think only with the head. 4. The unconscious must do what it is told.

The arrogance of these academic exorcists is surpassed only by their impotence. They fail to understand that myths cannot be refuted by seminar papers, and that their bans on ideas have a very short reach. What help is it to them, for example, and what use to us, if for the hundredth time they declare any comparison between natural and social processes inadmissible and reactionary? The elementary power of fantasy teaches millions of people to break this ban constantly. Our ideologists only raise a smile when they attempt to obliterate such ineffaceable images as flood and fire, earthquake and hurricane. Moreover, there are people in the ranks of natural scientists who are in a position to elaborate fantasies of this kind in their own fashion and make them productive instead of banning them: mathematicians drafting a topographical theory of catastrophe, or biochemists who have ideas about certain analogies between biological and social evolution. We are still waiting in vain for the sociologist who will understand that, in a sense that is still to be decoded, there is no longer any such thing as a purely natural catastrophe.

Instead of this, our theorists, chained to the philosophical traditions of German idealism, refuse to admit even today what every bystander has long since grasped: that there is no world spirit; that we do not know the laws of history; that even the class struggle is an "indigenous" process, which no vanguard can consciously plan and lead; that social evolution, like natural evolution, has no subject and is therefore unpredictable; that consequently, when we act politically, we never manage to achieve what we had in mind, but rather something quite different, which at one time we could not even have imagined; and that the crisis of all positive utopias has its basis precisely in this fact. The projects of the nineteenth century have been discredited completely and without exception by the history of the twentieth century. In the essay I already mentioned, Eric Hobsbawm recalls a congress held by the Spanish anarchists in 1898. They sketched a glorious picture of life after the victory of the revolution: a world of tall shining buildings with elevators that would save climbing stairs, electric light for all, garbage disposers, and marvelous household gadgets. . . . This vision of humanity, presented with messianic pathos, now looks strikingly familiar: in many parts of our cities it has already become reality. There are victories that are hard to distinguish from defeats. No one feels comfortable in recalling the promise of the October revolution sixty years ago: once the capitalists were driven out of Russia, a bright future without exploitation and oppression would dawn for the workers and peasants. . . .

Are you still with me, Balthasar? Are you still listening? I am nearing the end of my letter. Forgive me if it has gotten rather long, and if my sentences have taken on a mocking undertone. It's not me who injected this; it's a kind of objective, historic mockery, and the laugh, for better or worse, is always on the losing side. We all have to bear it together.

Optimism and pessimism, my dear friend, are so much sticking plaster for fortune-tellers and the writers of leading articles. The pictures of the future that humanity draws for itself, both positive and negative utopias, have never been unambiguous. The idea of the millennium, the City of the Sun, was not the pallid dream of a land of milk and honey; it always had its elements of fear, panic, terror, and destruction. And the apocalyptic fantasy, conversely, produces more than just pictures of decadence and despair; it also contains, inescapably bound up with the terror, the demand for vengeance, for justice, impulses of relief and hope.

The pharisees, those who always know best, want to convince us that the world would be all right again if the "progressive forces" took a strong line with people's fantasies; if they themselves were only sitting on the Central Committee, and pictures of doom could be prohibited by decree of the party. They refuse to understand that it is we ourselves who produce these pictures, and that we hold on to them because they correspond to our experiences, desires, and fears: on the motorway between Frankfurt and Bonn, in front of the TV screen that shows we are at war, beneath helicopters, in the corridors of clinics, employment offices, and prisons—because, in a single word, they are in this sense realistic.

I scarcely need reassure you, dear Balthasar, that I know as little of the future as you do yourself. I am writing to you because I do not count you among the pigeonholers and ticketpunchers of the world spirit. What I wish you, as I wish myself and us all, is a little more clarity about our own confusion, a little less fear of our own fear, and a little more attentiveness, respect, and modesty in the face of the unknown. Then we shall be able to see a little further.

Yours, H.M.E.

Translated by David Fernbach

Notes

The Industrialization of the Mind

1. This delusion became painfully apparent during the Nazi regime in Germany, when many intellectuals thought it sufficient to retreat into "inner emigration," a posture that turned out to mean giving in to the Nazis. There have been similar tendencies in Communist countries during the reign of Stalinism. See Czeslaw Milosz's excellent study, *The Captive Mind* (London, 1953).

2. Karl Marx, *Die deutsche Ideologie* (Part I, 1845–46).

3. A good example is the current wave of McLuhanism. No matter how ingenious, no matter how shrewd and fresh some of this author's observations may seem, his understanding of media hardly deserves the name of a theory. His cheerful disregard of their social and political implications is pathetic. It is all too easy to see why the slogan "the medium is the message" has met with unbounded enthusiasm on the part of the media, since it does away, by a quick fix worthy of a cardsharp, with the question of truth. Whether the message is a lie or not has become irrelevant, since in the light of McLuhanism truth itself resides in the very existence of the medium, no matter what it may convey: the proof of the network is in the network. It is a pity that Goebbels has not lived to see this redemption of his œuvre.

4. The importance of the transistor radio in the Algerian revolution has been emphasized by Frantz Fanon, and the role of television in the political life of Castro's Cuba is a matter of common knowledge.

5. A good example of this instinctive sense of security shared by the most entrenched political powers is offered by Senator Joseph McCarthy's lunatic crusade against Hollywood producers, actors, and writers. Most of them had shown an abject loyalty to the demands of the industry throughout their careers, and yet no abnegation of their talents could free them from suspicion. Much in the same way, Stalin never trusted even his most subservient lackeys of the intellectual establishment.

6. Among those who blithely disregard this fact, I would mention some European philosophers, for example Romano Guardini, Max Picard, and Ortega y Gasset. In America, this essentially conservative stance has been assumed by Henry Miller and a number of Beat Generation writers.

Poetry and Politics

1. Plato, *The Republic,* in particular 377–401 and 559–608.

2. For this and what follows I am indebted to *European Literature and the Latin Middle Ages* by Ernst Robert Curtius (Princeton, 1967). *Cf.* in particular Chapters 8 and 9.

3. Lachmann 26, 10.

4. Ibid., 17, 6. For what follows, *cf.* above all 19, 17; 17, 11; 31, 23; 26, 23; 26, 33; 28, 1; 28, 31.

5. From the complex of the *Venezianische Epigramme,* Artemis-Ausgabe II, 177 (Zürich, 1950).

6. *Sämtliche Werke und Briefe,* edited by Helmut Sembdner, Vol. I, 28 (Munich, 1961).

7. Written on July 31, 1898. Quoted from the Jubilee Edition, Vol. I (Berlin, 1919).

8. Quoted from *Die Zeit* of February 9, 1962. Some critics have questioned the existence of Gerd Gaiser's and Hans Carossa's Hitler poems. Gaiser's poem *"Der Führer"* can be found in his first book, *Reiter am Himmel,* published in 1941; Carossa's poem is contained in a *Tornisterschrift des Oberkommandos der Wehrmacht (Abteilung Inland). Zum Geburtstag des Führers 1941. Heft 37*; the work bears the title *Dem Führer, Worte deutscher Dichter.*

9. *The Republic,* 378; 391; 607.

10. Curtius, *European Literature and Latin Middle Ages.*

11. In the ironic *Lobgesänge auf König Ludwig* (1841), for example, the moment the ruler's name is mentioned, the lines degenerate to the level of a mediocre cabaret or beerhall joke.

12. The name Hitler appears in only two of Brecht's poems, in the *"Lied vom Anstreicher Hitler"* and in the *"Hitler-Choräle"* (*Gedichte* III, p. 35ff, Frankfurt, 1961). Both were written in 1933. Later Brecht consistently avoided the name and instead used paraphrases like *der Trommler* or *der Anstreicher.* (Cf. op. cit. IV., p. 10, 16, 100, etc.). The difference is not superficial. Brecht's most effective poems on fascism avoid all allusion to Hitler (*Die Erziehung der Hirse,* Berlin, 1951).

13. The poems mentioned are to be found in my *Museum der modernen Poesie* (Frankfurt, 1960).

14. In *Die Heilige Familie,* Chapters V and VIII (Frankfurt, 1845).

15. Draft of a letter to Margret Harkness in *Über Kunst und Literatur,* Karl Marx and Friedrich Engels (Berlin, 1949).

16. Ibid. Concerning *Marx, Engels und die Dichter,* see the book with this title by Peter Demetz (Stuttgart, 1959); it contains a comprehensive chapter on Lukács.

17. Georg Lukács, *Wider den missverstandenen Realismus* (Hamburg, 1958).
18. Two great exceptions are Benjamin and Adorno. Benjamin's treatise on *Der Begriff der Kunstkritik in der deutschen Romantik* (*Schriften* II, Frankfurt, 1955) and Adorno's essay *"Zum Gedächtnis Eichendorffs"* (*Noten zur Literatur* I, Frankfurt: 1958) could form the basis of a true understanding of German romantic poetry.
19. *Journaux intimes*. "*Mon cœur mis à nu*." LXXXIII.
20. *Auswahl in sechs Bänden*, I (Berlin, 1959).
21. *Fülle des Daseins*, p. 106 (Frankfurt, 1958).
22. *Ausgewählte Gedichte*, p. 49 (Frankfurt, 1960).
23. *Gesammelte Werke* III, p. 656 (Hamburg, 1961).
24. *The Republic*, 424. In accordance with the Greek notion, Plato conceives music to include what we would call rhythm and metrical figuration, as well as accent and phrasing. This is clear from the context; cf. in particular 398–401.

Commonplaces on the Newest Literature

1. A number of publications should be mentioned in reference to these commonplaces. Particularly worth mentioning are: *Kritik: Eine Selbstdarstellung deutscher Kritiker,* edited by Peter Hamm (München: Hanser, 1968); *Kürbiskern* 4/1968; Martin Walser, postscript to *Bottroper Protokolle,* by Erika Runge (Frankfurt: Suhrkamp, 1968); Karel Teige, *Liquidierung der "Kunst,"* Analysen und Manifeste (Frankfurt: Suhrkamp, 1968). The Breton quotes are from *The Second Surrealist Manifesto* of 1930. Régis Debray's letter is dated September 20, 1967, Camiri. The sentence from Walter Benjamin can be found in his *Versuche über Brecht.*

Constituents of a Theory of the Media

1. Bertolt Brecht, *Theory of Radio* (1932), *Gesammelte Werke,* Band VIII, pp. 129 seq., 134.
2. *Der Spiegel* (October 20, 1969).
3. El Lissitsky, "The Future of the Book," *New Left Review,* No. 41, p. 42.
4. *Kommunismus, Zeitschrift der Kommunistischen Internationale für die Länder Südosteuropas,* 1920, pp. 1538–49.
5. Walter Benjamin, *Kleine Geschichte der Photographie,* in *Das Kunstwerk im Zeitalter seiner technischen Reproduzierbarkeit* (Frankfurt, 1963), p. 69.
6. Walter Benjamin, "The Work of Art in the Age of Mechanical Reproduction," *Illuminations* (New York: Schocken, 1969), pp. 223–27.
7. Ibid., p. 229.
8. Op. cit., p. 40.
9. Benjamin, op. cit., p. 42.

Toward a Theory of Treason

1. Quoted from Günther Weisenborn, *Der lautlose Aufstand. Bericht über die Widerstandsbewegung des deutschen Volkes 1933 bis 1945*, p. 250ff. (Reinbek, 1962).
2. Margret Boveri, *Der Verrat im 20. Jahrhundert. I: Für und gegen die Nation* (Hamburg, 1956), p. 12.
3. With respect to the following, compare Sigmund Freud, *Totem and Taboo*. New York: Norton, 1952.
4. J. G. Frazer, *The Golden Bough*, Part II. *Taboo and the Perils of the Soul*. Third Edition (London, 1911), p. 132.
5. Montesquieu, *L'Esprit des Lois*, XII, 7.
6. Hannah Arendt provides a very trenchant analysis of the concept of the "objective opponent" in her book *Origins of Totalitarianism* (New York: Harcourt, Brace, Jovanovich, 1973).
7. Ibn Batuta, *Die Reise des Arabers Ibn Batuta durch Indien und China*. Bearbeitet von H. von Mzik. (Hamburg, 1911). Quoted from Elias Canetti, *Masse und Macht* (Hamburg, 1960), p. 497; English transl., *Crowds and Power*, New York: Continuum, 1978). Canetti's work is indispensable for the study of the connection between sovereignty and paranoia.
8. The figure 150,000 is based on data of Dieter Posser, a lawyer from Essen, who has made a name for himself as a defense attorney in political trials. Compare the *Süddeutsche Zeitung* of April 30, 1964.

Reflections before a Glass Cage

1. Eleventh edition, Vol. VII, p. 447.
2. *Leviathan*, XXVII chapter.
3. Chapter 5 in *Totem and Taboo*. Freud's argument is not necessarily dependent on the teachings of psychoanalysis. It makes sense even if one deletes motivation through the Oedipus complex and the question of incest.
4. Malinowski's investigation of *Sex and Repression in Savage Society* is a good characteristic example of the scientific criticism of Freud's hypotheses. Malinowski attempts an empirical reconstruction of fratricide and its consequences, an undertaking that has led to hypotheses *ad absurdum*. His critique shows the limits of Freud's presentation; Freud, however, who expressly called it a "scientific myth," was fully aware of these limitations himself. A refutation in this manner is just as impossible as is proof. The question of the priority of crime and social organization leads to philosophical and semantic conundrums into which anthropology can enter but which it cannot solve.
5. Canetti, *Crowds and Power*.
6. "The Taboo and Emotional Ambivalence" in *Totem and Taboo*.

7. Canetti, *Crowds and Power*.

8. *Politik* (Leipzig, 1897).

9. *Fischer Lexikon*, Volume 12: *Recht* (Frankfurt am Main, 1959), p. 137f.

10. *"Zeitgemässes über Krieg und Tod"* (1915), in *Das Unbewusste. Schriften zur Psychoanalyse* (Frankfurt am Main, 1960), p. 191f.

11. Gerhard Schoenberner, *The Yellow Star*, rev. ed., trans. Susan Sweet (London: Corgi, 1969), p. 12.

12. *Es gibt keinen jüdischen Wohnbezirk in Warschau mehr*. Facsimile edition of the Stroop Report English trans. Jürgen Stroop, *The Stroop Report: The Jewish Quarter of Warsaw Is No More*, trans. and annotated by Sybil Milton, intro. by Andrzej Wirth [New York: Pantheon, 1979]).

13. Felix Kersten, *Totenkopf und Treue*, p. 144. Quoted from Joachim C. Fest, *Das Gesicht des Dritten Reiches* (München, 1963), p. 169f.

14. Internationales Militärtribunal, *Der Prozess gegen die Hauptkriegsverbrecher* (Nürnberg, 1947), Volume XXIX, p. 145ff.

15. *On Thermonuclear War*, p. 21.

16. Op. cit., p. 133 and passim.

17. *Der Spiegel*, Nr. 47/1963, quoting the *Journal of Abnormal and Social Psychology* (Boston, October 1963).

18. In reference to this compare Eric J. Hobsbawm, *Primitive Rebels: Studies in Archaic Forms of Social Movements in the 19th and 20th Centuries* (New York: Norton, 1965).

Berlin Commonplaces

1. The *Fallex Bunker* is where the West German government went when it exercised the suspension of the Basic Law (the constitution) under the emergency laws.

Tourists of the Revolution

1. Heberto Padilla, *Ausserhalb des Spiels* (Frankfurt, 1971), pp. 113–15.

2. Leon Trotsky, *The Revolution Betrayed* (New York, 1973).

3. Victor Serge, *Memoirs of a Revolutionary 1901–1944* (Oxford: 1967).

4. Franz Jung, *Der Weg nach unten* (Neuwied, 1961), p. 169ff.

5. Victor Serge, *Memoirs of a Revolutionary*.

6. Arthur Koestler, *Arrow in the Blue* (New York: Macmillan, 1970).

7. Panait Istrati, quoted from Jürgen Rühle, *Literatur und Revolution* (München, 1960), p. 402.

8. André Gide, *Retuschen zu meinem Russlandbuch*, in *Reisen* (Stuttgart, 1966), pp. 413–15.

9. Bertolt Brecht, *Kraft und Schwäche der Utopie,* in *Gesammelte Werke,* VIII (Frankfurt, 1967), pp. 434–37.

10. André Gide, op. cit., p. 404. Gide is referring here to a pamphlet by M. Yvon, "Ce qu'est devenue la Revolution Russe."

11. *Nouvelle Revue Française* (March 1936).

12. André Gide, op. cit., p. 8.

13. Leon Trotsky, *Revolution Betrayed,* p. 8.

14. Umberto Melotti, in *Terzo Mondo* (Milano, March 1972), pp. 93ff. The book by Maria Macciocchi that he criticizes appeared in Milano in 1971 under the title *Dalla Cina, dopo la rivoluzione culturale.*

15. Susan Sontag, *Trip to Hanoi* (New York, 1969).

16. Jan Myrdal, *Report from a Chinese Village* (New York: Pantheon, 1965).

Critique of Political Ecology

1. *Ecology and Revolutionary Thought,* by Murray Brookchin (New York, 1970), p. 11. Brookchin argues that asking an ecologist *exactly* when the ecological catastrophe will occur is like asking a psychiatrist to predict exactly when psychological pressure will so affect a neurotic that communication with him will be impossible.

2. *An Inquiry into the Sanitary Conditions of the Labouring Population of Great Britain,* Report from the Poor Law Commissioners to the Home Department (London, 1842), p. 68. Quoted in *The Politics of Ecology,* by James Ridgeway (New York: Dutton, 1971).

3. Examples of this are not lacking in the ecology movement. In France there is an organization for environmental protection that has an extremely right-wing orientation. The president of these "Eco-fascists" is none other than General Massu, the man responsible for the French use of torture in the Algerian war.

4. *Profitschmutz und Umweltschmutz,* in *Rote Reihe* (Heidelberg, 1973), vol. I, p. 5.

5. *Capital* (Moscow, 1961), vol. I, p. 510 n.

6. Ridgeway, op. cit., pp. 22–25, sees Chadwick as an archetypal utilitarian bureaucrat, whose function was to secure the interests of capital by achieving peace and order among the poor. Better sanitation would produce a healthier and longer-living working force. Sanitary housing would raise workers' morale, and so on.

7. Ridgeway, *Politics of Ecology,* p. 15f., shows that over 150 years ago the Benthamites had evolved a theory of protecting the environment to promote production. As he also points out, the measures taken in the advanced, capitalist United States in the late 1960s fail to reach the standards of water and air cleanliness proposed by the utilitarians.

8. *Der Spiegel* (8 January 1973), p. 38.

9. Ridgeway, *Politics of Ecology,* pp. 207–11, analyses the "eco-industrial complex," i.e., the growing role played by business in promoting

ecological campaigns, such as Earth Day, and the liaison between business, politicians, local government, and "citizen campaigns."

10. For an illustration of the "eco-industrial complex" in West Germany see *Profitschmutz,* p. 14, and the pamphlet *Ohne uns kein Umweltschutz.*

11. "Primera Conferencia de Solidaridad de los Pueblos de América Latina," in *América Latina: Demografía, Población indígena y Salud,* vol. 2 (Havana, 1968), pp. 15f.

12. Ibid., pp. 55–57.

13. Claus Koch, *Mystifikationen der "Wachtumskrise": Zum Bericht des Club of Rome, Merkur,* Heft 297 (January 1973), p. 82.

14. *La morte ecologica,* Foreword by Giorgia Nebbia (Bari, 1972), p. xvf. (Italian edition of *The Ecologist, A Blueprint for Survival* [Hammondsworth, 1972]).

15. Club of Rome, *Limits to Growth* (New York, 1972), p. 13.

16. *Kapitalismus und "Umweltkatastrophe,"* by Gerhard Kade, duplicated manuscript, 1973.

17. "Die sozialistischen Länder: Ein Dilemma des westeuropäischen Linken," by Rossana Rossanda, *Kursbuch* 30, 1973, p. 26.

18. Cf. "Marx und die Öologie" in *Kursbuch* 33, 1973, pp. 175–87.

19. Rossana Rossanda, op. cit., p. 30.

20. André Gorz, "Technique, Techniciens et Lutte de Classes," *Les Temps Modernes* (August–September 1971), vol. 30–12, p. 141.

21. Anne H. and Paul R. Ehrlich, *Population, Resources, Environment* (San Francisco, 1972), pp. 322–24.

22. *Före-efter, En Diagnos,* by Gösta Ehrensvärd (Stockholm, 1971), pp. 105–7.

23. Ehrlich, *Population,* p. 322.

24. *Öffentlichkeit und Erfahrung. Zur Organisationsanalyse von bürgerlicher und proletarischer Öffentlichkeit* (Frankfurt, 1972), p. 242.

25. Ibid., pp. 283f.

26. *Economic and Philosophical Manuscripts of 1844,* by Karl Marx, ed. D. Struik, (London, 1970), p. 137.

ACKNOWLEDGMENTS

The sources of the translations contained in this volume are as follows:

"The Industrialization of the Mind," "Poetry and Politics," "Commonplaces on the Newest Literature," "Toward a Theory of Treason," "Reflections before a Glass Cage," "Berlin Commonplaces," "Tourists of the Revolution" all appeared in *The Consciousness Industry* and *Politics and Crime,* both copyright © 1974 by The Continuum Publishing Company.

"Las Casas, or A Look Back into the Future" appeared in Bartolomé de las Casas, *The Devastation of the Indies,* copyright © 1974 by The Continuum Publishing Company.

"Constituents of a Theory of the Media" and "A Critique of Political Ecology" are copyright © 1974 by the *New Left Review;* "Notes on the End of the World" is copyright © 1978 by the *New Left Review.*

The original German sources are as follows:

"Bewusstseins-Industrie" and "Poesie und Politik" from *Einzelheiten,* copyright © 1962 by Suhrkamp Verlag, Frankfurt; "Zur Theorie des Verrats" and "Reflexionen vor einem Glaskasten" from *Deutschland, Deutschland unter anderem,* copyright © 1964 by Suhrkamp Verlag, Frankfurt.

"Gemeinplätze, die neueste Literatur betreffend" copyright © 1969 by Kursbuch Verlag, Berlin; "Baukasten zu einer Theorie der Medien" copyright © 1971 Kursbuch Verlag, Berlin; "Berliner Gemeinplätze" copyright © 1968 Kursbuch Verlag Berlin; "Revolutions-Tourismus" and "Zur Kritik der politischen Ökologie" copyright © 1973 Kursbuch Verlag, Berlin; "Zwei Randbemerkungen zum Weltuntergang" copyright © 1978 Kursbuch Verlag, Berlin.

"Las Casas oder ein Rückblick in die Zukunft" copyright © 1962 Insel Verlag, Munich.

"Von der Unaufhaltsamkeit des Kleinbürgertums" copyright © 1976 by the *Frankfurter Rundschau.*